Language and Mind

Hyderabad Studies in Philosophy

1. **Philosophy of Wittgenstein** — Indian Response; by R.C. Pradhan; ISBN 81-86921-15-X
2. **The Philosophy of Language in Classical Indain Tradition**; edited by K.S. Prasad; ISBN 81-86921-20-6
3. **Indian Philosophy of Religion**; by A. Ramamurthy; ISBN 81-86921-22-2
4. **Language and Mind**; edited by R.C. Pradhan; ISBN 81-86921-34-6

Hyderabad Studies in Philosophy no. 4

Language and Mind

Volume - 1

A Western Perspective

edited by

R.C. Pradhan

Decent Books
New Delhi

Cataloging in Publication Data — DK
[Courtesy: D.K. Agencies (P) Ltd. <docinfo@dkagencies.com>]

National Seminar on Language and Mind (2004 : Hyderabad, India)
Language and mind / edited by R.C. Pradhan.
v. 1 23 cm. — (Hyderabad studies in philosophy ; no. 4)
Papers presented at the National Seminar on Language and Mind, held at Hyderabad in 2004.
Includes bibliographical references.
Includes index.
Contents: v. 1. A Western perspective.
ISBN 8186921346 (v. 1)
ISBN 8186921354 (set)

1. Language and languages — Philosophy — Congresses. 2. Philosophy of mind — Congresses. I. Pradhan, R.C. (Ramesh Chandra), 1950- II. Title. III. Series: Hyderabad studies in philosophy ; no. 4.

DDC 401 22

ISBN 81-86921-34-6
First Published in India in 2006

Published and printed by:
Decent Books
D-36/A-1, Mohan Garden
Najafgarh Road
New Delhi - 110 059
Ph. (011) 2535-3435

Distributed by:
D.K. Printworld (P) Ltd.
Regd. office : *'Sri Kunj,'* F-52, Bali Nagar
New Delhi - 110 015
Phones : (011) 2545-3975, 2546-6019; *Fax* : (011) 2546-5926
E-mail : dkprintworld@vsnl.net
Web : www.dkprintworld.com

Acknowledgement

THE essays included in this volume except the last one were presented in a National Seminar on "Language and Mind" held in 2004 in the Department of Philosophy under the UGC-SAP/DSA. We are thankful to the authors for their permission to include their essays in this volume. We express our thanks to the UGC for providing the necessary funds for the publication of the volume. We also express our thanks to the Vice-Chancellor, University of Hyderabad for providing all necessary help in undertaking this publication. To the Co-ordinator, SAP/DSA, Professor Amitabha Das Gupta and all the colleagues in the Department of Philosophy, we owe special thanks for their constant encouragement and help in this endeavour.

Contents

Introduction

THIS book is a collection of papers dealing with the problems of language and mind. The thrust of these papers is to highlight the recent developments in philosophy of language and mind in the West. These problems centre around the nature of the relationship between language and mind which is the central focus of cognitive science, artificial intelligence, cognitive psychology and cognitive linguistics. Philosophy of language and mind has been struggling with these problems since time immemorial. From Descartes to Davidson and Jerry Fodor, there has been a continuous struggle to locate mind and language in a close nexus so as to explain the possibility of cognition and communication.

In these papers there is emphasis on the cognitive competence of language — use and related matters of cognitive processing. There is also added emphasis on the nature of mental representations and intentionality, cognitive meaning and computationality, besides the analysis of non-linguistic thoughts.

Language and Mind: the Interface

Contemporary research on the interface of language and mind has revealed that there is a broad consensus on the fact that language and mind are interconnected at a deeper level. Language is not a mere means of communication, nor is thought a mere pre-linguistic mental entity. Thought and language are connected inseparably such that every thought has an echo in language and every linguistic expression has a thought-counterpart. That is to say that we cannot have a structured thought without a structured language and vice versa.

In the debate over whether language is prior to mind or mind is prior to language, there are philosophers who take one side or the other. But the fact of the matter is that there is no way we can escape the fact that every time we think a piece of thought, we are necessarily led to involve language at least to express the thought or in Frege's words, to grasp the thought. Even if thoughts have an ahistorical existence in a Platonic realm, as Frege advocates, they have to be grasped in a medium which is a logically structured language. There is no denying the fact that language has as pervasive a presence as thought itself so far as their logical structure is concerned. Wittgenstein, Davidson and Dummett endorse the view that language is indispensable for making thoughts intelligible in view of the fact that man is basically a language-using being. To have beliefs and thoughts is to have necessarily a language wherein these beliefs and thoughts are expressed.

It is necessary to admit that language and thought are of the same logical structure as they both have the same logical capacity to represent the world. Thoughts as the representations of the world are necessarily embedded in language which has the same capacity to represent the world. Hence to hypothesize that thought is prior to language is to put the cart before the horse. There can be no thought in the logical sense if there is no language — some language — to embed it. Language is the most primitive system of communication known to man. To think of a pre-linguistic stage of human existence is a misnomer as it posits a stage of human existence which could not be conceived in the absence of language.

It will therefore be justified to contend that the non-linguistic thoughts are a mere abstraction from the actual situation of thoughts being linguistically grounded and conditioned. The counter-example of the animals and the infants having thoughts without language does not cut much ice because there are no thoughts worth the name which we ascribe to animals and infants. It is only by extension of our thoughts that we ascribe thoughts to animals and the human infants. It is, however, not denied that animals communicate and have an evolved form of sign-language that helps them survive. Thus that animals and human infants have some rudimentary capacity for thinking and planning cannot be denied.

In this connection, it is worthwhile to mention the cognitive scientific discoveries regarding the innate capacities of cognition embedded in the human brain. The natural language processing and the information processing which the human brain undertakes give ample evidence of the fact that human mind/brain has an embedded language or grammar to facilitate the information processing. Fodor and Chomsky have done well to draw our attention to this fact in their Language of Thought Hypothesis and the Innate Universal Grammar, respectively. Fodor's idea is that the cognitive architecture of the human mind is embedded in a Language of Thought (LOT) which is a system of cognitive functions and symbols called the Mentalese. This language very different from the natural languages is a unique system of symbols which cannot be replaced by the natural symbols system. It is innate to the cognitive mind with an evolved cognitive architecture. Chomsky's Universal Grammar re-emphasizes the fact that the grammatical rules which regulate the function of the symbols are genetically embedded in the mind/brain. This explains how human beings are competent to use natural languages which follow the innate rules of the Universal Grammar.

Necessity and Contingency in Language

In this context the problem of necessity in grammar is very pertinent because language is embedded in a system of necessary rules of grammar. That language is a rule-governed system of symbols cannot be denied. But there cannot be any regularity in language if there were no necessary grammatical rules in the operation of symbols. This requires a logical syntax of language which specifies the rules of grammar. This has been well argued by Frege, Chomsky and Fodor in different ways. While Frege makes syntax the basic structure of language in general, Fodor makes it the mainstay of the computational language which is the Language of Thought. The paradigm of computational language is the model language that Fodor suggests for the natural languages to emulate. Chomsky makes the syntax the Universal Grammar on which all natural languages are based and from which they are derived. Thus they espouse the necessity of the grammatical structures underlying languages.

Richard Rorty and many others believe that language has no necessity of any type so that we cannot give any account of their so-called regularity and normativity. Rorty maintains that language is a contingent system of symbols which accidentally develops in the human community. The linguistic community is the source of the conventions and rules of language. These conventions arise in response to the need of the community and hence there is no *a priori* necessity about them. This argument for the contingency of language emphasizes the fact that language has no centre or central structure that can have it hinged on a firm foundation. There is no foundation of language except the linguistic conventions evolved by the human community. This foundation is the human solidarity that is a natural product of the human evolution in nature.

Now the question arises, How can there be contingency in language without there being necessity which cannot be bargained away by the human community? Can the human community evolve a language without following rules? If there are rules which regulate language-use, can these rules themselves be made by the community? In order to avoid an infinite regress, we must admit a bedrock of language that sustains the regularity and normativity of language. Mere contingency is not enough, there is something more to language than we can see on the surface. If we are in search of a cognitive architecture, we need a foundational source of this architecture. That source cannot but be necessary so far as language is concerned.

The cognitive processes underlying use of language do need a rule-bound architecture. That is the reason why Fodor has emphasized the necessity of a computational mechanism that accounts for the universality and the necessity of the rule-structure. Computational psychology espouses the need of necessity in language thus throwing open the possibility of a necessitarian model of grammar or logical syntax. The contingential model of grammar does not account for the primacy of the rules in language and the cognitive processes undertaken by the human mind.

Intentionality of the Cognitive and the Linguistic Structures

The phenomenon of intentionality has been a significant indicator of the inner structure of language and mind. Both language and mind have intentional structures which account for their not only being about the world, but also their being meaningful structures. Intentionality is associated with meaning in the sense that all that language and mind have as contents are meaning-embedded. The contents of the mental acts and the linguistic acts are the thoughts which are the objects of the beliefs and belief-expressions. The linguistic acts as well as the mental acts are intentional for the reason that they are directed at the thoughts or propositions. There is a world-directedness which characterizes these acts.

Intentionality is not a natural property in the way the brain process is a natural event. It is a normative property of how language and mind are related to the world. Though Searle believes that intentionality is a biological phenomenon, it is not the case that biology alone can explain the intentional mental phenomena. Intentionality itself is supervenient on the brain processes without being reducible to the latter. Intentionality brings in meaning into language because without it the linguistic symbols cannot be taken as meaningful. Searle is right in telling us that mere syntax of language is not enough. His Chinese Room experiment shows that even if a machine can operate symbols according to rules, it fails to understand the meaning of the symbols because it has no intentionality. Thus intentionality is a semantic feature of language and mind and hence has to be given a normative status.

The tendency to naturalize intentionality as it has been found in Drestke and Dennett is not always successful because there is always a gap between the intentional process as a brain process and the intentional character of the mental phenomena because the latter is a normative property while the former is a physical event. We cannot confuse the two. The natural physical order of things does not contain the intentional meaning of the symbols. The latter is an additional feature of the linguistic expressions. It can be protected only as a normative entity.

The intentional realists are right in holding that the intentional mental phenomena are real in addition to the natural processes of the brain. No brain science can explain how intentional experience is possible. Intentional experience is part of the human cognitive process. Fodor is right in recognizing that mental activities, though computational in nature, are intentional in character. This goes to prove that mental activities are intentional even if they appear to be mechanical. Dennett's contention that there is only an "intentional stance" and not intentionality proper is not sufficient to explain why there should be intentionality at all. The intentional stance is a pragmatic notion which needs a basis in the nature of the mind itself. Thus a defence of intentional realism is possible against intentional instrumentalism.

Meaning in the Mind

Intentionality prepares the ground for making meaning mental in view of the fact that the mental processes account for the meaning of the expressions which represent them. The mental representations constitute the broad spectrum of the mental activities which cry for meaning and other semantic properties like the linguistic representations. Both the mental and the linguistic representations constitute a single block for semantic treatment and for semantic evaluation. Meaning therefore qualifies for being an entity "in the head."

Philosophy of mind inspired by the later Wittgenstein and Ryle discouraged the idea that meanings are in the mind and that there are no such meanings like the mental contents to be deciphered by introspection. But this theory has been put aside by the recent philosophers of mind who espouse the idea that meaning is a mental content and that it can be traced back to the mind underlying language. Searle, Fodor and many other mentalists argue that meanings are "in the head" and that they are part of the mental contents. Meaning and contents have been brought together and so there is the claim that where there is meaning, there is content as well. This revives the old idea that meaning originates in the mind and spreads to language and the world. This gives a new lease of life to the theory that mind is real and that it is the seat of all semantic powers of language.

The theory of narrow contents has been the best candidate for the semantic theory explaining meaning. Fodor provides a robust account of how the narrow contents individuate meaning in the mind. The new psychosemantic theory goes to the extent of saying that meanings as the narrow contents are both psychological and semantic in character. As psychological entities they are part of the mental processes which are computational and representational in character; as semantic they are evaluable in the context of their relation to the world. The wide contents are world-directed and hence have a direct semantic relation to the world. The narrow contents do not have a direct relation to the world and so have to be indirectly semantic by being dependent on the wide contents.

Fodor's objections to meaning holism are based on his theory of narrow contents which shows that the narrow contents are individualistic and are not liaisoned with other contents. His attack on meaning holism is aimed at those who believe that contents are interconnected and are given in a package. He believes that meanings cannot be packaged together in any relevant sense as they are part of the mental representations which work piece-meal and not in a cluster. Putnam, on the contrary, shows that meanings come as wholes or packages since they are integrated into systems of wide contents and are hooked onto the world. His argument is that meaning holism follows precisely from the fact that meanings are widely diffused over the vast canvas of language which is linked with the world. Under the circumstances, it is necessary that both mental contents and meanings should be taken as holistic rather than individualistic.

Meaning and Computationality

Fodor's computational view of mind enforces a new way of looking at the meaning of the mental representations. Mental representations being computational in character are formal in structure. This therefore requires semantic evaluation for finding out their truth-conditions. Truth-conditions themselves along with intentionality take care of meaning. Fodor's argument is that meaning cannot be dispensed with even in a computational framework. Computationality, though syntactic, requires semantics for facilitating meaning. Therefore he never dispenses with intentionality which is the gateway to meaning.

However, it is a matter of grave concern for the semanticists that meaning cannot be attributed to machines or to any system that largely depends on mechanical devices. Searle's Chinese Room argument shows that machines do not understand language as they are not meaning-sensitive, while the human minds do understand meaning, however complicated it may be. The idea that semantics requires meaning-sensitivity itself is self-justified. That also ensures that intelligent machines cannot replace the human minds contrary to what the AI programme intends to say. AI programme is based on the notion of machine intelligence introduced by Turing. It has established itself as a practical programme without solving the conceptual issues surrounding machine intelligence and the mechanical concept of mind. However, it is being realized by the philosophers that the mechanical conception of mind has only a limited value and so cannot go very far in explaining the nature of human consciousness.

Consciousness is a basic datum that needs no explanation since it is at the basis of all explanations of the mental phenomena. All mental activities including the use of language presuppose consciousness. Therefore the effort to explain consciousness in terms of the mechanical processes of the brain is not successful. The brain activities and the resulting information processing are conscious activities to say the least. Hence there is no reason to make information processing itself the constitutive condition of consciousness. Roger Penrose has rightly pointed out that consciousness has to be posited as non-mechanical and non-computational. Computationality presupposes a conscious mind.

A Survey of the Problems in this Volume

This volume tackles a host of issues ranging from meaning theory, structure of language and other linguistic issues to the problems concerning mental contents, intentionality, etc. All these issues cluster around the central problem of the relationship between language and thought.

B. H. Boruah in his paper "Pain in the Neck of a Theory of Meaning" has taken up the issue of the semantics of the pain-language and offered the theory that the language of pain has a semantics that it is embedded in the "common affective humanity" which provides the broad framework in which human feelings and sensations can be understood. Following Wittgenstein, Boruah suggests that there is no need of a private language to justify the first-person experiences of pain and other sensations. The public language embedded in the common human life is capable of expressing the inner feelings of pain. He rejects the internal semanticist view that pains are internal and private accessible only to the sufferer. He sees no gap between the so-called inner phenomenological contents of experience and their public manifestation. The neo-behaviourists are wrong in attempting to reduce the inner experiences to outward behaviour. Boruah advocates a semantics that retains both the phenomenological experiences and their manifestations in human life. This semantics need not sacrifice the inner reality of pain and other sensations and thus it reconciles the phenomenological reality of pain with its relation to the outer physical setting.

Amita Chatterjee in her paper, "Thinking Without Words: A Possibility or Myth?" has argued that the relation between language and thought is such that only in the case of human beings we can establish a necessary relation between the two. That is, only in the case of humans we can say that thought is possible because of language and that a thinking being is necessarily a language-using being. This view advocated by

Wittgenstein, Davidson, Carruthers and others who emphasize the primacy of language is countered by a theory which argues that it is the mind which is primary and that language develops much later in the process of evolution. This view partly endorsed by Fodor, and others allows for the possibility of thoughts without the natural languages. However, Fodor accepts a language of thought in order to explain that the innate thought-structures have a language, though not a natural language, embedded in them. Chatterjee critically examines both these theories in course of her paper.

What Chatterjee pleads for is the view that there can be thoughts without language as in sub-human animals and human children. In these cases, unlike the case of the developed human beings, there are pre-linguistic thoughts and reasoning which are established by the study of animal behaviour. There are proto-thoughts which are not exactly like the logical thoughts expressed in human languages. She argues that animals are capable of full-fledged thoughts, even though they lack the sophistication of the human thoughts. This is, however, not to deny the crucial role of language in the formation and development of thought in human beings.

Tista Bagchi in her paper "The Sentence in Computation and Cognitive Science" has argued for a theory of sentences in cognitive science which can account for the process of computation involved in human cognition. The natural language sentences are so grammatically structured that they represent the cognitive processes occurring in the human mind. Sentences are the media through which the cognitive processes of the mind are represented in language. She further argues that the sentence is a computational device in the sense that it is meshed with all the computational processes. Computation as a mental process is linked with the formation of the sentence. She argues that both cognition and computation are the two aspects of the same human mental activity. She also argues that sentences, ontologically speaking, are real in language. In this context, she takes into account the natural languages as well as the computer programming languages.

V. Harinarayanan and C.A. Tomy in their paper "The Nature of Mental Representation: Classicism versus Connectionism" have discussed the recent developments in cognitive science from both the classicist and the connectionist points of view. They have argued that the mental representations are central to our understanding of the cognitive architecture of the human mind. The classicist point of view is represented mainly by Jerry Fodor who has shown in his works that the mental representations are computational in character and are basically expressed in a symbolic language called the language of thought (LOT). Fodor's hypothesis of a language of thought called the Mentalese consists of symbols which have both a syntactic and a semantic structure. Mental representations which are computational in character are therefore necessarily formal and symbolic. Thus the entire cognitive architecture of the human mind is endowed with an innate linguistic structure very different from the structure of the natural languages.

The classicist point of view has been systematically challenged by the connectionists like Smolensky, according to Harinarayanan and Tomy, on the ground that the mental representations are not serial but parallel and are distributed over many units. The connectionist network of the cognitive processes is modelled on the neural network of the human brain consisting of many neural units. The information processing is distributed over many units simultaneously to effectively produce the output. This approach dispenses with the serial order of the symbolically articulated mental representations and thus is free from the constraints of an innate mental language. However, by giving up the advantages of a mental language, this approach suffers from inadequacy in dealing with the cognitive structures of the human mind. The authors have argued that both classicism and connectionism have advantages and disadvantages, but on the whole both need to be taken as complementary to each other.

S. Panneerselvam in his paper, "Fodorian Folk Psychology and Computational Theory of Mind: An Analysis" has discussed the Fodor's defence of folk psychology and the computational representational theory of mind. Fodor is well known as an advocate of folk psychology of desires, beliefs and other mental states. He accepts the intentional character of these mental states against the eliminativists who argue that there are no such intentional states like beliefs and desires. Panneerselvam discusses the Fodorian computational theory of mind which is based on the idea that mind is like a computer and is a "semantic engine." He also points out how Fodor's syntactic approach to mental representations has been challenged by the connectionists who hold that cognition takes place through a neural network without involving computations and symbol manipulations as pointed out by the classicists. In recent times the idea of a computational mind has been challenged notably by John Searle who through his Chinese Room argument has shown that mind is not just a Turing Machine but a biological system having intentional mental states. There have been many attempts in recent years to go beyond the computationalist view of mind. Panneerselvam has hinted at this possibility while discussing the arguments against functionalism and Artificial Intelligence.

P.R. Bhat in his paper, "Mind and Language: Their Inter-Dependence" has argued that language and mind are inter-related and inter-dependent in view of the fact that both the mental and the linguistic acts go together and that one implicates the other. He argues for the autonomy of mind and language in view of the fact that they are not accountable to reality as such for their activities. However, they are not autonomous from each other as they are involved in each other. Mind in itself is not a substance but a dynamic system of activities, according to Bhat, since it can be compared with a form of energy. Language, for that matter, is not a static entity as such but is a dynamic system of activities governed by rules. He claims that this view of diversity of language and rules does not imply any sort of relativism which allows "anything goes."

N. Sreekumar in his paper "Reason and Language: An Appraisal of Richard Rorty's Pragmatic Post-Modern Approach" has discussed Rorty's post-modern approach to language and reason. Rorty's philosophy of language and mind is influenced by the developments in the post-modern thinking in the West. He takes language as a contingent phenomenon with no stable and eternal structure. Language is more a social practice with an assortment of conventions and rules devised by the linguistic community. Thus there is no reason to search for *a priori* foundations of language. Rorty further argues that language of mind are not "the mirrors of Nature" because of the fact that there is no essential structure of mind to mirror the structure of the world. Sreekumar goes into the whole question of why language mind have lost their metaphysical character in view of the post-modernist attack on the ahistorical reason as the source of the *a priori* ideas. He shows that Rorty combines his native pragmatism with post-modernism to arrive at the deconstruction of the modernist ahistorical conceptions of language and mind.

Ranjan K. Panda in his paper "Naturalizing Intentionality: A Searlean Critique" has discussed the nature of intentionality and its place in the world of Nature. Arguing from Searle's point of view, he holds that intentionality is an intrinsic feature of the human mind and therefore it cannot be identified with a property of the human body the way the reductionists take it to be. Though it is basically a biological property, it cannot be identified with a physical property in the reductionist sense of the term. For that reason, not physicalism, but dualism of some sort is needed to accommodate intentionality in the world. Panda argues that Searle is right against the physicalists in admitting an ontology of intentionality along with a first-person perspective within the broad framework of biological naturalism. It goes to the credit of Searle for showing that intentionality, though natural and biological in origin, yet has functional and ontological autonomy within the realm of Nature.

R.C. Pradhan in his paper "Fodor on Meaning Holism: Why Narrow Contents Do Not Hold Promise for a Meaning Theory" has discussed Fodor's arguments against meaning holism, as expounded in *Psychosemantics*. In this work Fodor held that the mental contents are narrow and that they are so structured that they do not support a holistic meaning theory. Pradhan's argument is that the contents need not be narrow and that even if content holism is rejected, that does not amount to a rejection of meaning holism. Fodor himself has realized that broad contents are part of the mental representations and that they need be taken into account while discussing meaning of the mental representations. He further realizes that mind cannot be taken as computational all the way down in view of the fact that there are mental processes that are not precisely computational because the mind does not work that way. Fodor's work *The Mind Does Not Work That Way* shows the limitations of the computational approach to mind and meaning. In this context, it can be said that meaning itself is not a computational property of the mental contents and that mind must be intrinsically capable of meaning and intentionality.

Amitabha Das Gupta in his paper entitled "Meaning and Mental Mechanism: A Critique" has developed a critique of the contemporary theory of meaning developed within the framework of the functionalist and cognitivist model of the mind. The contemporary cognitivist theorists of mind and meaning, especially Jerry Fodor, have construed meaning in terms of mental mechanisms. Central to Fodor's theory is his language of thought hypothesis according to which mind is basically a computational representational system. Meaning is situated in this system in terms of the causal and the functional properties of the symbols used in the language of thought. Das Gupta has given a detailed analysis of Fodor's functionalist semantics of meaning and intentionality and argued that the naturalization and functionalization of meaning is not possible. He has shown that meaning cannot be naturalized and that mind does not function as an information processing system.

Das Gupta has argued for the thesis that meaning is normative, holistic and autonomous. Taking the clue from Frege and Wittgenstein, he has shown that meaning is normative in character and that it cannot be reduced to the natural and causal properties of language. Besides, meaning is organic to language and has to be treated holistically and not atomistically. Thus, according to him, meaning is not reducible to any non-semantic property of language and hence is to be treated as autonomous.

Rakesh Chandra in his paper entitled "Kant and Kripke Reading of A Priori" has discussed the nature of the *a priori* propositions from Kant's and Kripke's points of view. He has discussed the distinction between a prioricity, analyticity and necessity in this connection. Kant had made this distinction in course of his epistemological inquiry. Kripke has made a revision in the Kantian notion of necessity by introducing the metaphysical notion of necessity. Thus there has been a revival of interest in the concepts of necessity and possible worlds thanks to Kripke. Chandra has a wide ranging discussion on this issue and has critically evaluated Kripke's concept of contingent *a priori.*

This volume takes into account a number of issues philosophers are grappling with in the area of philosophy of mind and language. It is hoped that these issues will continue to dominate philosophical discussions in the near future and this volume in a limited way may provide ideas in this direction.

1

Pain in the Neck of a Theory of Meaning

Bijoy H Borua

A Matter of Negotiation

That there is a natural language in a human community means that there is a relational feature that is essentially true of the language — of any natural language. A natural language is naturally world-directed. We might call this feature the *intentionality* of natural language. Of course we can play with language just for the sake of language, without using it in the world-directed mode. The intentional object of language may be bracketed out and language can be manipulated so as to relate it to language itself in an attitude of indifference to reference. But such a use of language would be parasitic on the world-bearing use that is more fundamental to language.

It would seem right to interpret this relational or world-directed character of language in terms of language's *negotiation* with the world. If the world, or any aspect of it, is utterly resistant to linguistic negotiation, then the world, or that aspect of it, will be inaccessible to language. Such aspects of the world or reality would be real, but *ineffable*. Thus, a natural language carves out a reality that becomes the object of inter-subjective communication. And the segment of reality so carved out becomes a *common communicative fact* of the human beings who share that language.

One of the clearest examples of language's negotiation with the world is the case of physical objects observably located in physical space. What is clear about this kind of negotiation is that such objects in space are accessible to the linguistic act of *reference* performed through the gesture of *ostension*. The object makes its "entry" into the domain of language by being designated as something, and the "internalisation" of the object by designation or denotation is quite smooth because of the smoothness of the act of publicly ostending the object. Of course a denotative move, made through the gesture of public ostension, occurs in a setting that embodies familiarity with the convention of designation and ostensive definition.

Ostensive definition of words given in a publicly observable context is therefore a prime instance of how, as it were, "lifeless" words acquire the life of meaning. And a language into the fabric of which are woven such words may be said fully to satisfy the terms of negotiation with the world of objects referred to by these words. Consequently, interpersonal communication concerning such a world of objects attains maximum *transparency* of meaning.

Obviously, not everything in reality is so unproblematically accessible to linguistic reference as physical objects of the publicly observable kind are, and hence we can very well anticipate contexts of real life in which the way a fact of life relates itself to language eludes referential understanding and ostensive gesture. It may actually be a most common fact of life, and thus a most talked-about phenomenon of the human condition. And yet, upon reflection, it may strike us as a surprising fact how our spontaneous talk about the fact in question could ever find its place in the network of communication. More precisely, we may wonder how the language in which we communicate facts about the given phenomenon actually manages to fulfill the required communicative task at all. The phenomenon itself may be inherently transparent to us, but it may then be quite *opaque* to the reach of language.

The Opacity of Sensations

Sensations are mental phenomena with an intrinsically inner nature specified in terms of their distinct qualitative subjective content. They consist in specific felt qualities directly cognized by the subject having the sensation. The what-it-is-like mental content of a pain, for example, is graspable only from the first-person perspective, or the perspective of the pain-suffering subject. This "first-person internality" of a painful sensation makes the mental state of pain essentially private. The reality of pain is thus irreducibly first-personal, intrinsically inner and constitutively phenomenological.

Can language successfully negotiate with a piece of reality that is real solely from the first-person perspective? Can the intrinsic privacy of pain, the first-person internality of its inner content, "enter" into the framework of language that is by nature a framework of public, inter-subjective communication? Is the referential apparatus of language adequate to making inroads into the inner recess of one's pain-sensational content? What would possibly be the gesture of ostension by virtue of which reference to pain is to be made, and how would that alleged referential link be recognized by the community of language-users, who would then grasp that "pain" means the *hurtful feeling* that the pain-sufferer undergoes?

It should rather be clear why a state of pain is opaque to the reach of language, whereas a physical object, say a football, is quite transparent to what might be called the "semantic gaze" of language. Unlike the football, a pain, considered as a state with a specific kind of felt content, is not a publicly observable phenomenon. Linguistic reference being a third-person-centred mechanism for linking a word with its target-object or state-state, it is not possible for someone to deploy the word "pain" with a referential intention of linking it with the pain-state that someone else feels. For the target-object of "pain," unlike the target-object of "football" that lies open to all in outer space, is hidden in the private mental space of the sufferer. What would one point to in trying to fix the reference of "pain" when one uses the word for the ascription of pain to someone else?

Is the target-object of "pain" transparent to the sufferer herself in an act of self-ascription of pain, so that, in this case at least, the referential arrow successfully hits the private pain-content of one's own? Is the gesture of ostension to the phenomenologically circumscribed reality of pain the exclusive privilege of the subject of pain-experience? If the answer is in the affirmative, then there is no opacity to the semantics of "pain," but *no* opacity *only* with regard to the referential intention of the sufferer. Pain is a self-intimating state and is never an "other-intimating" state of human reality. The general truth in this context is that any phenomenologically contentful mental state intimates its reality only to the subject experiencing the state.

On an Allegedly Private Semantics of Pain

I think that the general belief about first-personal intimation of phenomenologically contentful states is indisputably true. The question, however, is the "shape" of the semantics of terms for phenomenological states, especially sensations like pain. Must the semantics of "pain" be directly attuned to the ontic privacy of pain, analogous to the determination of the semantics of "football" by direct reference to the publicly accessible (hence ontically public) football? This question seemingly invites a consideration of the relation between metaphysics and semantics, that is, between the existential status of the object or state in question and the meaning-theoretic character of the language that is intended to represent the object or state. If the metaphysical or ontic status of the object or state is private, is it necessary that the term for the object or state be invested with private meaning? Does the fate of semantics depend on metaphysics?

The questions raised above bears on the general relation between language and reality. If language's negotiation with reality is governed by terms of constraint imposed by reality, then the negotiation would be a matter of subordination on the part of language to reality. Language would not then be autonomous, but a handmaiden of reality, in which case semantics would also be subordinated to metaphysics.

It surely would be a gross misunderstanding of the nature of language to deny it autonomy. The negotiation between language and reality is not an one-sided affair, in which language is to surrender itself fully to the demands of reality. Granted that language has to be appropriately sensitive to what apparently is the nature of reality, there is no denying the fact that language is governed by rules of constraint imposed by its own nature. One such constraint is that it must be a vehicle of inter-subjective communication of ideas and representations with shared meanings.

However, the mistaken idea that language is a handmaiden of reality, and that semantics is subordinated to metaphysics, is worthy of being considered with some seriousness. This is because the mistake is instructive in shedding light on the nature of language and its complex relation with reality. And the complexity of this relation is effectively revealed in an imagined attempt to develop a language of sensations in terms of semantic privacy. It is this abortive attempt that gets succinctly exposed by Wittgenstein in what is famously known as the Private Language Argument. The private linguist is projected as holding the view that the meaning of "pain" is private for the reason that the word is assigned its meaning on the basis of the sufferer's inner ostensive reference to the privately real phenomenological content of pain.

This way of assigning meaning to "pain" and other sensation words would of course render the whole of sensation language an "odd man out" in the field of natural language. For sensation language would then be a sub-field of *intra*-subjective private language within the wider *inter*-subjective field of language. More devastatingly, the rules for the correct use of sensation-terms would then lack any objective basis. If the sufferer of pain focuses her attention on the quality of the sensation, and then promised to call just that kind of sensation "pain" in the future, her use of the term in any subsequent occasion would have to depend for its correctness entirely on the subjective criterion of what *seems* to her to be the recurrence of a sensation with the same phenomenological content. But if what *seems* to be right is indistinguishable from what indeed *is* right as far as the rules for the use of "pain" is concerned, the required linguistic convention of objective confirmation of rule-following is flouted.

The Persuasiveness of Semantic Externalism

If the so-called privileged introspective access to the first-personal reality of pain and the gesture of ostensive reference cannot constitute the basis of the meaning of "pain," this evidently indicates that the semantic determinant of the word must be something external and third-personal. The natural external candidate for playing this role is pain-behaviour, or, broadly speaking, the physical setting of stimuli and responses in which pain occurs. The sense of "pain" is determined by reference to publicly observable pain-behaviour, which fixes objective, public-criterial rules for the correct use of the term in inter-subjective communication. The implication is that pain-behaviour has a non-contingent link with pain, which is why it can justifiably be treated as *criterial* of the occurrence of pain.

This way of accounting for the possibility of inter-subjective pain-talk has its grounding in the general theory of semantic externalism. The positive content of semantic externalism is that it is by reference to typical observable behavioural effects of a mental state that a satisfactory account of the meaning of mental terms can be given. The meaning of a word is logically tied to publicly available features of circumstances that are generally held to constitute sufficient grounds for its correct application. We cannot properly determine what we are talking about when we use mental vocabulary without adverting to the sorts of public circumstances in which such a vocabulary is mastered, and subsequently employed, by us. For these circumstances have a *definitional* role in articulating what we *mean* when we employ mental vocabulary.

Semantic externalism with regard to the meaning of sensation-terms is advocated by Wittgenstein with great persuasiveness in his anti-private language argument, and in his general account of the rule-governed character of language. Wittgenstein has made the convincing point that the independent references to sensation-types that two people, *A* and *B*, make by inner ostension when they individually feel sensations of that type, say pain-type, do not really play any role in their communication with one another. Since *A* and *B* both do not share each other's direct awareness of the sensations, one does not get to know what exactly is the target-object that the "internalized" arrow of reference hits in the case of the other, and vice versa.

But the fact of the matter is that in real life people do communicate with one another about their pains and other sensations. Sensation-words are very much part of a common, inter-subjective language, and hence our use of these words do conform to communally agreed upon rules. The truth therefore has to be that, when *A* and *B* actually confer with one another about their pain experiences, the conference is not in fact sustained by the putative private object — the inner pain-phenomenological content — allegedly referred to by each in their internalized acts of ostensive gesture. In *Philosophical Investigations (Section 239)*, Wittgenstein emphasizes the externalist standpoint by making the strong claim that the "[private] object drops out of consideration as irrelevant" to what might be called the semantic adequacy of the sensation-term in question. As Peter Hacker puts it, "the private object allegedly referred to is a piece of idle machinery and plays no part in the mechanism of communication" (p. 270).

An Internalist Worry about Semantic Externalism

Even though semantic externalism is vindicated by the inescapable constraints of communication, it does not seem fully to settle the problem of meaning of sensation language for reasons pertaining to the *nature* of sensations. There is no doubt that any philosophical theory about the meaning of "pain" must not conflict with the commonsense view that it is, as Galen Strawson says, "simply the general term for a certain class of unpleasant sensations, considered just as such and hence considered entirely independently of their typical causes or typical behavioural effects or expressions" (p. 214). Given this ordinary and correct view, it seems rather odd to endorse, wholeheartedly, the third-personal, public criteria-based approach to the meaning of "pain." Indeed, it seems quite hard to believe that the private phenomenological content of pain — the unpleasant physical sensation as such — drops out of consideration as semantically irrelevant.

The ordinary or commonsensical view appears to conflict with semantic externalism because there is a strong "internalist" implication in this view, i.e. that "pain" means nothing other than the inner state of painful feeling of the sufferer. Since the reality of pain is first-personal in that it consists in the what-it-is-likeness of pain accessible to the first-person perspective, the meaning of the term for this real state of mind would somehow have to be "anchored" to the first-person point of view. And from the first-person point of view what figures most prominently is the pure and private pain-phenomenological content, which is, as it were, sandwiched between pain-causing stimuli and pain-expressive behaviour responses. How, then, can we define "pain" in such a way that the definition relegates to irrelevance the inner reality "held up" between the outer contexts of stimuli and responses, while choosing the outer contexts as semantically decisive?

Scepticism about the semantic externalist standpoint with regard to the meaning of "pain" and its relation to pain might encourage the contrary standpoint of semantic internalism — a standpoint that directly results in the advocacy of a private language of sensations. Even though this advocacy is doomed to lose the case, the theoretical inspiration that motivates the adoption of this standpoint is well understood and can be sympathized with. The so-called standpoint of semantic internalism derives its motivations from what might be called the *ontic* concern with pain, i.e. what it is for something to *be* pain. Since the being of pain consists in the private, first-personal intimation of *what it is like* to be in a pain-state, and it does not consist in the third-personally accessible antecedent stimuli or consequent responses of the internal state, any attempt to define "pain" by adverting to the outer, causal-physical context of the inner phenomenological content is likely to evoke doubt about semantic propriety.

The Inner and the Outer: A Semantic Predicament

Although Wittgenstein has championed the widely acknowledged claim that meaning is primarily a matter of use, the Wittgensteinian account of the publicly observable circumstances of stimuli and responses, in which the use of the word "pain" is mastered, is not the whole story of the meaning of this word. There is a true "inner" story of the word's reference to private experiential content as much as there is the true "outer" story of the mastery of the word's use in public, inter-communicative context. I think this is the spirit, if not the letter, of the internalist motivation, and the message underlying the spirit cannot be undermined.

It seems to me that a viable theory of meaning for sensation language has to conceive of a delicately balanced relation between these two stories. Of course these are not parallel stories simultaneously running together in the life of the meaning of "pain." Rather, the two stories mesh with one another so as jointly to get over a predicament that would otherwise loom large in each story taken in isolation. The predicament with the inner story is that independent, context-free, private reference made by each person to his or her own sensation of pain would not support a common language in which people could communicate with one another about pain. With the outer story the predicament is that inter-communication of the sensation of pain is possible only if the word for the sensation is allowed to latch on to the physical setting of stimuli and responses, at the cost of rendering the phenomenological essence of pain semantically gratuitous.

Does Wittgenstein ignore the inner story while highlighting the communicatively salient features of pain-behavioural expression? There are many remarks and examples in his writings (especially in *Philosophical Investigations*) that would encourage the (perhaps entirely wrong) opinion that the thrust of the Wittgensteinian argument is behaviouristic. Galen Strawson complains about what he calls Wittgensteinian neo-behaviourists who profess the view that "the notion of behaviour is central and indispensable in discussing the nature of the mental, simply because it has a central and indispensable place in any correct analysis of the nature of our *language* of the mental" (p. 221). Describing the alleged neo-behaviourist position as "W-theoretic argument" (alluding to Wittgenstein's externalist heritage), Strawson adds that once it is accepted that reference to publicly observable occurrences is all that enters essentially into any satisfactory account of the meaning of the word "pain," the strange conclusion then follows that our language is utterly incapable of talking in any way about pain as such (*ibid.* p. 223-4).

Certainly, any argument that leads to such a conclusion would be absurd, and the W-theoretic argument tends to lead to it. Ordinarily we do talk about pain and mean by that talk nothing other than publicly unobservable experiential episodes of a certain quality occurring within us. Is Wittgensteinian neo-behaviourism, therefore, really a brainchild of Wittgenstein himself, or it is the emergence of a cult of distorted Wittgensteinianism? Given that Wittgenstein himself was emphatic on the denial of any allegiance to behaviourism, I should think that the so-called W-theoretic account of sensation-semantics is a pernicious distortion of the legacy of Wittgenstein. Unlike the neo-behaviourist, Wittgenstein is acutely aware of the "inner" story of the meaning of "pain" as much as he is eager to delineate the "outer" story concerning the public context of private pain as providing the semantic locus of the word.

A something about which nothing could be said

Consider the following remark that Wittgenstein imagines his adversary making towards him:

> "But you will surely admit that there is a difference between pain-behaviour accompanied by pain and pain-behaviour without any pain?" — Admit it? What greater difference could there be? — And yet you again and again reach the conclusion that the sensation itself is a *nothing* (*ibid., Section 304*).

Here the adversary is imagined to react to Wittgenstein on the suspicion that his (Wittgenstein's) externalist semantic construal of "pain" dismisses any connection of this word with the private *feeling* of pain, and keeps the necessary connection confined to pain-behaviour alone. To this reaction he then responds with a cryptic and enigmatic disclaimer:

> Not at all. It is not a *something*, but not a *nothing* either!

This apparently is a paradoxical disclaimer that demands a close interpretative attention. While it has been categorically denied that there is nothing like a phenomenological content — a raw feel — that attaches to sincere pain-behaviour, it has also been added expressly that this subjectively real content is not *a* something. It is the latter disclaimer that is really enigmatic. Perhaps some light is thrown upon the whole problem by the immediately next remark with which Wittgenstein continues to complete the assertion:

> The conclusion was only that a nothing would do just as well as a something about which nothing could be *said* (emphasis added).

The implication in the last remark is that there is something real — the pain-sensation sandwiched between stimuli and responses — but this reality, considered as detached from the physical context of stimuli and responses, is as good as *no* reality at all inasmuch as it remains unsaid *in principle*. Any attempt to talk about it in its contextually detached condition would be thwarted by the constraint of inter-subjective communication. Even though the *feeling* of pain itself, conceived of independently of the antecedent condition of bodily damage and the consequent condition of behavioural manifestation, is a robust reality from the first-person standpoint of the sufferer, it is in itself *virtually nothing* when considered from the third-personal standpoint of the members of the community of inter-communicative language-users, including the sufferer. The implication here is that nothing that has irreducibly first-personal reality and is conceived entirely independently of its natural place in the nexus of publicly accessible context can be of any substantive use in the business of linguistic communication.

Of course something that is *virtually* nothing is not necessarily *actually* nothing. The context-independent reality of pain is undeniably something, but Wittgenstein insists that it would be an error of logical grammar to construe this reality on the model of the reality of physical objects. A physical object is rightly countable as *a* something in that it can be named and referred to by the use of that name, and the designative-referential link between the name and the object is accessible to grasp from the third-personal point of view. And it is a condition of communication that wherever there is a link between "object and designation," the link is inter-subjectively open to grasp. It is in this sense that the model of being "a something" conforms to the logical grammar of physical objects — which is the grammar of "object and designation" in Wittgenstein's words. Wittgenstein thus concludes his argument aimed at assuaging the sceptical worry of his adversary: "We have only rejected the grammar [of "object and designation"] which tries to force itself on us here."

What alternative construal of the reality of pain is called for? What would the significantly different grammar of "pain" be as contrasted with the grammar of, say, "football?" David Pears seems to me to have provided us with an ingenious interpretation of Wittgenstein's construal of sensations *vis-ā-vis* our talk of sensations. The reason why, according to Pears, a sensation is not to be counted as *a* something is that "a sensation is part of the sufferer, because he does not sit back and take it in like a spectacle, but lives through it" (1987, p. 50). This "living through" of sensations by the sufferers explains why sensations "cannot be treated as detached apparitions on an inner screen." There is a "fusion" of the sensation with the sufferer, which is why it would be wrong to count the sensation as *a* something to which the sufferer stands in an internal world, analogous to the way a subject stands to the football he sees lying on the ground in the external world.

How is the sensation to be described so that the description fits into the communicative framework of language? Pears's ingenious suggestion, which takes the form of an innovative description, is that it should be construed as "a spreading structure, with its roots in the stimulus and its ramifications in the subject's responses" (*ibid.*). What this description is intended to do is capture the "narrow" phenomenological reality of sensations in the "wider" non-phenomenological (physical) setting in which the experience of a sensation occurs, and with which the experience is non-contingently tied up. It actually is a redescription of sensation as a "spread-out structure" of which the middle part is phenomenological, while the two outer ends are parts of physical reality. This redescription avoids the introspectionist's predicament of having to construe a sensation as a kind of inner object detached from outer reality and hence condemned to epistemic privacy and linguistic incommunicability.

With the above redescription of sensation Pears articulates the important point that we can make reference to a sensation of pain (or pleasure) only in the physical setting (of stimuli and responses) on which it depends. This he thinks is the point that Wittgenstein is trying to drive home in so many ways: "All that he is trying to get rid of is pain construed as something completely detached from all physical criteria" (1988, p. 350). This means that Wittgenstein is not only trying to avoid going on the mistaken way that the behaviourist takes, but also the equally mistaken path of the introspectionist. Surely a sensation of pain is a reality additional to the reality of pain-behavioural phenomena, but *talking* about pain, and therefore *referring* to pain, is possible only when we "visualize" the reality of pain as structurally hooked on to pain-inflicting stimuli and pain-behavioural expression.

When it comes to referring to physical objects and their properties, it is not necessary to make any reference to the background contexts of those objects and their properties. This is because physical objects stand out from their background and endure, and thereby they become amenable to independent, context-free reference. But context-free reference to sensations and their properties is not possible because they do not stand out as "objects" detached from their "roots" in stimulating conditions and their "ramifications" in behavioural responses. The "roots and ramifications" of sensations are an integral part of the conditions of adequacy for reference to them. Not being able to recognize this condition of adequacy for talk about or reference to sensations is failing to identify the correct "grammar" of the language of sensations.

Inside and Outside the Limits of Language

Despite Pears's impressive interpretative gloss on the enigmatic remark of Wittgenstein's discussed above, there still lingers the suspicion whether the so-called "context-bound" reference to pain satisfies the condition of a true definition of pain. If what the word "pain" really means has to do with the *essence* of pain, and the essence of pain consists in the inner phenomenological content — the raw feel of hurtfulness — that lies in between the outer contexts of stimuli and responses, then something is surely amiss if the reference of "pain" is inevitably bound to latch on to the outer context. It is as though the referential apparatus of language is inherently incapable of reaching beyond the external circumstances of pain, while pain itself is confined to an internal region enclosed by physical boundaries that are boundaries of language as well. Given the limits of language demarcated by external physical boundaries, it would seem that the real essence of pain is something that falls outside the limits of language, while what comes within the limits of language is not quite the real thing but only its "roots and ramifications." And what the sufferer feels has intrinsic subjective properties that cannot be captured by any physical criteria drawn from the outer regions of the boundary line.

Is language, then, doomed to fail to negotiate with the inner reality of pain, which in turn is to be acknowledged as an ineffable phenomenon of the human condition? Do we really end up referring to the "roots and ramifications" of pain when we actually intend to refer to pain itself? These questions arise because the foregoing discussion does not seem to have laid to rest the problem of how the true semantic link between "pain" and pain is established. Whatever might be the general internal constraints of language and communication, it is unquestionable that the ordinary, commonsensical meaning of "pain" is a hurtful inner state irrespective of what stimulating condition and response behaviour might constitute its outer periphery. It is in conformity with this commonsensical intuition that Galen Strawson argues that unless the meaning of "pain" transcends the public circumstances in which mastery of this word is standardly transmitted, the word "pain" would fail to mean what it is intended to mean, namely "a certain kind of unpleasant sensation, considered entirely independently of any of its behavioural or publicly observable causes and effects" (p. 245).

Strawson admits the Wittgensteinian point that understanding the meaning of "pain" involves mastering the technique of using the word appropriately. And learning how to use the word would require having recourse to public circumstances of stimuli and responses. But the word's latching on to public circumstances of cause and effect in the process of learning how to use it is only *instrumental* to the semantics of "pain." Dependence on public circumstances in the process of mastering the rules of application of the word is to be understood as an inevitable, but subsequently dispensable, *modus operandi* that culminates in the word's assuming its true meaning. Strawson writes:

> The word "pain" kicks away the ladder of the publicly observable circumstances that allow it to get going, and takes on its actual meaning as a word that refers only to experiences — yours, mine, theirs — that are entirely private (p. 246).

Once the word actually gets going on the rails of language, it no longer needs to depend on the crutch of publicly observable setting. Thenceforth, the word is invested with public-context-free semantic life.

It is not that Pears has nothing to say about this "transcendence" of dependence on public circumstances. He does say something that is quite analogous to Strawson's assertion:

> After it [i.e. the use of the word "pain"] has been mastered, it operates with an independence from external world that appears to be complete, and it strikes us as the paradigm of an internalized sector of language (1988, p. 344).

The "post mastery" independence of the use of "pain" from any reference to outward criteria seduces one (namely, the solipsist and the classical phenomenalist) into the mistaken belief that, even while learning the meaning of "pain" the word has the same independence from the external world. Against this illusion Pears states the truth:

> The truth is that this impressively independent linguistic competence can be achieved by someone who starts by exploiting the connections between sensations and the external world. It is a language with an internal field of

> application but though it is not learned at the interface between body and the external world, it does owe its development to something that happens there (*ibid.*).

Two distinct semantic facts seem to have come to light from the foregoing discussion. One (call it the *external* semantic fact) is the fact of *learning* how to use the word "pain" with the support of publicly observable concomitants of the experience of pain. The other (call it the *internal* semantic fact), subsequent, fact is that of the word "pain" taking on its true *meaning* without requiring any public-criterial support. Pears's gloss on the internal semantic fact about the word "pain," or about pain-talk, is that the language of pain (or sensation in general) has "an internal field of application." This semantic fact is "internal" in that it belongs to "an internalized sector of language," as Pears puts it. I think what this characterization means is that the word "pain" finds its external-context-free application directly to the inner state of hurtful feeling and thereby means just that feeling, quite independently of external cause and effect.

Presumably Wittgenstein's own discourse on the semantics of sensation language lays greater emphasis on the former semantic fact and says hardly anything explicitly on the latter fact. Pears's discussion, I think, seems to suggest that a deeper and extended reflection on what Wittgenstein is trying to say in so many ways should, in addition to the former fact, also bring to light the latter semantic fact. But the latter is not an *independent* semantic fact, because the semantic link between "pain" and the *inner* state of pain could not be grasped by someone who does not go through the initial process of learning the use of "pain" by linking it to the *outer* circumstances of pain.

It is at this juncture that Strawson's contention on the semantics of "pain" becomes worthy of critical deliberation. For Strawson the only genuinely semantic fact about "pain" is the internal semantic fact, and the so-called external semantic fact is actually about a "pre-semantic" mechanism unavoidably made use of in acquiring the meaning of the word. Since the pre-semantic mechanism has an extraneous role to play, it cannot be part of the semantics of "pain." The language of pain and other sensations therefore has only the "internal field of application." In other words, the word "pain" applies only to a publicly unobservable inner state of hurtful feeling. And yet, the word that has only the internal field of application is very much part of the common language in which we intercommunicate our private experiences of pain. What, then, is the basis of the possibility of the word "pain" having an inter-subjective meaning, or intercommunicative use in language, given that what it means is an *intra*-subjective, private state of ours?

Semantic Attunement to Common Affective Humanity

Strawson's answer to the question mentioned above is that "the possibility of our possessing the word "pain" that we actually do possess . . . is fundamentally grounded in the simple fact of the existence of a certain sort of interpersonal congruence in the character of our (private) experience — in something quite independent of any facts about behaviour," namely the fact that we all have experiences that are hurtful (p. 243). That is, the common *semantic* fact of our pain-talk is supervenient upon the common *metaphysical* (or ontic) fact of our having private experiences of a hurtful quality. It is, in other words, an ontological truth about us and creatures like us, that individual members of these species *share* the ontic plight of experiencing hurtful feelings that are entirely private. Indeed, "*the* PRIVATE *experience of pain is itself (and specifically as private) a fact of* COMMON *experience*" (*ibid*, emphasis original). This private experience of pain is said to be a "fundamentally given fact" that we access with our talk of pain.

Apparently this argument is somewhat perplexing because we are likely to be intrigued by the acclaimed combination of a fact about *private* experience with a fact of *common* experience. Usually one would find the phrase "common private experience" to be an oxymoron: one would think that privacy and commonality are exclusive of each other. However, Strawson claims that his argument is in conformity with commonsense realism about pain-talk. If commonsense realism about the language of pain — involving the belief that "pain" means something entirely inner and private, and something that is believed to be true of *all* of us — is far from being counterintuitive, then it follows that the alleged fact of "common *private* experience" is no more perplexing than the platitudinous fact of "common *public* experience." There indeed are irreducibly first-personal, ontologically private, facts of common experience, much as there are third-personal, ontologically public, facts of shared experience. And commitment to the former species of facts, to the extent that this commitment is attested by commonsense realism, does not result in solipsism or phenomenalism. To enunciate this argument, Strawson adds:

> The publicly observable is not all that is shared among us. We are not only fundamentally similar in general observable physical form. We are also, no doubt, fundamentally similar in respect of the general character of our private experience. The reality of private experience is also something shared among us, in such a way as to be available to be talked about in the way it is (p. 245).

But how do we know, or establish, the alleged commonality of private experience that is supposed to underpin the common use of the word "pain" with unitary meaning? What support is drawn for the realist claim that we are internally, experientially similar to one another, given the fact that there can be no third-personal verification of an essentially first-personal fact? Strawson is candid in admitting that the *de facto* general, inter-personal congruence in the character of our private experiences of pain is beyond objective verification. It is held to be a "large, simple, immoveable, unprovable truth" (p. 234). Nevertheless, this verification-transcendent fact of similarity in our private experiential lives is not something we merely *believe* to be true, but "something we *know*, and so we have to think about *how it is possible*" (p. 247, emphasis added).

The last statement above is a clear indication of a transcendental argument. It is said that we *do* know, without any confirmation by objective verification, that we are fundamentally similar in respect of our pain-experiential inner lives. If indeed this is so, then there must be conditions for the possibility of this knowledge. Strawson does not set himself to an investigation of this transcendental argument. No suggestions are therefore made with regard to what these conditions might be. However, he seems to be pointing, unwittingly perhaps, to something quite important and pertinent to the issue in question when he adds: "We know it before we begin to do philosophy, and we know it again when we close our books, even if philosophy has made us doubt it in between" (*ibid.*). Evidently, what this last remark implies is that this knowledge of ours is pre-philosophical and hence *pre-theoretical*.

If our knowledge about inter-personal pain-experiential similarity is pre-theoretical, then the conditions for the possibility of this knowledge must lie in some pre-theoretical *belief* that is deeply ingrained in us conceived of as conscious agents of a human community. I think that there is such a belief, and it is a belief about, what I would like to describe as, our *common affective humanity*. It is part of our being conscious, socially interactive agents, with individual lives of affective experiences, that we view one another as human subjects who are, in respect of our affective subjectivity, *mirror images* of one another. Although as distinctly individuated embodied subjects each one of us is "impenetrable" or subjectively non-transparent to the other, we still believe that we are actually quite transparent to one another in respect of the general character of our internal and private affective subjectivity.

There is, of course, a question that forces itself on what I have said above. It concerns our *embodiment* and the subjectivity that, as it were, inhabits it. How is it that the enclosure of embodiment that individuates us as spatially distinct persons does not actually render us subjectively impenetrable to one another? If we were pure spirits or Cartesian souls, there would have been no question of doubting the possibility of inter-personal subjective transparency. Since we in fact are not such spirits or souls, the fact of transparency is not obvious enough to need no explanation.

It seems to me that this problem — which is part of the general problem of *other minds* — is so complex and deep that it would be most difficult to arrive at an adequate explanation. But I think that any attempt to tackle this problem would have to address itself to the actual character of the phenomenon of inter-personal relation at the level of affective inter-communication. What I mean is the character of the human *"form of life"* within which our affective experiences are in fact shared in an environment of inter-subjective transparency. We need to apprise ourselves of the real "shape" of this form of life and thereby seek an understanding of the possibility of transparency despite the impression of opacity caused by our embodiment.

In a typical situation of inter-personal affective communication, a person approaches another person with a gesture of affective concern — sympathy, for instance — on the belief that the other is in a state of sorrow. The other person responds to the gesture of sympathy with another gesture that is appropriate to the context in which the sympathy is expressed. The sympathizer understands the communicative response because the response is in accord with the expectation and anticipation of the sympathizer. There is then a further response, on the part of the sympathizer, to the response of the person sympathized with, as an acknowledgement of a successful affective communication between the two persons. The gestures of response on both sides fit the expectation and anticipation of either of the interlocutors. In this way, the entire situation of inter-communication of private affective states or attitudes seems to complete a kind of "hermeneutic circle." Perhaps this kind of a hermeneutic circle uniquely characterizes the form of life that is a testimony to genuine affective inter-subjective transparency.

It is not that, when we enter into such hermeneutic circles as fellow participants, we *infer* the presence of affective states in others of the kind we ourselves experience *on the basis of* external responsive gestures that are in accord with our expectations and anticipations. Our firm belief that others are in states affectively similar in kind to our own states is not inferentially acquired through observable responses. In point of fact, we *already* have this belief in such a way that we do not persist in a state of doubting whether the other person is really in an affective state *until* we secure confirmation in terms of objective manifestation of expected responses. We do not wait for these gestures of response to establish the truth of our belief. Rather, these responsive gestures are palpable expressions of our *embodied subjectivity* that *structure* our interpersonal affective form of life. The truth of our belief does not rest on these objective expressions. On the contrary, the validity of these expressions presupposes the truth of our belief.

What is the nature of the relation between our individualized, embodied subjectivity on the one hand, and our humanity constituted of these individual embodied subjects on the other? I think there is something important in the nature of this relation that speaks for the possibility of inter-personal affective transparency. It is true that our embodiment makes each of us individual subjects, or agent-selves, spatially separated from one another. However, I contend that the enclosure of embodiment that individuates the agent-self does not have the consequence of making each agent-self an *island of subjectivity* in the ocean of humanity. Because, the ocean of humanity is made up of a type of subjectivity that permeates every embodied agent-self, and that also finds its unimpeded expression even through the enclosure of embodiment. When affective experiences and attitudes of fellow members of humanity find public expression, verbal as well as non-verbal, we fellow sympathizers do not take such expressions as *symbolic representations* of affective states. We rather cognize the affective states of other persons more directly *in* the expressive gestures. It is, for example, the inner agony itself that we "perceive" in perceiving the harrowing cry of the fellow sufferer.

Human *fellowship* is a significant indicator of what is being suggested above. Our capacity for non-symbolic *direct apprehension* of the affective experiences of other fellow human members is perhaps *innate*, and the truth of this cognition is unprovable because of its innateness. The directness of this cognition would also imply that it "penetrates" the enclosure of embodiment that spatially separates us one from another. But — and this is the pivotal point of importance — the objective physical separateness between any two of us is, as it were, neutralized by *subjective unity* at the level of experiences that are kind-identical across individual subjects. Our common humanity is sustained by this unity of experiential subjectivity, and our affective form of subjectivity is a central part — perhaps the core — of our common humanity.

I now want to submit the claim that the belief in our common affective humanity is tacit and deeply entrenched in our attitude towards other human beings as well as in our relations with others. So, when we use affective terms, like "sad" or "pain," in ascribing affective states of sadness or pain to another person, we take these terms to be directly referring to, and meaning, those inner states, even though the referents of these terms are unobservable and private because of being intra-subjective to the other person. The affective states referred to by these terms are internal to a *different* circle of subjectivity that is circumscribed by the enclosure of embodiment. In this sense, these states are external to *our* own circles of subjectivity. Nonetheless, the affective states of another circle of subjectivity are not quite outside our cognitive reach. Because any circle of subjectivity, whether that of ours or of others, is really identifiable within the unitary overall space of human subjectivity that constitutes what I have called our common affective humanity.

One vital point still remains obscure behind the metaphor of "unitary overall space of human subjectivity," and this point is the question, raised earlier, of how the enclosure of individual embodiment does not render us subjectively invisible to one another. Strawson's contention, that we are fundamentally similar in respect of our subjective experiences much as we are so in respect of objective physical constitution, seems to me to espouse a rather strong type of dualism of the subjective and the objective, the private and the public, and thus it leaves the original problem dangling. While I think that the spirit of this dualism is quite right, the dualism needs to be reconstrued in "lighter" terms. The reason why we know that we are fundamentally similar in subjective experiential respect is that our objective physico-behavioural expressions are an *undetached,* though significantly different, part of the experiences we undergo. These two aspects — the subjective and the objective — are in a single *continuum;* that is, there is no Cartesian divide between the two. Unless we have any good reason to believe that what we see as another person manifesting pain behaviour of a certain type is actually a robot, we *do* see that she is in pain *in* noticing her pain-behavioural expression. And our common physical make-up, our common physiology, that underlies our common expressive patterns of pain-behaviour, also sustains the qualitatively common subjectivity of our individual experiences of pain.

Conclusion

When Wittgenstein talks about the "mental object" of pain dropping out of consideration as irrelevant to the semantic essence of "pain," this talk must be interpreted as having reference to the mental object construed as something ontologically *sui generic* subjective counterpart of its objective behavioural counterpart. This is perhaps a Cartesian metaphysical fiction about subjective states that forms the shadowy basis of the private language argument. But the rejection of this fiction is hardly a definitive reason for preferring a neo-behaviourist semantic externalist turn that downplays the subjective counterpart altogether in defining the meaning of "pain." There is a non-Cartesian way of construing the reality of pain-experiential subjectivity that makes it an undetached aspect of a genuine pain-behavioural expression. On this construal, the inner content of pain phenomenology is the subjective end of a continuum of which the object end is the outer dimension of behaviour. Hence, the spirit of semantic internalism is duly imbibed by a theory that allows us to say that "pain" refers to the subjective content of a state which is *ontically* tied up with its objective behavioural counterpart.

Bibliography

Hacker, P.M.S., (1986), *Insight and Illusion: Themes in the Philosophy of Wittgenstein*, second edition (Oxford: Clarendon Press).

Pears, David (1987), *The False Prison*, Volume I (Oxford: Clarendon Press).

———, (1988), *The False Prison*, Volume II (Oxford: Clarendon Press).

Strawson, Galen (1994), *Mental Reality* (Cambridge, MA: Harvard University Press).

Wittgenstein, Ludwig (1953), *Philosophical Investigations*, ed. E. Anscombe (Oxford: Basil Blackwell).

2

Thinking Without Words
A Possibility Or A Myth?*

Amita Chatterjee

1

Cognitive Science is no longer concerned merely with the high-level activities of human beings. Studies of ever-increasing number of species and ever-earlier stages of humans are being included within its ambit. In the western tradition, right from the days of Thomas Aquinas, non-human animals were thought to be devoid of soul. When Descartes replaced the earlier notion of soul with the mind, animals were equally deprived of mind. In the medieval Europe, animals were thought to possess no soul because they didn't have the capacity of ratiocination, though they were said to be endowed with several other capacities. Descartes, on the other hand, equated animals with automata, having no speech and hence no mind or thought. He proved by abductive reasoning (the process

---

* Research for this paper was partly funded by the UGC Scheme of the University with Potential for Excellence. I had the opportunity of presenting the first draft of this article when I was invited by the Department of Philosophy, Central University of Hyderabad as a Visiting Fellow. I was immensely benefited by the comments of the faculty members who were present in my lectures. I express my indebtedness to all of them. Special thanks are due to my colleague Ms. Maushumi Guha for carefully reading the entire manuscript.

of inferring, from certain phenomena, the best explanation of those phenomena) that if a creature is born human, there is no escape from language (speech) and if, on the other hand, a creature is not born human, then there is no entry into language (speech). Descartes holds that human speech behaviour cannot be predicted or explained from bodily clues. Speech expresses thought and therefore speech must be explained by appeal to the mind. Non-human animals do not have any speech hence we need not ascribe mind to them. Thus in the hands of Descartes speech became a human-centric faculty.[1] Under the Cartesian influence, therefore, all animal actions were thought to be capable of being explained in terms of physical laws, innate releasing mechanisms, sensory-motor schema or classical and instrumental conditioning. Recently, however, cognitive ethologists and animal psychologists have drawn our attention to the fact that some complex animal behaviours cannot be explained mechanically. If we are not ready to grant thinking capacity to dumb animals, we simply fail to explain animal behaviour satisfactorily. Side by side, many developmental psychologists point out, as opposed to the Piagetian theory of cognitive development that pre-linguistic infants behave like little scientists processing, testing and fine-tuning their theories of the physical world. All these new findings have led philosophers and cognitive scientists to review the relation between thought and language. In this

---

1. This was not the perception of the Indian theorists. In the *Ṛgveda* we find the Goddess Speech speaks thus: I move with the *Rudras* and the *Vasus*, with the *Ādityas* and all the gods . . . the one who eats, who truly sees, who breathes, who hears what is said, does through me. Listen what I tell you should be heeded . . . I gave birth to the father on the head of this world . . . I am the one who blows like the wind, embracing all creatures. Beyond the earth, beyond the sky, so much have I become in my greatness. . ., translated by D. O'Flaherty, Penguin Classics, Penguin, London, 1981, p. 26.

article I propose to present a critical survey of the representative views on the relation between thought and language and examine the issue of the possibility of thinking without words from an inter-disciplinary perspective.

2

Both "thought" and "language" have been used in various different senses. So at the outset I must lay down, albeit tentatively, in what sense we are going to use these two words. Thinking is a kind of mental state, which includes believing, knowing, desiring, fearing, etc. and contents of such states are called thoughts. Language is a system of arbitrary as well as conventional symbols — spoken or written, iconic or non-iconic. Any language has a syntactic and a semantic side and these features distinguish a language from a very efficient signalling system. Consider for a moment the non-verbal communication system of dogs. There is nothing arbitrary about their means of communication since all signs in this system are directly related to their meaning, e.g., a snarl means aggression, a wagging tail means happiness, etc. There is some amount of arbitrariness in the communication system of vervet monkeys. They use different warning calls to alert their conspecifics about different types of predators, e.g., a "chutter" for snakes, a "chirp" for leopards and a "kraup" for eagles.[2] But monkeys use these signs only in the presence of predators. They do not use these for small talk or pleasant conversation in the parties. That is, these signs will not mean anything if dissociated from particular contexts. Honeybees' signalling system, however, is much more efficient because honeybees use certain signals to communicate over time and distance. When a honeybee returns to a hive after locating some distant food source, it dances a particular type of dance consisting of

---

2. See *Cognitive Psychology And Its Implications*, Sixth Edition, John R. Anderson, Worth Publishers, New York, 2004.

a straight run followed by a turn and circle to the left and so on. The length of the run indicates the distance of the food source and the direction of the run relative to the vertical axis indicates the direction of the food source relative to the sun. Though signals used by bees are characterised by arbitrariness and also the feature of displacement in time and space, their signalling system lacks one of the important marks of natural language, viz. productivity. Productivity of any language is due to its discrete units, which can be combined to produce infinite number of phrase structures to mean infinite number of situations. It is this productivity resulting from compositionality of symbols that distinguishes human language from the communicating system of any other social species. Thought and language thus explained, we are now ready for a discussion on the relation between them.

3

The question of the relation between thought and language has been addressed from so many different perspectives that it is almost impossible to provide the reader with an exhaustive field-guide. I shall therefore take up a strategic short cut. Since the main issue facing us here is the possibility of thought without language, I shall begin by sketching the possible contentions of the opponents: (a) thought is reducible to language and (b) language is necessary for thought.

It is well known that the behaviourists held the extreme reductionist position mentioned above. While explaining away human thought within the stimulus-response paradigm, Watson identified thought with sub-vocal speech, i.e., thinking is just talking to oneself. When deaf-mute children were presented as counter-instances to his theory, Watson extended his thesis and said that humans think with their whole body and hence thought is to be identified with some other muscle, if not with the vocal cord. In support of his thesis he provided the evidence that deaf mutes actually use sign language when they dream and this, Watson thought, was proof enough to establish that thought is reducible to some kind of language. When the behaviourist influence was on the wane after ruling the world of American psychology for more than three decades, some crucial experiments were performed to refute the Watsonian thesis that thought is either implicit speech or some motor activity. Smith, Brown, Toman and Goodman conducted one such experiment in 1947. Smith offered himself as the subject whose entire muscle system was paralysed by using a curare derivative. Smith was put on an artificial respirator and it was absolutely impossible for him to use any of his body muscles. But even in that state, Smith could observe what was happening around him, comprehend speech of others, understand the implications of his observations and remember everything. This shows that thought is not to be identified with any motor activity rather it is an internal non-motor activity.

Cognitive psychologists offered other experiments to disprove Watson's theory. J.S. Sachs[3] (1967) made the following experiment on semantic memory. Subjects listened to paragraphs on various topics, such as Galileo's work on the telescope. After a little time gap, they were presented with the following four sentences and were asked to identify the sentence that they heard before.

1. He sent a letter about it to Galileo, the great Italian scientist.
2. He sent Galileo, the great Italian scientist, a letter about it.
3. A letter about it was sent to Galileo, the great Italian scientist.

3. "Recognition memory for syntactic and semantic aspects of connected discourse," *Perception and Psychophysics* 2, pp. 437-42.

4. Galileo, the great Italian scientist, sent him a letter about it.

The actual sentence that was read to the subjects was 1. When asked to identify the sentence they had heard before most subjects failed to point at 1. None of the subjects confused 4 with 1. But they were unsure about 2 and 3.They frequently thought that they heard either 1 or 2 or 3. Thus under the conditions of Sach's experiment subjects could remember the meaning of the sentences without remembering its linguistic form. So it was surmised that the meaning was represented in an underlying non-linguistic form that could be translated in a variety of linguistic paraphrases. Hence thought may be identified at least with some abstract, non-verbal propositional code.

Cognitive psychologists also mentioned patients with Williams' syndrome (who do not have any language), purposeful behaviour of non-verbal animals and pre-linguistic children as counter-evidences to behaviourist reductionism.

Let us now consider the second counter-position (b): language is necessary for thought. This thesis, contrary to its appearance, is open to a large number of interpretations some of which are mentioned below:

1. Language is necessary for communicating thought
2. Language is necessary for understanding or facilitating thought
3. Language is necessary for thinking as such, i.e., language is constitutive of thought
4. Language is necessary for all kinds of thought for all kinds of beings
5. Language is necessary for all kinds of thought for some kinds of beings

6. Language is necessary for some kinds of thought for all kinds of beings
7. Language is necessary for some kinds of thought for some kinds of beings
8. Language is conceptually necessary for thought
9. Language is metaphysically necessary for thought
10. Language is naturally necessary for thought
11. Some formal language is necessary for thought
12. Some internal language is necessary for thought
13. Some natural language is necessary for thought.

Some of these interpretations require a bit of explanation. Interpretation 1 is known as the communicative conception of language. This interpretation concedes that thought may be independent of language. Language is necessary only for expressing and communicating thought. Interpretation 2 is popular with the mentalists like Edmund Husserl and John Searle. Both of them think that intentionality is the mark of the mental states, hence of thinking too. But to understand the nature of thought/consciousness, they have used natural language as a heuristic device. Searle, for example, explains the nature of intentional mental states by using the analogy of speech acts. Interpretation 3 is called by Carruthers[4] the cognitive conception of language. On this interpretation natural language is constitutively involved in our thought. Interpretation 8 implies that the concept of natural language is involved in the concept of thought. Therefore it is inconceivable that creatures without language can have "thought" in the true sense of the term. Whoever wants to

4. Peter Carruthers, *Language, Thought and Consciousness*, Cambridge University Press, Cambridge, 1996.

explain the notion of thought must explain it by invoking the notion of natural language. Later Wittgenstein, Donald Davidson, Michael Dummett are amongst the illustrious exponents of some version of this interpretation. Interpretation 9 highlights the fact that the nature of human thinking is such that it cannot but essentially involve natural language in all possible worlds. Such a conception of necessity is prevalent in Kripke and Putnam. The claim involved in the interpretation 10 is weaker than that of the ninth interpretation. It only asserts that the nature of thought being what it is, language is essentially implicated in thought in all such worlds, which resemble the actual world in their initial conditions. Carruthers claims such a naturally necessary connection between human thought and natural language.

The alternative interpretations mentioned above may be combined with one another to generate historically representative positions. Take, for example, Frege's view: *Begriffsschrift* is metaphysically necessary for understanding/grasping all kinds of human thought — which we can get by combining 2, 5, 9 and 11. On the other hand, Fodor's view that Mentalese is naturally necessary for all kinds of thinking as such for all kinds of beings can be obtained from the following combination — 3, 4, 10 and 12; Carruthers' view that some natural language is naturally necessary for some kinds of thinking as such for some kinds of beings is obtainable from the combination of 3, 7, 10 and 13. In the next few sections I propose to discuss in brief the views of Frege, Davidson, Fodor and Carruthers to have a better grasp of the debate because though their take-off point is the same, they have tackled the issue from different angles.

4

No discussion into the nature of thought can be pursued without referring to Frege's theory,[5] though apparently it is irrelevant for the issue at hand. While we have been interested in the role of thought, as the content of a mental state, Frege's theory is out and out anti-psychological. Yet as a strong counterpoint it may suggest how to deal with non-linguistic thought.

To Frege, thought is nothing but the sense of an assertoric sentence. He identifies thought with proposition. Thought, in this theory, does not arise as a result of a psychological process, say, thinking. Rather in the psychological process of thinking a thinker gets related to a thought, which has a mind-independent existence. Thought in this theory, therefore, is not subjective but objective and ahistorical. Thoughts exist in a third realm — neither in the physical world like material objects nor in the mental world like ideas. Like ideas these are non-amenable to external senses; like material objects these are mind-independent. The Pythagorean Theorem, for example, can exist independently of any mind; it holds even if nobody ever knows it. Thoughts thus have a necessary and space-time transcendent existence. Relations that obtain amongst thought, viz. inconsistency, entailment, etc. — all are logical and hence mind-independent.

Is language necessary for grasping thought or is it just a contingent tool? Frege holds that thought may be mind-

---

5. For understanding Frege' View I have consulted the following articles and books. (i) "Thoughts," Frege (1918), tr., P. Geach and R.H. Stoothoff in B. Mcguiness (ed.) *Collected Papers on Mathematics, Logic and Philosophy*, Blackwell, Oxford, 1984. (ii) *Frege: Philosophy of Language*, M. Dummett, Duckworth, London, 1973. (iii) *Frege and Other Philosophers*, M. Dummett, Oxford University Press, Oxford, 1991. (iv) "Language and Communication," M. Dummett in A. George (ed.) *Reflections on Chomsky*, Blackwell, Oxford, 1989.

independent but understanding language is necessary for understanding thought. Thought is inherently structured and this structure is isomorphic to the structure of a formal language, viz. the concept-script or *Begriffsschrift*. This language is a vehicle of our thought. Both from the explanatory and epistemological point of view thought is language-dependent but these two are not identical.

Frege had two modes of writing about sense — the first when he was concerned with the relation between sense and reference and the second — when he was invoking the mythology of the third realm in order to elaborate the ontological status of senses.

Frege's theory of thought has to be understood in its historical setting. He was against Brentano's psychology from an empirical standpoint. According to Brentano, any mental act is always to be considered as enjoying only mental inexistence, but represents the external object, if there is one. Brentano, however, maintained that the object of a mental act is intrinsic to the act, but insisted that it is external to the mind. "I intend to marry a woman" — a real woman, he says, in flesh and blood and not an *ens rationis.*

Frege tried to do away with the apparent inconsistency of Brentano's theory by admitting, three realms: the inner world — private to each individual; the external world of material objects which is objective; the world of thoughts and their constituent senses, which like the external world is accessible to all in common, but whose contents, though they are grasped by the human mind, are immaterial, immutable and causally inert.

Frege believed that it is possible in principle to grasp a thought otherwise than as expressed linguistically but his account of sense does not show how it is possible. The metaphor used in speaking of the structure of a thought relates to what is involved in grasping it. This idea has an obvious intuitive force: to grasp the thought that *239 is a prime number* requires possession of the concept of a prime number. Only when understanding the form of words used requires a grasp of what belongs to the structure of thought do these words express the thought. The structure of a sentence corresponds to the structure of thought it expresses. To grasp a thought is to have a particular way of conceiving what determines it as true, just as to grasp the thought expressed by a sentence is to have a particular way of conceiving what determines the sentence as true. There is a distinction between grasping a thought as being the sense of a particular sentence, and grasping a thought that happens to be expressed by that sentence, without necessarily recognising that the sentence has that sense.

Frege allowed that while thoughts are not mental contents, grasping a thought is a mental act directed towards something external to the mind. It is the sense that is the logical notion; grasping the sense of an expression is a psychological process. Since Frege was interested in the nature of sense, he never paid any attention to the psychological process of grasping a sense. Although sense is not a content of consciousness, a thought may be an object of conscious attention.

Frege accepted that thought is directly graspable in principle, though we generally grasp it via language. It is not intrinsic to thoughts to be expressed in language, but it is necessary for us, human beings, that a thought of which we are conscious is connected in our consciousness with one or another sentence. Human mind can handle complicated thoughts only when expressed in language; for we can attend to words without paying attention each time to all their senses. Grasping a sense, according to Frege, is not a practical skill but is a piece of knowledge.

Like all analytic philosophers, Frege has admitted priority of language over thought in the order of explanation. Since thoughts are not contents of consciousness, a thought requires a vehicle. The priority thesis contains no assumption that there is no such thing as languag-less thought. He only says that at present we do not know how to characterise thoughts of creatures devoid of language. Most unverbalised thought of an adult human is related to fully verbalised thought as a sketch to a finished picture; it can therefore be explained only in terms of that of which it is a sketch.

Frege's theory, therefore, belies our expectation. Though it grants the possibility of thought of non-linguistic creatures, it does not tell us how we can be sure of existence of thoughts where the putative thinkers are animals or children. Besides, Fregean thoughts, being inert, cannot have any causal role in explanation of apparently purported behaviours of creatures without language. We shall come back to this point later.

5

Donald Davidson,[6] in consonance with his general theory of mental states, explains the relation between thought and language by taking an interpretationalist stance. Admission and ascription of beliefs, desires and other thoughts to our fellow beings are necessary for explanation of their actions. Thought, says Davidson, can best be ascribed on the basis of others' speech behaviour. That is why he maintains that language is conceptually necessary for thought. Let me give a summary exposition of Davidson's theory as we find in his article, "Thought and Talk."

Davidson begins his article by categorically asserting that though thought and language are closely intertwined, neither

6. "Thought and Talk," D. Davidson, *Essays on Truth and Interpretation*, Oxford University Press, Oxford, 1980.

is reducible to the other. He upholds that desire, knowledge, belief, fear, etc. all are thinking states, being intentional and intensional. Belief, according to Davidson, is the paradigm of thought since all intentional states depend upon some belief state. A man usually has innumerable beliefs forming a network and the system of such beliefs identifies a thought by locating it in a logical and epistemic space. Having a language, maintains Davidson, consists largely in being able to speak and speaking plays an indirect part in thinking.

Having thus set the parameters of his discourse, Davidson puts forward his central interpretationalist thesis and arguments supporting it. Simply stated Davidson's thesis is: A creature cannot have thought unless it is an interpreter of the speech of another. So a speaker must be interpreter of others' speech. But why does Davidson think so? The reason can be explained as follows. An interpreter knows the conditions under which utterances of sentence are true, and often knows that if certain sentences are true, others must be. The pattern of relations among sentences is very much like the pattern of relations between thoughts. This parallel is an indicator of interdependence of thought and language, not primacy of any one. Intentional states are characterized by intensionality and that is why it is impossible to ascribe beliefs to others without any linguistic clue. Suppose a man shows his preference by choosing an apple when he is offered both an apple and a pear. But in fact he may be expressing a preference for what is on his right rather than what is on his left, what is red rather than what is yellow, what is seen first or judged more expensive. Repeated tests may make some readings of this man's actions more plausible than others. It, therefore, follows that attribution of belief, desire and other thoughts go hand in hand with the interpretation of speech and neither the theory of decision nor of interpretation can be successfully developed without the other.

Following Quine's paratactic analysis, Davidson also upholds that when a speaker attributes an attitude to a person what he does is ape or mimic an actual or possible speech-act of that person. If I affirm, "Jones believes that snow is white," my utterance of "snow is white" may have no actual utterance of Jones's to imitate. Still we could say what I affirm is that Jones would be honestly speaking his mind, were he to utter a sentence translating mine. Only someone with a language could have a thought because to have a thought would be to have a disposition to utter certain sentences with appropriate force under given circumstances.

But this is still no argument for the position that only creatures with speech can have a thought. For, when I say, "Jones believes that snow is white," I describe Jones's state of mind directly. Jones would honestly assert "snow is white" if he speaks English but that may be a state which a language-less creature could also be in. So language is not necessary for thought.

The argument that Davidson has offered to counter this point is relevant for the issue we are interested in. Davidson categorically states that a creature cannot have a belief **unless it has a concept of belief** and to have the concept of belief a creature must be a member of a linguistic community. Hence Norman Malcolm's dog, which chases the cat up the maple tree cannot have belief since it cannot have the concept of belief not being a member of a linguistic community. But what does it take to be a member of a linguistic community? Membership of a linguistic community depends on one's ability to interpret the utterances of the members of the group, and a method of interpretation is at hand if one has and knows one has a theory, which provides truth conditions for all sentences, a la Tarski. Of course, Davidson is not assuming that speakers never have false beliefs. What makes interpretation possible is the fact that we can dismiss *a priori* the chance of massive error. An effective method of interpretation enables an interpreter to count a sentence true just when the speakers hold it to be true. Without ruling out the possibility of error, a good theory of interpretation optimises the agreement between the speaker and the interpreter. Easy communication has survival value. A good theory of interpretation tries to optimise communication across linguistic communities.

Davidson has mentioned two general constraints within which any interpretation should operate. These he called (a) the principle of charity which says, "Try to make most of the subject's belief come out true" and (b) the principle of rationality which exhorts us to assume that the subject will act so as to maximise the expected utility. Adherence to these principles ensures that an interpreter will be able to determine the thoughts of the speaker in the long run from within the holistic network of the speaker's thoughts.

Let me sum up Davidson's position on thought and language. Someone cannot have a belief unless he understands the possibility of being mistaken and this requires grasping the contrast between truth and error, between true belief and false belief. But this contrast, thinks Davidson, can emerge only in the context of interpretation, which alone forces on us the idea of an objective, public truth. One may wonder what the role of language is in the whole scheme. Davidson says that language is not directly in the picture; it is a part of the frame. The notion of a true belief depends on the notion of a true utterance and this in turn is impossible without a shared language. It is evident that to Davidson having a thought exhausts in being interpretable in the light of a holistic web of beliefs. It, therefore, follows that creatures without language are also creatures without thoughts because mere non-linguistic behaviour cannot be a sufficient warrant for ascription of thought.

Peter Carruthers has offered two external criticisms against Davidson's position from the point of view of intentional realism. Carruthers questions the contention that one cannot have belief without having the concept of belief. It is one thing to say that we lack sufficient evidence to ascribe any particular desire or belief in the absence of linguistic behaviour, and quite another thing to say that belief etc. cannot exist in the absence of language. The latter, points out Carruthers, does not obviously follow from the former.

Since according to Davidson having thought is constituted merely by the fact that the subject is interpretable as acting out of belief-desire, Searle's Chinese Room objection[7] can be levelled against Davidson's thesis too. Some system may just pass the Turing Test by mimicking intelligent human behaviour; still the system may lack thought. That is why intentional realists believe that a thinking subject must also possess a suitable internal structure of interacting mental states and events. Davidson's anomalous monism, we all know, makes him anti-realist about mental states and events, though at the conceptual level he has refused to reduce thought to language.

6

Jerry Fodor[8] is probably the staunchest supporter of realism of internal states, contents of which we have branded as thoughts. Fodor's main argument in support of realism of internal states or propositional attitudes is derived from the

---

7. "Minds, Brains and Programs," John Searle, *The Behavioural and Brain Sciences*, vol. 3, 1980.

8. Fodor is a prolific writer so to understand Fodor one needs to consult at least his following works:

   (1)*The Language of Thought*, Harvard University Press, Cambridge, MA, 1975; (2) *Representations*, Harvard University Press, Cambridge, MA, 1981; (3) *Psychosemantics*, MIT Press, Cambridge, MA, 1987; (4) *A Theory of Content and Other Essays*, MIT Press, Cambridge, MA, 1990.

immense success of folk psychology. Huge explanatory and predictive success of human behaviour in terms of attribution of belief and desire to the agent makes realism about propositional attitude a highly plausible position. Surely, we would not have been so successful in predicting and explaining human behaviour, had our theory of human mind been largely incorrect.

Fodor's thesis can be best understood within the framework of the computational representational theory of mind (CRTM). In developing this theory he was equally influenced by the Church-Turing thesis of computation and Chomskyan linguistics. Theory of computation helped him to understand how syntactic manipulation of symbols accounts for the causal power of a symbol-manipulating system as well as preserves the semantic properties of the symbols. Following Chomsky he explains how linguistic processing is done on internal representations by virtue of possessing some innate culture-invariant syntactic principles. Fodor combined both these strands in his controversial theory.

Given that thoughts are contents of real internal states of the agent and these states causally interact with one another to produce further thoughts and behaviour, it is natural to ask how those thoughts are carried out and by what mechanism they interact. There may be two alternative theories: (a) imagist theory and (b) sententialist theory.

Imagist Theory: Thoughts consist of images only (mostly visual images in case of sighted persons) and interaction takes place by means of association (mostly learned) between those images. Many philosophers starting with John Locke endorsed this imagist position. In the modern times, the most important support for this view comes from none other than Albert Einstein. Einstein reported[9]:

---

9. As reported by K. Devlin in *The Math Gene*, Basic Books, New York, 2000, p.124.

> Words and language, whether written or spoken, do not seem to play any part in my thought process. The psychological entities that serve as building blocks for my thought are certain signs or images, more or less clear, that I can reproduce and combine at will.

Despite such a categorical account given by Einstein, we have to admit that the imagist theory is not without problems. The first problem is: not everything can be imaged. Second, no image carries even the content of such a simple thought, such as "All tangerines are orange." Besides, we have many concepts, especially functional concepts, which may be regularly associated with some images, but which do not represent them by virtue of those images.

The **sententialists,** therefore, uphold that the medium of thought is a sentence of some sort. Fodor's arguments for this position are as follows. According to the realist view of propositional attitudes, beliefs, desires, etc. interact with one another causally to produce behaviours in ways, which preserve their semantic content and semantic value. Propositional attitudes are systematic, productive and inferentially coherent like sentences. Hence the best hypothesis is to uphold that their nature is sentence-like and mental states are relations to such internal sentences, which are encoded in the neural structure of the brain in some distinctive way. For sentences have contents that are systematically determined by the contents of their component words, together with rules of combination. If we suppose in addition that the mind is so arranged as to effect computations on these sentences in some ways, which respect their syntax, then the causal role of the sentences will respect their semantic properties, for usually in case of a formal language syntax takes care of semantics. This thesis, however, is not sufficient to establish that internal sentences are sentences of a public natural language. Fodor forcefully argues that such sentences belong to an innate, universal language of thought, the Mentalese, and not any natural language. This internal language consists of an innate lexicon and an innate set of combinatorial rules for the production of completed sentences, held in common by all human beings, and perhaps by all creatures sharing the basic features of human psychology.

Fodor is not ready to admit that beliefs and desires are relations to sentences in a natural language, native to the believer or desirer because it cannot explain (1) how two persons belonging to two different linguistic communities may possess the same belief; (2) what should count as the identity condition of a belief. (For example, "The dog bit the man" and "The man was bitten by the dog" are two different natural language sentences, but do they express two beliefs? Obviously not. How are we then supposed to individuate beliefs? Will Frege's intuitive criterion help? Can we simply say that these two sentences have the same sense? Can we maintain by the same logic that "There are 9 planets" and "The number of planets is 2 larger than the smallest prime number larger than 5" stand for the same belief? No, because someone may commit calculating error and fail to realise that the content of these two sentences are the same; again the second sentence introduces a new concept of prime number, which was not a part of the sense of the first sentence. Fodor, therefore, claims that the only acceptable principle of individuation of belief is that sentences in question must both translate into the same sentence in the language of thought or the Mentalese). Besides, our language of thought must be an internal language encoded in the brain, for animals and pre-linguistic infants think, though they lack natural language.

Here intervenes Peter Carruthers and tries to establish that some human thought is necessarily carried out in some natural language though he does not deny that some of our thoughts may involve images too. Carruthers understands this necessity as natural necessity and distinguishes between two types of natural necessity. Accordingly he offers two theses. The weak thesis says: some human conscious thinking (viz. conscious propositional thinking) is such that, of natural necessity, it involves public language, in virtue of the given architecture of human cognition together with causal laws. The strong thesis may be formulated thus: Some human conscious thinking is such that, of natural necessity, it involves public language (in virtue of the given architecture of human cognition, together with causal laws); and necessarily, some of these propositional thoughts belong to types which (for us at least) constitutively involve such language. The weak thesis of Carruthers is not incompatible with Fodor's thesis. Though this point deserves elaborate discussion, I will just point out briefly why this is so. According to the modularity thesis of Chomsky and Fodor,[10] human beings have an innately structured language faculty, which is modular in nature and is governed by the rules inherent in the module. The modularity hypothesis also implies that information processing within the module is autonomous, since any module is informationally encapsulated. The language which is developed within this module and which is permitted by the innate structure of the module is a natural language. Human thinking, however, is carried out by the non-modular central system which is informationally unencapsulated. The language in which concepts are manipulated in the central system may be Mentalese, which can never be grasped through our introspection. But when results of these subpersonal processings are brought forward as conscious thought, these cannot but involve natural language. This explanation evidently requires that all our concepts must be duplicated both in a natural language and in the lexical items of the Mentalese. Such duplications are not at all required, if one upholds the

10. See *The Modularity of Mind, Jerry Fodor,* MIT Press, Cambridge, MA, 1983.

strong thesis suggested by Carruthers, since on this thesis many of our concepts are tied to their natural language expressions only. Carruthers, therefore, recommends the strong thesis on the ground of economy.[11]

7

Carruthers claims that his thesis can be supported by the findings of the cognitive scientists. So in this section my main task will be to see whether evidence from cognitive psychology can really establish Carruthers' theory. For the convenience of the reader, I have presented the arguments in favour of and arguments against Carruthers' thesis separately.

Let us begin with evidences from normal developments. It has been found that linguistic and cognitive abilities of young children develop together. If a child's language is advanced, so will be its ability across a range of tasks including the false belief task.

Con: Such data at the most reveals that language is a necessary condition for certain kinds of thinking but not that it is constitutively involved in thinking. These facts fit in well with the communicative conception of language too; since according to the latter, language is a necessary condition of normal enculturation.

Pro: But what if a child's language development often lags behind its conceptual and cognitive development? For example, an 18 month-old utters, "Mommy, shoes" to mean both "Those are Mommy's shoes" and "Mommy, put my shoes on." Though the baby can think two thoughts, it cannot express them in two different sentences.

Con: Such cases do not prove that thought is independent of language. Even Chomsky distinguishes between the ability

---

11. Carruther position has been delineated mainly depending on Carruthers (1996).

of language comprehension and the ability of language production. The child may not be able to produce two different sentences, yet the child definitely understands the difference.

Cognitive psychologists often put forward evidences from abnormal development to show that thought depends on language. We have heard about children reared by wolves, Jane strapped to a chair till the age of 13 in solitary confinement, congenitally deaf children using their own signing system to communicate. All lack natural language and show some abnormal cognitive development. One may argue that these are not sure proofs of thoughts depending on natural language. It only proves that normal cognitive development depends on enculturation and enculturation depends on the ability to communicate in some natural language. However, Carruthers suggests that if a congenitally deaf child, who is developmentally ready to acquire full-blown language (5-6 years), learns to sign extremely fast and thereafter display dramatic change in her cognitive ability, then that may count strongly in favour of the cognitive conception of language.

One may still object that language is necessary for acquisition of some concepts and modes of thinking without thereafter being necessarily implicated in those thinking. Hence Carruthers cannot uphold that language is necessarily involved in all conscious human thinking.

Even evidence from disorders like aphasia is not sufficient to establish Carruthers' theory and he was aware of that. Let me elucidate this point. Aphasic people are those who were previously normal but have lost their capacity for language due to some injury or stroke. Global aphasics are those whose production ability and comprehension ability are impaired. Though it is very difficult to devise non-linguistic tests of cognitive ability for global aphasics, cognitive psychologists have come up with some jigsaw puzzle-type tests by application of which they noted that in some severely global aphasics a variety of non-verbal cognitive abilities are quite well preserved. But how do we know that the ability in question is not language involving? Maybe, language faculty consists of three distinct sub-systems — production system, comprehension system and a linguistic ability system. A global aphasic may retain the last ability even when he is incapacitated in respect of the first two abilities. Chomsky (1995)[12] theorised that in addition to production and comprehension system, there is a distinct knowledge base, which underpins both the former systems. But this theory is yet to be fully verified.

So we regret to say that none of these evidences is conclusive.

Carruthers next offers evidence from introspection in favour of the thesis that inner thinking is mostly done in inner speech. Here too he relies mainly on data derived from cognitive psychologists.

Russ Hurlburt[13] (1990, 1993) devised a method for sampling people's inner experience. Subjects of Hurlburt wear headphones during the course of the day, through which they hear a randomly generated series of bleeps. When they hear a bleep, subjects are asked to "freeze" and report what was passing through their consciousness at that time. Although frequencies vary widely, all normal subjects report experiencing inner speech on more than half of the occasions sampled.

We often find ourselves thinking entirely in natural language, especially, when I meticulously consider the pros

---

12. Language — Natural Object, *Mind,* vol. 104, 1995; included in *New Horizons in the Study of Language and Mind,* Cambridge University Press, Cambridge, 2000.

13. *Sampling Normal and Schizophrenic Inner Experiences,* Plenum Press, 1990; *Sampling Inner Experience with Disturbed Effect,* Plenum Press, 1993.

and cons of a thesis. Though in many cases we introspect to employ a combination of natural language and mental images, in most cases there is some implicit sentential embedding.

Some people report that thought occurs in the form of different heard voices. Isaac (four-and-a-half year old), for example, reported, "I can hear myself speak in English." These considerations might entail that it is images of natural language sentences, which are the primary vehicle of our conscious thoughts. However, it is not the image as such which carries the content of thought but what is imaged, viz. a natural language sentence. This position is endorsed by the fact that very often in our discourses the multi-lingual thinkers shift from one natural language to another without any break in thought. If thought were not natural language-involving, and each piece of thought involved act of translation from one natural language to another, then there would have been felt hiatus between two expressed thoughts. But that does not happen.

Anti-introspectionists might correctly point out that we are not aware of all our thoughts. Hence introspective evidence can be cited only in favour of some of our episodic thoughts. That is, only some of our episodic thoughts involve natural language.

If my conscious thinking takes place in English, it does not take place in any other natural language or in a supposedly innate, universal symbolic system like the Mentalese. Here I cannot but intervene in favour of the Mentalese. If the language of thought hypothesis does not hold, smooth transition between thoughts involving two different natural languages becomes more difficult to explain.

Carruthers has anticipated and answered many more objections against the introspectionist position. I will mention some of them very briefly.

A thought fully determinate in content can surely occur to us in a flash without there being any time for any sentence expressing that thought to be formulated, and without any such sentence being introspectively accessible.

Without denying the possibility of lightning-like thought occurring in public speech as well as in private thinking, Carruthers strongly believes that even such thought involves natural language.

We do choose things without using any natural language. When a dress displayed in the right side of a big departmental store simply suits my taste and I pick it up ignoring everything else in the display windows, I do not seem to use a natural language at all. Carruthers thinks that such choices are mostly unconscious. On the other hand, our conscious choice cannot but involve natural language.

How are we supposed to account for various tip-of-the-tongue phenomena? Isn't thought here prior to natural language? There may be two alternative responses to this objection. Some may point out that in such a phenomenon, a determinate thought is present involving some other language. Or some may say that prior to its linguistic formulation there cannot be any determinate thought at all hence this is just an illusion.

Sometimes we are found to struggle while choosing between alternative natural language expressions to represent a thought. A plausible reply would be: what seems to be choosing between alternative words to express some prior thought is most probably choosing between two thoughts involving two expressions.

Creative thinkers often insist that their thinking is done without words. But in our creative enterprise two tiers might be involved. One tier may be of creative, non-discursive, non-conscious idea-generating tier and the second may be a judgmental, logical, discursive and consciously planned idea-assessing tier. According to Carruthers, the second tier must involve natural language.

The most problematic of all the cases, I think, is our metaphorical understanding. Suppose somebody says, "This young gentleman has a green mind," meaning thereby that his ideas are quite immature. Which of these concepts are tied to our natural language? Can it be the case that the thought has occurred in the Mentalese and has been given its public expression in a different natural language? Carruthers attempts to explain such metaphorical understanding without invoking the Mentalese. He says that the token occurrence of that thought has been inseparably bound up with its non-literal linguistic expression.

Introspective evidence has always been suspect in the post-behaviourist era. However, now cognitive psychologists are ready to grant that we are generally right about our introspection, according to which most of human conscious thinking involves some natural language. So, thinks Carruthers, to defend his LOT hypothesis, Fodor will have to prove that all our introspections are false. That is not an easily defensible position. I don't think that Fodor has much to worry about *vis-ā-vis* the arguments from introspection because Fodor has always claimed that the Mentalese operates in a sub-personal level and hence does not ever appear in our introspection or any form of conscious reflection. The strength of Fodor's claim lies elsewhere. Children all over the world have been found to acquire a mastery over a natural language within first few years of their life. Explanation of this phenomenon in terms of a process of imitation or inductive extrapolation from the linguistic data to which they have been exposed is generally considered inadequate. Mastery of the first language can be explained easily once we grant that children know implicitly the syntactic principles of their mother tongue. Fodor thinks that such tacit knowledge of syntactic principles must be represented in brain code of some sort. Otherwise, we are likely to face the symbol-grounding problem. Either we will have to say that the phenomenon of the first language acquisition is a mystery. Or we will be faced with an infinite regress. Admission of the Mentalese successfully stops the infinite regress.

Moreover, assumption of a universal innate language a la Fodor can avoid many of our problems, e.g., how different language users can have the same thought; how we can account for thinking behaviour in animals and human infants. Maybe, Fodorian theory is better from an evolutionary perspective too. Besides, our being able to switch from one natural language to others may not be a proof for natural-language-involving thought. Rather, this might be an evidence of our having a background thought which we are capable of expressing in different natural languages, sometimes even better in one language than in another. Though apparently ascription of the Mentalese solves the problem of non-linguistic creature's capacity to think, yet one may raise doubt here too. What is the guarantee that animals also have the same system of representation? The case of pre-linguistic infants is of course more problematic, since they appear to think before they have any grasp of natural language. But one question still remains, i.e., if early thinking involves the Mentalese, then why should that change later? Many children have reported that they hear themselves thinking in their first language.

Fodor's language of thought hypothesis, we know, relies heavily on the computer metaphor. But from analogical construal it does not become clear at all what actually are the units or the building blocks of the Mentalese. Are these non-linguistic concepts, directed schemas, virtual programmes? Any of the alternatives has some problem of its own. Besides, if there are really two languages, one internal language in which we think and a public language by which we express and communicate, then all the problems of translation crop up here. Besides, if thought does not necessarily involve language, then we should be able to train a being to think without giving that being training in language. But are the processes of language training and thought training of a child really different? These are formidable problems indeed; if, on the other hand, the distinction between inner and outer is downplayed, there is every possibility of a return to the behaviourist stance.

Both Fodor and Carruthers are realists about propositional attitudes. Reliance on introspective evidence and thinking partly through images and partly through natural language fit nicely with folk psychology. But explanatory power of Fodor's hypothesis, it appears, is more than that of Carruthers. It is extremely doubtful whether natural language can play the same causal role as the Mentalese.

8

Let us stop for a moment and take stock of the situation. We have discussed four important philosophical theories regarding the relation between thought and language. Of these, only Fodor's theory leaves some room for thought by non-linguistic creatures. But do we really need such a framework? Does the best explanation of animal behaviour really need such support? An overwhelming majority still insists that ascribing thoughts to animals is an instance of anthropomorphism. Animals cannot have thought simply because animals (also the pre-linguistic infants) lack *a theory of mind*. To have a theory of mind one must be in possession of some concepts — concepts that one ascribes to oneself, concepts that one ascribes to one's fellow creatures to understand and anticipate their moves and also to communicate with them. Like Davidson, many cognitive psychologists also uphold,

> . . . it needs to have something like a "theory of mind," and thus the concept of a *thought* or *belief* as a state of mind with a propositional content, which can be communicated from one thinker to another. This in turn entails that it must have some grasp of the concepts of *truth* and *falsehood*, since it must be able to conceive of the beliefs of another thinker as being correct or incorrect. It must even have some grasp of the concept of a *concept*, an ingredient of the propositional content of a thought or belief. But although some non-human primates, such as a chimpanzee, enjoy a fairly complex social life, it is very questionable whether they possess a theory of mind in anything like the foregoing sense. This, then, may help to explain why such creatures, despite their undeniable ingenuity, are incapable of learning to use language in the way that humans do.[14]

It is questionable indeed whether non-human primates have a theory of mind. This is one area of the hottest debates in different branches of cognitive science including cognitive ethology and primatology. There are scores of cognitive scientists who are ready to ascribe some sort of theory of mind to the apes and even other animals occupying a phylogenetically lower step of evolution, having observed their behaviour in their natural habitats. There are plenty of evidences of cheating/deceiving behaviour amongst animals in different stages of evolution and this probably shows that they are not as innocent of truth and falsehood as supposed by Davidson and the like-minded cognitive psychologists. What appears to me all the more questionable is their rash conclusion that non-language-using creatures necessarily lack concepts. Though it is impossible to use language without having any concept (I am not considering the imitative behaviour of some species of talking birds), the converse thesis that it is impossible to have concepts without language is controvertible. We can have reason and evidence galore in

14. E.J. Lowe, *An Introduction to the Philosophy of Mind,* Cambridge University Press, Cambridge, 2000, p.181.

support of the converse thesis from the standpoint of evolutionary psychology.[15]

Some thinkers hold that non-language-using creatures really lack concepts because we sometimes misconceive their fine-grained perceptual ability as conceptual ability. So we need to be extremely careful while ascribing thoughts to animals. Thus an orangutan's ability to track larger quantity of water when placed in a differently shaped physical container should not be taken as an instance of intuitive fluid mechanics but as a direct perceptual estimation strategy. Some minimalist theories in the area, therefore, ascribe non-propositional thoughts to animals. To understand the contention of the minimalists we need to remind ourselves of two well-known distinctions: (a) between propositional thought and perception and (b) between thinking how and thinking that.

Let us look at the second distinction first. *Thinking that* is about acquiring information about the environment. *Thinking how*, on the other hand, is a skill, which does not involve propositionally encoded representations of the environment. Hence thinking how cannot be easily put into words and some cannot be expressed at all. Bermudez[16] has listed five types of thinking, all of which allow one to adjust oneself to the environment without having recourse to propositional thought. These are:

---

15. M.D. Hauser, *Wild Mind: What Animals Really Think*, Penguin Books, London, 2000. Hauser mentions many cases which may not be construed as examples of possessing a full-fledged theory of mind but which shows that animals already possess some capacities that are useful for building such a theory. Take, for instance, plover. She feigns injury to a wing to distract predators from her nest by limping and taking them away from her young offspring. When a human being looks at her nest, she tries her antics harder to deceive them.

16. Jose Luis Bermudez, *Thinking without Words*, Oxford University Press, Oxford, 2003.

(1) Imagistic reasoning involving visual imagination, e.g., when one tries to think whether a computer table can be accommodated in the already crowded room of the head of the department;

(2) Empathic reasoning, i.e., putting oneself in other's shoes, e.g., one trying to imagine how much pain the accident-victim might have felt;

(3) Trial and error reasoning where there is an explicit representation of the goal but not how the goal is to be attained;

(4) Analogical reasoning where we just perceive the analogy between two situations without formulating it linguistically; and

(5) Reasoning involved in exercising complex bodily skills, e.g., whether one will be able to pass through a very narrow gap.

We have mentioned that according to the proponents of minimalism, non-linguistic thought is non-propositional in nature. In the linguistic account of thought, there is a sharp distinction between attitude and content and this enables different attitudes to have the same content and also the same attitude to have different contents. Some kind of thinking even involves entertaining some content without having any attitude towards them, e.g., when we deal in logical inferences. The second key element of propositional thinking is that propositions should be independent of the particular context of thinking, i.e., it should be possible to grasp a proposition without knowing its truth value and without grasping the state of affair which it expresses. Third, it should in principle be possible to find a sentence, which can express the content of a propositional attitude without remainder. Fourth, the content of a propositional thought must have a definite structure isomorphic to the sentence that enables it to be a part of an inference. Some minimalists maintain that non-linguistic thought may lack the third and the fourth trait mentioned above, but may possess the first and the second trait in common with linguistic thought. That is, in case of non-linguistic thought they allow the distinction between content and force and also independence from the context of thinking.

The minimalists also use the distinction between perception and propositional thought to clarify the notion of non-linguistic thought. They suggest that perceptual states represent the world in an analogue form while in propositional thought the world is represented in digital form. The content of perception, especially distance, seems unit-free but propositional thought can represent distances only in terms of specific units. The contents of perceptions are more fine-grained than the content of propositional thought. For example, I can perceive more colours than I can name. Perception being essentially perspectival, the content-attitude distinction cannot be made in perception. Since perceptual contents are fine-grained, they cannot be adequately expressed in sentences, though it is possible for us to express the content of perceptual belief through sentences. Pixellization of perception is possible but that does not have a structure isomorphic to the structure of a sentence. An analogy will help to understand the point. Just think of a computer scanning a document. It can scan and store the same document either as a picture or as a text. Though both methods store the same document faithfully, there is no isomorphism between the two stored documents and this fact becomes evident if one tries to edit the pieces.

Some philosophers have also entertained similar ideas. Michael Dummett,[17] for example, granted proto-thoughts,

---

17. M. Dummett, *The Origins of Analytical Philosophy*, Duckworth, London, 1993.

though not full-fledged thought to non-language — using creatures. Proto-thoughts are essentially tied to the possibilities the environment affords for action.[18] This makes them more similar to perception. According to Dummett, the vehicles for proto-thoughts are spatial images super-imposed on spatial perception. In perceiving the ambient environment, proto-thinkers visualise the possible ways it might transform. Proto-thinkers, however, exercise judgements (not expressible in language) like a car driver's judgement in a crowded street whether she can squeeze her car in the middle lane between two trucks. Usually we do not talk of truth/falsity of such judgements but of their correctness/incorrectness. Unlike that of linguistic thoughts correctness/incorrectness of proto-thoughts is to be understood ultimately in terms of success/failure of resulting actions.

Adrian Cussin,[19] being influenced by Gibson[20] attempts to explain proto-thoughts in terms of *affordances*. On this view, an organism perceives a distal environment structured in terms of possibilities it affords for action. To grasp affordances it needs experience-based knowledge, other than the propositional knowledge of objects. Affordances are context-bound and relativised to the organism's capacity of action and reaction. That is why proto-thoughts cannot be objective, since these are not independent of contingent characteristics of the subject and therefore necessary separation for attaining objectivity would not have been achieved.

---

18. *Aitareya Aranyaka*, which is a part of the Vedic corpus, also contains passages to the effect that birds and beasts cannot foresee events and hence cannot plan. Man alone knows tomorrow and can distance his speech and understanding from his immediate bodily needs.

19. "Content, embodiment and objectivity: the theory of cognitive traits," *Mind*, vol. 101, 1992.

20. J.J. Gibson, *The Ecological Approach to Visual Perception*, Houghton-Mifflin, Boston, 1979.

As a corollary of the theory of proto-thoughts, we have an alternative model of explanation of animal actions. In case of language-using creatures a three-template model is generally used: (a) X has desire for something; (b) X has some instrumental beliefs regarding satisfaction of the desire; and (c) X's instrumental beliefs are anchored in X's beliefs about the environment. In the context of human beings, environment consists of social roles, social routines and direct perception of emotional states of oneself and others. The minimalists hold that we can understand the behaviour of non-language-using creatures solely in terms of the goal-directed exercise of visual imagination, not belief. Since relevant environmental information forms part of one's current perception of the environment, we can do away with the correlative instrumental beliefs in case of explaining actions based on proto-thoughts. Hence a non-linguistic thought should be successfully explained in terms of a simple combination of a perceptual state and a desire. Non-linguistic thoughts are intentional simply by virtue of having a goal-desire, i.e., desire for a particular thing.

Bermudez rightly points out that this minimalist theory of thought together with its alternative model of explanation of actions is highly inadequate. He has offered three arguments to show the necessity of using three-template models even in the case of non-language-using creatures:

1. *The argument from planning*: On the minimalist view, since proto-thoughts cannot be dissociated from the current context, we should not ascribe any mediate thought or suitable planning to non-language-using creatures. But animals have often been found to act on goals they cannot immediately perceive, e.g., a predator lying in wait for a prey:

   Affordances become irrelevant when a creature is placed in highly unfamiliar surroundings unrelated to the creature's natural habitat. Yet much evidence for thinking in absence of language is derived from studying how non-human animals and human infants behave in precisely such unfamiliar surroundings.

Dealing with imperceptible goal and making of instruments involve planning, which the minimalist account cannot accommodate. Chimpanzees in the wild really devise such instruments, which is undoubtedly an instance of future planning. Consider wild chimpanzees that make two different types of wands for dipping into ant-nests and termite-nests much before they start for their nest-exploring expedition. Wands for dipping into ant-nests are made of strong twigs several feet long, while tools for plundering termite-nests are made out of flexible vines, shorter and with bitten ends, giving them a brush-like appearance.[21] Hence should we not extend the belief-desire model of explanation of action in such cases too?

2. *The argument from intelligent action*: Flexibility of response is a characteristic of thinking behaviour. But for that, a creature's responses must be abstracted from the present environment and its structure. A creature must also be able to distinguish between the feature-placing level[22] and the particular-involving level of experience. At the feature-placing level no distinction is to be drawn between one instance of a class and another. For example, when at dusk birds return to a tree, do they return to a particular tree, knowing its peculiar advantages and disadvantanges

21. R.W. Byrne, *The Thinking Ape,* Oxford University Press, Oxford, 1995.

22. This distinction was drawn by P.F. Strawson in *Individuals*, Methuen, London, 1959.

or would any of the neighbouring trees have been equally acceptable? A creature that operates at the particular-involving level is able to detect regularities of a completely different order, which is the enabling condition for re-identification of a persisting object. The minimalists cannot account for such thoughts; but such thoughts need to be attributed in explaining individual-involving representation of the environment which non-language-using creatures can recognise.

3. *The argument from psychological explanation*: It is a constraint on explanation in general that it supports counterfactuals. This requirement entails that the creature possesses structured motivational states, i.e., desires with contents that are sensitive to various satisfaction conditions. This type of explanation is sometimes needed in the context of behaviours of non-language-using creatures too. Suppose a bird is delivering food to its chicks in the nest. It lands at the edge of the nest and delivers food to the nearest chick. The question may be raised: whether the bird is motivated to give food to a particular chick or by a desire to give food to the nearest chick or by an even more general desire? It is clear that our prediction would depend on the counterfactual situation in which chicks were in different positions of the nest. Had the bird still sought out the same chick when it was removed from the edge of the nest, it would be plausible to hold that the bird was motivated by the desire to feed that particular chick.

9

In the preceding paragraph, I have given some justification for attributing full-fledged thoughts to non-linguistic creatures and for using the three-template model of explanation of some animal actions. But that should not lead one to think that a two-template model will always be inadequate. In fact, the latter would suffice in many cases where actions of non-linguistic creatures are guided by proto-thoughts. Like Bermudez, I am also in favour of multi-modal representation of the environment both in the context of language-using and in the context of non-language-using creatures.

One may wonder how much does this position concede? Can non-linguistic creatures have extremely complex thoughts, logical thoughts, higher-level thoughts? My answer will be different in all three cases. Thoughts by non-language using creatures never attain much sophistication. Sophisticated thoughts definitely need linguistic support; but animals are capable of many simple thoughts. Non-linguistic creatures cannot use rule-governed formal logic but many of their actions are definitely guided by proto-logic in which basic laws of formal logic have situation-based non-verbal representation. To make this point clear, I shall once again borrow some examples from Bermudez. Forms of reasoning that animals can identify at the non-linguistic level involve three propositional operators of disjunction, material conditional and negation of the standard propositional calculus.

Non-linguistic creatures understand negation through experience of some incompatible situations. This is definitely not a propositional negation. Suppose a hare observes absence of a gazelle at a waterhole where at other times it has seen the drinking gazelles. The hare can somehow grasp that these two situations are incompatible. Thus animals learn to recognise contrary situations — safe and dangerous, characterised by absence and by presence. We cannot simply deny that animals can discriminate between contrary situations; otherwise, their survival would have been at stake. Animals can also reason from an excluded alternative. A creature that is as threatened by the presence of a lion as a gazelle is seen to avoid a waterhole which is frequented by the gazelle. From experience it has come to know that two situations — a gazelle is at a waterhole and a lion is at a waterhole exclude each other. So from the absence of a gazelle at a waterhole at a usual hour, it concludes that the lion is at the waterhole or nearby and it keeps its distance from that waterhole. This is a counterpart of disjunctive syllogism. Similarly, animals somehow understand conditional dependence between two states of affairs. A creature that knows that if gazelles see the lion they will run away, and recognises that the gazelles will soon detect the lion, can predict that the gazelles will soon take flight. If this is *proto modus ponens*, we can also show instances of *proto modus tollens*. For example, an observer (maybe, a fellow predator) who is too far away to have a view of the visual perspective of the gazelles can infer from the fact that the gazelles are happily feeding where they are that they have not yet detected the lion.

About attributing higher-order thoughts to non-linguistic creatures I have strong reservations. Our reflexive thinking on thoughts definitely requires language as a vehicle. Whenever we try to think consciously on thoughts, first-level thoughts are represented through some imaged sentences. It holds both in cases of propositional and non-propositional thoughts. Even when a first-level thought is represented through images, it can be the content of some higher level-thought if and only if it is somehow converted to its sentential counterpart. Within imagistic representation the distinction between the first level and the higher levels gets blurred. Fodor, of course, claims that his language of thought being iterative can account for reflexive thinking. But as on this view the entire operation is conducted at the sub-personal level, we shall never be aware of our thinking about thinking. However, the fact is — we are aware of our thinking about thinking. Besides, acceptance of this hypothesis does not enhance our explanatory ability unlike the case of the first-order thoughts; therefore it is unwarranted to hold that the vehicle of our reflexive thought is the Mentalese. According to Bermudez, reflexive thinking requires semantic ascent, i.e., thinking about words and therefore it is not available to non-language-using creatures. This point, I think, can be made more convincingly. Look for instance at the phenomenon of pain and suffering which pervade the entire sentient world but only language-using creatures can entertain reflective thoughts like "why pain?"

Behind attribution of full-fledged thought to non-language-using creatures, there is a big presupposition that contents of thoughts are somehow encoded in their brain. Does it mean that language-using and non-language-using creatures possess the identical code, the same system of representations? Maybe, because of species-specific mode of grasping the world, different non-linguistic creatures cut up their world differently. How can we then confidently infer the background, belief and desire of such creatures from their behaviour? Cognitive psychologists and ethologists are therefore trying to devise suitable experiments to determine in what ways member of a particular species apprehend its environment and cut up the world where they inhabit. Progress in this area is expected to reduce the level of indeterminacy, even if it may not eliminate indeterminacy altogether. Though we may never grasp what it is like to be a dolphin, yet through imaginative experiments possibly we shall be able to guess, more or less correctly, to what object-properties dolphins are sensitive.

10

Granted that non-language-using creatures are capable of full-fledged thought, am I suggesting that language has no role to play in our thinking? Certainly not. I only want to assert that natural language emerged at a very late stage of evolution but thought has preceded it. Before concluding this article, let me give an outline of the evolutionary story, which is in consonance with Fodor's Mentalese Hypothesis.

According to some evolutionary psychologists,[23] thought is the execution of special computer code that composes the "mind." This program results from execution of a highly compact programme that has been trained through evolution to compress a vast amount of interaction with the world and thus has extracted the semantic coordinates functionally.

Evolution started with simple reactive systems like *E coli*. With the progress of evolution through bees and rats, dogs and apes to man, more and more complex reactive systems developed, capable of communicating through mechanically computed subroutines. The nature of evolution is such that given an intermediate subgoal, these reactive systems can construct a new programme. In many cases, animals and humans learn many new routines just by watching others. In this evolutionary picture, words are labels for computational modules, the semantically meaningful units out of which the programmes are built. It does not, therefore, follow that merely having labels for concepts facilitates thinking. So dogs without language may have a concept as we do.

However, having attained this stage, the process of evolution was in a rut until language arrived at the scene and that brought about a significant qualitative change in the cognitive abilities of language-using and non-language-using creatures. Before this stage, "evolution was trapped in a local optimum where creatures could not evolve powerful language because it was fitter to use non-scalable methods for communication." Then, perhaps, some initial genetic mutation

---

23. Vide Eric B. Baum, *What is Thought?* A Bradford Book, MIT Press, Cambridge, MA, 2004.

made us speak and slowly to acquire rules of grammar. Language has allowed human beings to build a huge database of useful codes on top of the programmes that evolution wired into the genome. Human thought processes are more powerful because we have been programmed with some of the programmes from this vast accumulated library. According to this story, therefore, the difference between humans and non-humans is largely due to more powerful nurture made possible by language. Nevertheless, even before language evolved, simple animals have developed mechanisms adequate for simple thoughts. Hence, the possibility of thinking without words cannot be simply discarded.

3

The Sentence in Computation and Cognitive Science*

Tista Bagchi

Introduction: Computation, Cognition, and Sentencehood

Sentences provide the model for computer programming statements and instructions. Sentences, however, also impart structure and clarity to our thoughts and enable us to communicate these to other people (and, increasingly, to computers), and to a great extent we acquire items of knowledge in the form of sentences that we encounter in the process of growth and development from early childhood on. This paper, therefore, takes a look at these roles of the sentence in shaping the nature of computation and human cognition, and puts forward the claim that these roles are ultimately different facets of the same unitary nature of the sentence as the human "unit of ratiocination" *par excellence*.

---

* This is a somewhat revised version of the paper that I presented at the National Seminar on Language and Mind organized by the Department of Philosophy, University of Hyderabad. I am particularly grateful to Amitabha Dasgupta for his insightful comments as discussant for that version, to Ramesh C. Pradhan for helpful ideas and especially for his support of the endeavour, and to several other participants at the Seminar, too numerous to mention individually by name here, for their probing questions and comments during and after the presentation. Needless to say, the responsibility for any errors remains with me.

Computation and the Sentence

It is interesting to speculate whether computing codes, or at least high-level programming languages, could have been created in the absence of the sentence as a fundamental cognitive and communicational unit. To quote from Sebesta (1999) on the commonality of the notion of sentencehood in both natural and formal language:

> Languages, whether natural (such as English) or artificial (such as C++), are sets of strings of characters from some alphabet. The strings of a language are called **sentences** or statements. The syntax rules of a language specify which strings of characters from the language's alphabet are in the language. English, for example, has a large and complex collection of rules for specifying the syntax of its sentences. (Sebesta 1999: 107)

Of course, for a linguist (or for any cognitive scientist interested in natural language), a sentence is more than simply a "string of characters from some alphabet." Nonetheless, the instructions and control statements in a programming language share many crucial features with natural-language sentences.

Moreover, phrase and sentence structure, along with (crucially) propositional and predicate logic, have been topics of interest in the phase in cognitive science that came to be known as artificial intelligence (AI) during the 1980s (into the early 1990s), as the chapters devoted to those topics in Winston (1999) testify. The term *sentence* in AI, however, is used in more than one sense, depending on the domain of research and implementation. In the domain of "logic and resolution proof" (Winston 1999: 283-304), for instance, the following definition appears:[1]

---

1. From Winston (1999: 288).

> A wff [well-formed formula] in which all the variables, if any, are inside the scope of corresponding quantifiers is a sentence. These are sentences:
>
> $\forall x[\text{Feathers}(x) \Rightarrow \text{Bird}(x)]$
>
> $\text{Feathers(Albatross)} \Rightarrow \text{Bird(Albatross)}$

A "sentence" in this domain of AI, then, is a proposition without any unbound variables. However, in the domain of "language constraints" (Winston 1999: 575–98), the sentence is essentially the composite unit with which so-called *language-generation procedures* and *language-understanding programs* operate (*ibid.*: 596-8). Language-understanding programs are based heavily on the notion of the sentence as being either an IP (inflectional phrase) or a CP (complementizer phrase), as assumed by mainstream syntacticians in the area of theoretical linguistics.[2]

What does Sentencehood Have to Do with Computer Programs?

A legitimate question that anyone is perfectly entitled to raise at this point is: What *is* the connection between sentences and computer programs? After all, we speak in sentences as *human* beings, whereas the ordinary personal computer is simply an electronic *machine* (no matter how apparently sophisticated) that can process only mechanical instructions fed into it through keystrokes, mouse or trackpad movements and clicks, touch on touch-sensitive screens, or pre-programmed routines hard-wired or plugged into it.

The question of whether there is any connection at all between the sentence and what has been called *computability* (Boolos & Jeffrey 1989) needs to be pitched at a much deeper

2. The categories IP and CP recur in various incarnations in work in Chomskyan linguistics especially during the decade or so of linguistic research leading up to Chomsky (1995).

level of philosophical inquiry, however. In particular, one might ask the following question: Is computability supervenient on the existence of the sentence as a natural unit, or is it the other way round, i.e., is the sentence as a natural unit supervenient on the phenomenon of computability?[3] In other words, is it the case that computability cannot even be conceived without sentencehood, or is it instead the case that sentencehood would in itself have been impossible without the *a priori* possibility of computability itself?

A prerequisite to finding an answer to this question is for us to first understand exactly what one means by *computability*.[4] Ironically, this is not a concept that computer scientists *per se* seem to treat with any particular interest.[5] Even the well-known *Computability and Logic* (Boolos & Jeffrey 1989) addresses the concept of computability in relation to number systems and other mathematical systems rather than the kinds of input and output formulae and expressions that we human beings operate with. We therefore have to turn to work on the philosophy of mind — such as is represented by Searle (1979), Penrose (1989), and Chalmers (1996) — to gain any kind of understanding of the notion of computability as relating to the human mind and human language.

---

3. Here I draw upon the excellent treatment of the notion of supervenience to be found in Chalmers (1996, ch. 2), which is crucial not only to Chalmers' analysis of consciousness as a phenomenon but in fact to any meaningful exploration of ontological issues in the philosophy of science and (by extension) the philosophy of language construed broadly, to include fundamental issues in linguistics.

4. See Penrose (1994: 24-25, 61n.8) on the issue of computability as "Turing computability."

5. *The Penguin Dictionary of Computers*, for instance, does not seem to possess any entry for *computability*; nor do technical works on computing such as Malvino & Leach (1991) and Sebesta (1999) make any mention of the term.

Sentencehood and the Structure of Programming Languages (Assembly Language and Higher-Level Languages)

Programming languages are crucially structured around the "human" concept of the sentence. Even a cursory look at some of the basic "syntax" of the lowest-level programming language, namely, Assembly Language, makes this patent (the comments explaining each line of code occur following a colon):

```
(1)   MOV     EAX, I        : LOAD I INTO EAX
      ADD     EAX, J        : ADD J TO EAX
      CALL    B             : CALL PROGRAM B
```

(From Tanenbaum 1997: 410, 419)

As one can see, although the convention of ordering is different for the commands to the left of the colons (the actual Assembly Language code), the commands themselves relate systematically to the natural-language comments to their right. For higher-level languages such as PASCAL or C, the sentence-like character of each line of code is even more evident, even if the syntax of the code is conventionalized differently on the surface from natural-language sentential syntax. Typically, in these languages, there is a predicate or function expression (such as "readln," "scanf" or "add") occurring with one or more argument slots to be filled in by variables or pointers to variables (such as *x*, *y*, or *&x*, **y*). These can be seen as direct programming-language analogues of natural-language predicates and arguments that make up clauses and sentences.

The Computational Parsing of Natural-Language Sentences

Enabling the computer to parse sentences from one or more natural languages has become a key part of much of mainstream industrial computing today, and especially so in recent years, both with the spread of computing technology worldwide to an unprecedented degree and with the increased movement of speakers of a wide variety of languages across the globe. The creation of computer hardware devices and software programs that can parse natural-language sentences has therefore already become central to such technology-based functioning, both in order to facilitate automated user interfaces (as is being done in the case of airline reservations, for example, in many parts of the world) and to facilitate data processing and mining in human-readable format (as is also being done increasingly with professional and commercial databases worldwide). In view of all of this, the processing of natural-language sentences through computational means has taken on a particularly crucial role on the information superhighway around the world. Commonly used parsers for a number of typologically distinct languages are based on linguistic frameworks such as Lexical-Functional Grammar and Head-driven Phrase Structure Grammar: the implementation is often done through what is called Unification-Based Grammar (Kay 1992, Ginzburg & Sag 2000). A full overview of all such parsers in current use or under development would be too much of a digression from the major focus of this paper, but it is worth noting that these parsers crucially work on the analysis of *sentences*, in isolation or in connected discourse.

The Sentence in Cognition

The term *cognition* is something of a buzzword in our times: the term is from the Latin verb *cognoscere*, "to get to know, to learn; to recognize,"[6] but in English it has been listed in a dictionary as having the sense of "the mental action or process of acquiring knowledge and understanding through thought, experience, and the senses."[7] It might be worth noting that

6. The English glosses are based on the entry for Latin *cognoscere* in Betts (1986: 323).

7. See Hobson (2002: 78).

this rather recondite-sounding word has been used in the coining of a number of brand names modelled on the word *cognition* and its derivational cousins in part or whole[8] - not to mention the use of its derivative in the term *cognitive science* itself.

So what is special about the role of the sentence in cognitive science? Interestingly, what is special is precisely what is NOT special about the sentence in terms of what we can readily observe about it, namely, that it is possibly the most obvious and the most heavily used kind of composite unit of human language,[9] for both information gathering by the human mind and the sharing of information with other human minds.

Nonetheless, taking one's cue from the noted American structural linguist Edward Sapir (Sapir 1949), one can still ask whether there is any "psychological reality" to the sentence. More specifically, it remains a valid question to ask whether the sentence correlates with anything in the so-called "language of thought."[10]

This question takes on a particular significance in view of the fact that the sentence clearly does figure in some capacity

---

8. Examples of this are the CogNet e-resource hosted by the MIT Press website, the company Cognizant Solutions, and many others.

9. In Bagchi (2000), for instance, I have raised the matter of intentionality in the cognition of linguistic meaning, from which by implication the role of propositional content in capturing mental states can be deduced. In Bagchi (forthcoming), I demonstrate the significant role played by the organization of certain sentence types into their constituent clauses in the signalling of certain aspects of causality and temporality in natural language.

10. The notion of a "language of thought" is originally due to the philosopher Jerry A. Fodor. Pinker (1994) devotes a chapter to the concept under the rubric of "Mentalese" (Pinker 1994: 44-73).

in conscious, semi-conscious (e.g., hypnotic and REM sleep), and even sub-conscious levels of the mind (or beyond, as in the case of dreamless, non-REM sleep): aside from producing and recognizing sentences while fully awake, we also talk, often in complete sentences, in our sleep (or at least some of us do so), and can be woken up with a start from deep sleep by a spoken sentence, with usually at least partial, and often complete, comprehension of what has been said.[11] These observations demand a reconciliation with the kind of relationship that David Townsend and Thomas Bever (Townsend & Bever 2001: 406-8) have sought to establish between sentence comprehension and the kind of account of consciousness that David Chalmers (Chalmers 1996) has sought to provide.

Such a reconciliation can, in a sense, be achieved simply enough: Chalmers' focus is on *phenomenal* consciousness, as opposed to the *psychological* manifestation of consciousness (or "awareness," as Chalmers defines this) — whereas issues of *awakeness* (or its absence in varying degrees), which are of relevance to the discussion in the preceding paragraph, are to be located in the domain of *psychological* rather than *phenomenal* consciousness.

To this, however, another objection can in principle be raised, namely, that the sentence could *also* be held to be a *phenomenon* — an entity that, in addition to possessing certain formal and intentional properties of special kinds, also possesses the capacity to be "experienced." This objection, however wild it may appear at first glance, merits some

11. Of course, we can also be equally validly woken up by a sudden loud non-linguistic noise, shouted word of warning (such as "Fire" or "Earthquake"), or incomplete phrase (such as "Out of here!"). This does not detract from the comprehensibility of any full sentence by which we can be woken up, with partial or complete comprehension thereof, from deep sleep.

consideration. First, the speakers of a language have strong "gut reactions" regarding the well-formedness of sentences constructed in their language, as generative linguists can attest to in profusion. Such "gut reactions" are commonly termed "native-speaker intuitions," and get invoked when we hear an incomplete or grammatically erroneous sentence, for instance, especially from a speaker with native competence in the language (though we are sometimes prepared to make allowances for such grammatically imperfect sentences in the speech of foreigners and small children who are yet to achieve complete competence in the language). Second, these reactions also form a good part of the empirical basis for generative linguistic theory. Thus, sentences that are found to be not completely well-formed by native speakers provide significant clues as to the limits of what the faculty of language for any speaker of the language in question would allow — or not allow — as grammatical in the language (or in any natural language, for that matter).

Sentence Processing in Cross-Linguistic Perspective

In recent decades, with the awareness that results based on experiments in sentence processing among speakers of English cannot be assumed to hold good for languages that are typologically quite different from English, there have been significant studies of how speakers of other languages and language types process the sentences of their languages. Notable among such studies are those reported in MacWhinney & Bates (1989) and, more recently, Hillert (1998).

Li (1998), for instance, points out that, despite the fact that at first glance Chinese seems to be typologically similar to English in having unmarked SVO word order, there are marked differences in the typology of sentences as they are actually *used* in Chinese, and that therefore experimental results for sentence processing in Chinese can be expected to be significantly different from those for English (and European languages in general).

Different models of sentence processing have been proposed on the basis of cross-linguistic data from processing experiments. Two prominent models are considered here, namely, the *competition model* of MacWhinney & Bates (1989) and the *comprehension model* of Townsend & Bever (2001).

The Competition Model

The competition model of sentence processing is centred on the attachment of roles (arguments) to predicates. The system is based on lexical knowledge, which itself is an organized repository of auditory, semantic, and role-relational, i.e., syntactic, knowledge (see Townsend & Bever 2001: 126). According to the competition model, therefore, a "garden path" sentence such as (2) below would be processed roughly in the manner (3a) and would then have to be re-processed in the manner (3b) when the competing second predicate *fell* follows:

(2) The horse raced past the barn fell.

(3) a. ((the → horse)→ raced) → (past → (the → barn))

b. ((the →(horse → (raced → (past → (the → barn))))) →fell)

The sentence processing system supposedly arrives at this structure by linking a series of roles and cues that are associated with each word as it is encountered. The primary kinds of cues to role relations, according to the competition model, are word order and morphology. Each verb specifies a set of possible roles that it can assign to noun phrases, and then various cues combine to specify a particular role for the noun phrases in its argument domain. For instance, in the example above, *the* is specified as having a head noun that follows it, so when the noun *horse* appears next, it can be linked to that particular (head noun) slot specified by *the*. The verb *raced* is expected to have a subject argument and an optional adverb or prepositional phrase following it, and is accordingly initially linked up with *the horse* in its subject role and the prepositional phrase *past the barn* in the optional role following it; but as soon as the competing verb *fell* occurs, it competes with the verb *raced* and breaks down this initial linking as shown in (3a), so that *raced* along with *past the barn* is now delegated to the status of a relative clause modifying the noun *horse;* under the new linking scheme as in (3b), the entire phrase *the horse raced past the barn* is now selected by the verb *fell* to fill its subject role.

What is significant in this model, for our purposes, is the significance it accords to each *predicate* as having the power to "introduce" a *clause*, the syntactic correlate of the simple sentence. It thus captures the recursiveness of the sentence as a linguistic unit in a natural manner. Nonetheless, it is precisely because this model is far too exclusively "syntactic" in its basic spirit that Townsend & Bever assess it critically and then reject it as being inadequate to the task of fully accounting for language processing.

The Comprehension Model

According to Townsend & Bever, "any viable and behaviourally adequate model [of sentence processing] must have both an associative and a syntactic component" (Townsend & Bever 2001: 157). The comprehension model that they propose combines a probabilistic associative component and a largely deterministic syntactic component, and their account of how human beings process language in terms of individual sentences rests crucially on the case for the psychological reality of these two components.

Briefly, they outline their model of sentence comprehension as follows (pp. 157-85). Regarding the syntactic component of such a model, the "primary question" that they raise is "whether a syntactic structure can be constructed by direct left-to-right application of a grammar," which they go on to answer in the negative. "This conclusion motivates consideration of a model that "reconstructs" the syntactic derivation," according to them. By way of example, they point out that "lexical items in speech are not neatly segregated for auditory recognition," as in the case of the apparently unrecognizable string of segments (4a) representing the structured sentence (4b) (p. 158):

(4) a. Thuoarseraayseznwinz.

b. The horse races and wins.

The difficulties with mapping (4a) unambiguously on to the syntactic entity (4b) in a real comprehension model are described as follows:

> A listener might initially code *thuoarse* simply as an unrecognized noun phrase, based on the fact that it begins the sentence and the initial sequence *thu* is a reasonable pronunciation of *the*. This would allow for further processing. But then the *raysez* could either be a continuation of the noun phrase or the verb, requiring further suspension of a final analysis. In fact, the structure of the initial phrase is not really clear until the sequence *winz*, along with the fact that that is the end of the utterance. In certain instances, even the word *horse* may not be recognized until near the end of the sentence. Even worse, the sequence *winz* might be heard as the noun *winds*, in which case the entire sequence would be incorrectly analyzed as a noun phrase until its very end.

Simple cases like this show that the comprehension mechanism for auditory input cannot always work as the mere mechanical application of syntactic categories and frames from left to right. Rather, there must be a set of procedures for dealing with temporarily indeterminate information even at the acoustic level and using projected phrase and content information to guide comprehension both prospectively and retrospectively. That is, there must be a set of templates and processes that can predict likely sequences and structures from incomplete information.

This kind of information is partially structural, partially probabilistic. It is a structural fact that *the* introduces a noun phrase. But it is a probable fact that horses *race* more often than they *raise* or *erase*.

(Townsend & Bever 2001: 158-59)

According to this model of sentence comprehension, the internal parser forms a "pseudosyntax," a quick-and-dirty syntactic representation for every sentence based on probabilistic information, and then forms a "candidate real syntax" by taking the candidate meaning/form from the pseudosyntax and mapping it onto a corresponding set of structures that serve as the input to a syntactic derivation. The mapping principles are partly statistical and partly structural (pp. 164-65). What is noteworthy, however, is that the "pseudosyntax" that is formed by the model is not merely syntactic in nature but has a "likely meaning" assigned to it as an essential step (p. 165).

Conclusion: The Ontological Status of the Sentence

In the body of this paper, we have taken something of a wide-angle view of the ways in which the sentence figures both as a conceptual unit and as a structural exemplar in computation and in a significant area of psycholinguistic research and inquiry, namely, language processing. Having undertaken this, however, we are still under some obligation to try to address a significant question: what is the ontological status of the sentence with reference to all of these roles that it is found to play in computation and cognition, with special focus on the Western traditions of inquiry?[12]

To begin addressing this question, we might consider the sentence in relation to one of three distinct modes of inquiry identified by Amitabha Dasgupta (in Dasgupta 1996), namely, philosophy of language, linguistic philosophy, and philosophy of linguistics. The question raised here, it seems to me, relates the most fundamentally to philosophy of language and, I claim, at best derivatively to the other two modes of inquiry. What is at issue here is not whether the sentence is a unit that figures in linguistic philosophy (it does, alongside objects such as expressions and conceptions of being, definite descriptions, predicates, and arguments) or in philosophy of linguistics (here too it figures centrally, even if not recognized explicitly[13]), but whether it can be said to have any kind of basic reality in the sphere in which language occurs. The conclusion is that, given its ubiquitous occurrence in all of the various spheres of activity and application of the human mind that we just had an overview of earlier, the sentence does have such reality.

---

12. This latter qualification is significant, in my view, given that the kind of ontology that emerges from the sentence is rather different in the Indian linguistic and philosophical tradition, notwithstanding differences between its conceptions among key Indian figures such as Panini and Katyayana on the one hand and Bhartrhari on the other. Common to these conceptions seems to be a consensus on the sentence as both a *structured* and a *structuring* entity, whether in linguistic discourse or in thought in general.

13. Chomsky (2002), for instance, makes no special mention of the sentence as a unit of grammar.

Bibliography

Bagchi, Tista, 2000, Turing's "Computing Machinery and Intelligence" revisited: cognition from a linguistic perspective, In J.R. Isaac and Karuna Batra, eds. (2000) *Cognitive Systems: Reviews and Previews*, 728-33, New Delhi: NIIT-Phoenix.

———, Forthcoming, 2005, Causation and tense in subordinate clauses: conditionals and conjunctive participles in Bangla and Hindi, In *Polymorphous Linguistics: Jim McCawley's Legacy*, eds. Salikoko S. Mufwene, Elaine Francis, and Rebecca S. Wheeler, Cambridge, Mass: MIT Press.

Bates, Elizabeth, and Brian MacWhinney, 1989, Functionalism and the Competition Model. In Brian MacWhinney and Elizabeth Bates, eds. (1989) *The Cross-Linguistic Study of Sentence Processing*, 3-73. Cambridge and New York: Cambridge University Press.

Betts, Gavin. 1986. *Latin: A Complete Course*, London: Hodder & Stoughton.

Boolos, George S., and Richard C. Jeffrey, 1989, *Computability and Logic*, 3rd edn. Boston and London: Cambridge University Press.

Chalmers, David J., 1996, *The Conscious Mind: In Search of a Fundamental Theory*, Cambridge, Mass.: MIT Press.

Chomsky, Noam, 1995, *The Minimalist Program*, Cambridge, Mass: MIT Press.

———, 2002, *On Nature and Language*, Edited by Adriana Belletti and Luigi Rizzi. Cambridge: Cambridge University Press.

Dasgupta, Amitabha, 1996, *The Second Linguistic Turn: Chomsky and the Philosophy of Language*, Frankfurt am Main: Peter Lang.

Ginzburg, Jonathan, and Ivan A. Sag, 2000, *Interrogative Investigations: The Form and Meaning of English Interrogatives*, Stanford: CSLI.

Hillert, D., ed., 1998, *Sentence Processing: A Crosslinguistic Perspective, Syntax and Semantics*, vol. 31, San Diego: Academic Press.

Hobson, Archie, ed., 2002, *The Oxford Dictionary of Difficult Words*, New York: Oxford University Press.

Kay, Martin, 1992, Unification, In *Computational Linguistics and Formal Semantics*, eds. Michael Rosner and Roderick Johnson, 1-29, Cambridge and New York: Cambridge University Press.

Li, Ping, 1998, Crosslinguistic variation and sentence processing: the case of Chinese, In Hillert, ed., pp. 33-54.

Penrose, Roger, 1994, *Shadows of the Mind*, London: Vintage.

Pinker, Steven, 1994, *The Language Instinct: How the Mind Creates Language*, New York: Harper Collins.

Sapir, Edward, 1949, The psychological reality of the phoneme, In *Selected Writings of Edward Sapir in Language, Culture, and Personality*, ed. David Mandelbaum, pp. 45-60, Berkeley, Calif.: University of California Press.

Schiller, Eric, 1993, Autolexical Theory, http://www.chessworks.com/ling/papers/autolexical.htm

Searle, John R. 1979, *Expression and Meaning: Studies in the Theory of Speech Acts*. Cambridge: Cambridge University Press.

Sebesta, Robert W., 1999, *Concepts of Programming Languages*, Reading, MA, and Singapore: Addison-Wesley.

Tanenbaum, Andrew S., 1997, *Structured Computer Organization*, 3rd edition, New Delhi: Prentice-Hall of India.

Townsend, David J., and Thomas G. Bever. 2001. *Sentence Comprehension*. Cambridge, Mass.: MIT Press.

Winston, Patrick Henry, 1999, *Artificial Intelligence*, Reading, MA, and Delhi: Addison-Wesley.

4

The Nature of Mental Representation Classicism versus Connectionism

V. Harinarayanan and C. A. Tomy

WITH the passing of the behaviourist paradigm in the philosophy of mind, which attempted to do away with any intermediary between stimulus and response, the notion of representation as something that mediates between the two has come to play a central role in theories of cognition. It is now generally accepted that there are representational states within an organism that shapes its response to the stimuli. The most important argument for the existence of mental representation is based on what is known as "behavioural plasticity" — the adaptability and flexibility that complex organisms such as human beings exhibit in their interactions with the environment. It is argued that behavioural plasticity is not the result of organism's sensitivity to the physical appearance of the stimuli but to their informational content. This requires that there has to be a way for the organism to represent the informational content. This is possible only if there is a rich and complex system of internal representation that enables the organism to interact with the environment effectively. Similarly, it is argued that the relation between the organism and the environment cannot be direct in the case of imagination and contemplation because when we imagine or contemplate, there is apparently no direct stimulus effect. This again suggests that there must be a representational system available to the organism.

But the thesis that there exist representational states within the organism that mediate between stimuli and responses, by itself, does not make any commitments regarding the nature of the representations. Hence there has been intense debate among philosophers and cognitive scientists about the nature of the internal representations. The dominant view, in this debate, has been that the system of mental representation is language-like. This position, known as classicism or symbolicism, is well articulated and championed by Jerry Fodor. Of late, however, classicism has been challenged by another approach known as connectionism, which treats representation as being realized by a neural network. The purpose of the present paper is to articulate the conflicting positions of both classicism and connectionism with regard to the nature of internal representational states.

Symbolicist Approach

The symbolicist approach has its origin in the Representational Theory of Mind, which holds that mental states are representational states and that the mental processes are various transformations over them.[1] It is based on the assumption that the representational entities are a system of symbols. On this assumption, if mental states are representational, then they are symbolic and the mental processes are transformations over symbols. Moreover, it is held that the transformations over symbols involved in the cognitive mental processes do not take place at random but are governed by certain rules. The view that cognitive states are representational and that the cognitive processes are rule-governed symbol manipulations has given rise to what is

---

1. Kim Sterelny, *The Representational Theory of Mind: An Introduction.* Cambridge, MA: Blackwell, 1994, pp. 19-23.

known as the Computational-Representational Understanding of Mind as a major paradigm for the study of cognition. This paradigm is known as classicism in cognitive science.

The cognitivists conceive of language as the paradigm of a representational symbol system. Language has two important aspects: syntax and semantics. By semantics we mean the representational content or the meaningfulness of the symbols used in a language. What is meant by syntax, on the other hand, is the set of rules that structures the occurrence of a group of symbols conveying some meaning. The metaphor that guides research within the classicist paradigm is that of a computer. In a computer, there are always two languages. One is the input-output language in which the computer interacts with the environment and the other is the machine language in which it performs its computations. The machine is able to "understand" only the machine language and, therefore, the input-output language has to be translated into the machine language.[2] Thus, the computer is a paradigmatic case of a system that works in a medium of language different from the one it uses to communicate with the external world.

Language of Thought Hypothesis

A detailed account of the view that mental representation is symbolic appears in the works of Jerry Fodor. Since the publication of his book, *The Language of Thought,* Fodor has been advocating the thesis that the realm of mind is structured like a language.[3] He argues that there is an inner language, which he calls *mentalese,* in which the mental processes are carried out. In what follows, we shall briefly discuss Fodor's arguments in support of the language of thought (LOT) hypothesis.

---

2. There is a third language as well that mediates between the two, but we do not intend to consider it for the present purpose.

3. New York: Thomas Y. Crowell, 1975.

The nature of the cognitive processes shows that thought cannot but function in a language-like medium. For example, consider the processes involved in making a decision or perceiving a physical object. The processes involved require representations in a manipulable way. Decision making is based on computing certain hypothesis about the probability of actions and their consequences out of which some are preferred by the agent. This implies that the agent has to have the means for representing their behaviour and its consequences. This representational system has to have the capacity of infinite production from finite elements as there is no limit, in principle, to the representations one can entertain in the course of making various decisions. Similarly, the representational system has to exhibit semantic properties like truth and reference because the representational states refer to the states of affairs in the world outside, and the selection of the possibilities is normally based on the advantages it brings to the agent.

A second argument for a language-like medium for executing cognitive processes is based on an account of the processes involved in perception. According to Fodor, like decision making, perceptual processes also presuppose the availability of a rich representational system. Apart from the naïve realists, nobody thinks that perception is a simple matter of copying from the object. Rather, it is considered to be a process where high level cognitive processes such as hypothesis formation and confirmation play a role. It is now generally accepted that, in perceptual processes, an organism plays an active part and that this is not possible without there being a representational system similar to language.

Fodor further argues that the nature of the cognitive process that we call thought also shows that cognitive states and processes share some characteristics with language.[4] Thought is said to be systematic in the sense that any one who is able to entertain the thought, "John loves Mary" will be able to entertain the thought, "Mary loves John" as well. This is because both the thoughts have the same constituents. This kind of systematicity is exhibited in language use as well. Anyone capable of constructing the sentence, "John loves Mary" is equally capable of producing another statement that is systematically related to it, namely, "Mary loves John." The two sentences are systematically related because they share the same constituents. An expression x can be considered to be a constituent of another expression y if and only if the former is both syntactically and semantically part of the latter or in other words, the latter is, in part, composed of the former. So both thought and language are systematic because they are compositional in nature.

Another important feature that thought and language share is their productivity. From a finite set of resources, we are able to think, in principle, infinite number of thoughts. This feature of thought is closely related to its systematicity because the production of new thoughts is based on the systematic relation among the constituents of the concerned thoughts. Similarly, recursive infinity is a major characteristic of language use as well. Anyone capable of using language in a normal way is able to produce infinitely many sentences out of the finite resources available to him. In Fodor's view, the similarity between thought and language in terms of their productivity suggests that thought processes take place in a medium that is structured like language.

The systematicity and productivity of both thought and language leads us to another important feature that they share,

---

4. Fodor, *Psychosemantics: The Problem of Meaning in Philosophy of Mind*, Cambridge, Mass: MIT Press, 1987, pp. 135-54.

namely, compositionality. The systematicity and productivity of a representational system cannot be explained unless the representational realm possesses a compositional structure and the processes taking place within the system are sensitive to its compositional structure. The representations are compositional if and only if the atomic representations are constituents of the complex ones. If thought is systematic and productive like language, then it must possess a compositional structure and the thought processes must be sensitive to the structure. Given the constituent structure of symbols involved in the language of thought and the syntax-sensitive processes over them, LOT hypothesis claims that it can give an explanation of the systematicity and productivity that thought exhibits.

Language of Thought as Innate

It could be objected that if thought is to function in a language like medium, it could very well be the natural language itself and that there is no need to postulate a language of thought distinct from the natural language. Moreover, we have the intuitive feeling that we think in a natural language, mostly in our own mother tongues. But the view that we think in a natural language is not acceptable to Fodor. First of all, this view would imply that infra-human animals and children with undeveloped language would have no thoughts at all. But they exhibit striking behavioural similarities with adult humans which, in turn, point out that they have thought processes that function more or less similarly to human thought. To cap it all, the very process of acquisition of language requires a medium in which the understanding of the language being learned takes place. All this makes, in the Fodorian scheme, the inner language a *fait accompli.*

The inner language of thought, according to Fodor, is not acquired but innate. Had it been learned like a natural language, it would not have been able to carry out the functions it is required to perform. In Fodor's opinion, the view that the language of thought is acquired would lead to infinite regress, because its acquisition would require a language like system which if acquired or learned, in turn, would require another language prior to that and so on *ad infinitum*. Rather than being acquired, the inner language is supposed to be hardwired in the organism in a way that the physical operations and the linguistic processes go in tandem. Hence all that we can conceptually entertain is already there in the LOT. Thus the question of how the organism understands the inner language does not arise. This does not, however, mean that learning a natural language does not provide an organism with any definite advantage. On the contrary, the acquisition of a natural language helps the organism to certain internal advantages. The most important change that occurs in a system after the acquisition of language is that it is able to act in a more efficient manner due to language acting as a mnemonic device.[5] In other words, the acquisition of language has implications at the performance level, and not at the competence level.

It is to be noted that Fodor does not claim his thesis to be irrefutable. For him, it is the best available one as there is no other viable alternative. Moreover, it is an area where empirical evidence is hard to come by. However, Fodor believes that the LOT hypothesis is not empirically unsupported. In his view, there are linguistic and psychological evidence to substantiate his thesis. The poverty of stimulus (POS) argument and impossibility argument (IA) are well-known for their support for a strong innate basis of language. Following Noam

5. It is obvious that language provides a medium for communication without which the cognitive activity makes little sense. But the present point is about the internal advantages to the organism. Perhaps the debate of internal and external theories of cognition can get light from this.

Chomsky, who originally advanced the POS argument,[6] Fodor argues that the stimulus a child receives is too poor to elicit a complex response such as language. So the child's ability to use language can be properly accounted for only if it is assumed that the knowledge of language is innate to the child. Whereas Chomsky makes use of this argument to demonstrate the existence of universal grammar out of which the grammar of a particular language is derived, Fodor builds his LOT hypothesis upon it.

The most important psychological evidences that Fodor makes use of comes from the rationality and flexibility with which the organism is able to perform complex cognitive processes. An organism is always bombarded with different sorts of stimuli all of which do not end up receiving a full cognitive analysis. The organism represents only those stimuli that are useful for its purpose at hand.[7] This intelligent management of internal representation cannot take place without a powerful representational resource. However, this resource cannot consist of mere images as their representational capacity is limited. Images without description speak little and, therefore, cannot act as full fledged representations.

The Nature of Computation

From Fodor's point of view, the mental operation of thinking is carried out in the internal language of thought whereas an organism's external social interactions take place in a natural language or through some other means of communication. The various propositional attitudes like desire, belief, etc. are different computational relations that the organism bears to the linguistic formulae of the internal language of thought or mentalese. For instance, the desire that it is raining and the

---

6. See, *Rules and Representations*, Cambridge, Mass: MIT Press, 1980.
7. Fodor, *The Language of Thought*, pp. 159-63.

belief that it is raining constitute different relations to the same symbols or formulae of the internal code, namely, "F (it is raining)." That these mental states constitute different relations to the symbols shows that they are computationally different. The construal of various propositional attitudes as different relations to the formulae of the internal code does not, however, mean that the objects of mental states are language-like; rather each representational state is structured the way a sentence is structured within a language.

Fodor believes that cognitive mental processes are basically computational processes. In thinking, an organism operates upon its internal representations the way a computer acts on data structures. Whereas a computer has data structures and algorithms over them, the mind possesses a language-like representational system with its own syntax to govern the processes involved in thinking and other cognitive phenomena.

According to Fodor, it is a characteristic of the computational processes that they are both symbolic and formal.[8] By formal, what he means is that it is the form or shape of the representation, and not its content, that determines the operation to be carried out. Fodor contends that thinking also takes place in a formal way. The syntax that guides or regulates computational operations applies to the representational symbols in virtue of their form and not their content. Thus, only the formal aspects of symbols determine the nature of computational processes. Hence the semantic features of the symbols like truth and reference do not play any role in determining the cognitive processes. This, however, seems to give rise to some kind of tension between the formalist approach that Fodor adopts and the semantic features that need to be taken care of for an adequate explanation of our

---

8. Fodor. "Methodological Solipsism Considered as a Research Strategy in Cognitive Psychology" *Behavioural and Brain Sciences* 3 (1980); pp. 63-109.

cognitive behaviour. In other words, whereas the causal account of the mental processes and the production of behaviour demand a formal approach to the internal representation, the semantic considerations seem to demand a non-formal approach.

Fodor attempts to defuse the tension by claiming that the formal operations are capable of preserving the semantic aspects. That the syntax-sensitive processes preserve semantic features embedded in cognitive processes is elucidated by, once again, exploiting the metaphor of computer. Fodor observes: "computer shows us how to connect causal properties of a symbol with its semantic properties. This connection is done via its syntax."[9] The operations of the computer are sensitive only to the formal characteristics of the symbols involved and the computational outputs are meaningful only because the symbols upon which the operations are performed themselves are meaningful. Thus it is an important characteristic of the classicist approach that syntax-sensitive processes preserve semantics.

In proposing a computational representational account of cognitive states and processes, Fodor's primary objective is to establish the autonomy of psychology as a special science. Psychology, for him, is an extension of our folk psychology and he believes that the categories adopted by folk psychology for the prediction and explanation of behaviour are real. Folk psychology grants reality to representational states like belief, desire, etc. which cannot be reduced to mere neuronal functions. The folk psychological conception of mind cannot make sense without positing an autonomous realm of mind, which exists over and above the neuronal level. This gives ample space to formulate laws of psychology as a special science without being constrained by natural laws or laws of physics.

---

9. Fodor, *Psychosemantics*. p. 18.

Thus it grants a level above the neuronal one where cognitive processing takes place. Fodor believes that LOT hypothesis helps us locate the level of cognitive processing and explain how folk psychological categories work. Folk psychology and computational representational theory of the mind go hand in hand. To be more precise, the computational representational theory that is committed to language of thought hypothesis is an extension of our folk psychology.

Connectionist Approach

As has been stated earlier, Fodor's primary argument for the language of thought hypothesis is in the form of an inference to the best explanation. But arguments of this kind hold water only as long as there are no viable alternatives. With the emergence of connectionist models for the working of the mind, classicism no longer enjoys that privilege. Even though the history of the connectionist network can be traced back to the origin of the computer revolution, it received a boost only in the 1980s. The connectionist models are based on the observation that most of the common tasks that the brain performs require simultaneous execution of multiple tasks. This cannot be achieved as a result of serial processing, as in the case of classicist models, because this would require enormous amount of time. The connectionist networks are based on the assumption that the brain processes information parallelly and not serially. Several processing units are involved in a connectionist network. The members of the set of processing units share equal status in the sense that there is no executive unit, which oversees the activities of other units. Therefore, connectionism is alternatively known as parallel distributed processing (PDP) model of cognition. In this section, we shall discuss the connectionist theory with reference to the nature of mental representation and examine whether it is a viable alternative to the classicist approach.

Neurons and Nodes

Connectionist networks are modelled on the neuronal network in the brain. Even though there is no comprehensive account of the different brain processes, the basic functions in terms of interactions among the neurons is well accepted. The brain consists of billions of interconnected neurons. Their main function is information transfer, which happens both intracellularly and intercellularly. There are three main structural elements in a neuron. They are the axon, the dendrites and the synapse. In the axon, what takes place mainly is intracellular information transfer. The dendrite is the place where information is received by the neurons from the other neurons. The synapse is the connecting point between neurons where information from one neuron is transferred to another.

A connectionist network has various interconnected units or nodes corresponding to the neurons in the brain. However, the connectionist networks do not have elements corresponding to each and every element of the neuronal network in the brain. Yet, it is assumed that the connectionist networks share with neural networks the basic mechanism of information transfer. There are five assumptions about the kind of computation that takes place in the brain.[10] They are: [1] *Neurons process information*. Though there are different types of neurons, all of them perform the task of integrating information by means of accepting impulses through dendrites and if the input exceeds the threshold, it fires as a result of which information is sent to other neurons via the axon. [2] *Neurons pass information about the level of their input*. The output level of a neuron is directly proportional to its input level. [3] *Brain structure is layered*. For any type of activity to take place, for instance vision, there are multiple layers in which the

10. Peter Mcleod, Kim Plunkett, and Edmund T. Rolls. *An Introduction to Connectionist Modelling of Cognitive Processes*, New York: Oxford University Press, p. 11.

processing takes place and the final outcome is the result of the integration of all these levels. [4] *The influence of one neuron on another is dependent on the strength of the connection between them.* [5] *Learning is achieved by changing the strength of the connection between neurons.* It is supposed that learning in human brain is because of the changes in synaptic strength. The phenomenon of learning that an organism exhibits shows that nervous system exhibits some sort of plasticity. As the inter-neuron information transfer constitutes the central mechanism of brain functioning, the changes in the properties of synapse explain how the plasticity of nervous system is realized in learning.

It is pointed out that the connectionist models of cognition are based on the above five assumptions about the way the brain processes and transfers information. The assumptions at work in the connectionist networks that corresponds to those of the brain processes are the following: [1] *Connectionist models consist of a number of units* and these units do the work of *passing information* through an *input-output mechanism* similar to the one that is at work in the neural network of the brain. [2] Like neurons, connectionist units pass information about the *level of their input*, and the output level of a unit is directly proportional to its input level. [3] Just as the brain structure is layered, a connectionist *network* too is *layered*: in a connectionist model, normally, there are input, hidden and output layers. Cognition takes place due to the integration of all these layers. [4] The *influence* of one unit on another in a connectionist network is dependent on the *strength of the connection between them*. That is to say, the weight of the connection determines the level of information transfer. [5] It is assumed that, in connectionist models of learning, the changes in connection weight among units result in learning the appropriate output. If the response of an output unit is incorrect, then the connection among various units may be modified to correct that mistake. When this action is repeated, the *network learns* the correct output according to *several learning rules*. This is the most distinguishing aspect of a connectionist network.

There are eight important aspects to a connectionist model.[11] They are: a set of processing units, a state of activation, an output function for each unit, a pattern of connectivity among units, a propagation rule for propagating patterns of activity through the network, an activation rule that explains the combination of the input to a unit and its current state, a learning rule that explains learning as the modification of pattern of connectivity, and finally an environment in which the network operates.

A typical connectionist model consists of some input units, which receive data from the environment, and some output units, which give the result of the activity of the network to the environment. The activities of the input and output units are mediated by hidden units. When a stimulus is applied to a network, some of its input units are activated. As each unit is interconnected to others, the pattern of activity in the input units stimulates other units and the propagation of this activity results in the final output. The activities that take place in a connectionist network are mathematically described as follows.

The activity level of a unit is represented by the symbol a with a subscript, which identifies the unit that is activated. Accordingly, a_j means unit j is activated. Suppose unit j influences unit i by passing information to it. The influence exerted is proportional to the weight of the connection between the two units that is represented by the letter w. It

---

11. D.E. Rumelhart and J.L. McClelland, "PDP Models and General Issues in Cognitive Science," In D.E. Rumelhart and J.L. McClelland (eds.) *Parallel Distributed Processing: Explorations in the Microstructure of Cognition,* vol. 1 Cambridge, Mass: MIT Press, 1986. pp. 110-46.

will have two subscripts. The first one represents the unit which receives the influence and the second represents the unit that influences. If the weight is small, then the influence exerted will be negligible. The measure of the input from unit *j* to unit *i* is the product of the activity of unit *j* and the weight of the connection between them. That is,

$$\text{Input}_{ij} = a_j \, w_{ij}$$

The total input to unit *i* is the result of the sum of input from all units which send input to it. Thus,

$$\text{Net input} = \sum \Sigma \, {}_j a_j \, w_{ij}$$

This means that the net input to a unit is determined by the activation level of all the units that send information to it, and the weight of the connection between the unit whose net input is calculated and the units which send information. The relation between the net input to a unit and the activity level it produces is called the activation function. The simplest activation function is a linear relation between the net input and the activity level.

Models differ in treating the units regarding their representational capacity. In models where representation is conceived to be local, each unit represents a meaningful entity whereas in distributed models, meaning resides in the pattern as a whole. Since the network is the essence of a connectionist modelling, in order to know the status of a representation one has to look into the activation among units. Different models have different assumptions about the activation value of units. However, processing in a system is generally held to be the evolution of pattern of activity over the entire set of units.

It is the pattern of interactivity or connectivity that determines the knowledge encoded in a system as well as its various processes. In order to explain the interactivity among units, the output function of each unit is to be taken into consideration. The output of a unit is determined by its input as well as the degree of activation. The activation of a unit has to exceed a threshold value without which it cannot affect other units, i.e., emits output. Each unit is connected to many other units and so the overall input to a unit is the sum of various inputs. The input may be excitatory or inhibitory and the sum is to be determined after cancelling the inhibitory ones. Thus a matrix can be used to describe the connectivity to a unit which determines what that unit represents.

Distributed Representation: Smolensky's Approach

There are different types of connectionist networks. Among them, those which conceive representations as being distributed over the processing units are philosophically significant as the form of representation they adopt is radically different from the ones used in the symbolic approach to cognition. To put it in the words of Rumelhart and McClelland, there are connectionist networks where "each entity is represented by a pattern of activity distributed over many computing elements, and each computing element is involved in representing many different entities."[12] The notion of representation employed here is slightly difficult to comprehend for it is different from both linguistic (logical) and iconic forms of representation.

There have been some attempts to explain the way in which connectionist networks use representation as distributed over processing units. Among them, Smolensky's microfeatural analysis is the most significant one.[13] Smolensky's attempt is

12. G.E. Hinton, J.L. McClelland, "Distributed Representations," In D.E. Rumelhart and J.L. McClelland (eds.) *Parallel Distributed Processing: Explorations in the Microstructure of Cognition,* vol. 1 Cambridge, Mass: MIT Press, 1986, pp. 77-109.

13. Paul Smolensky, "On the Proper Treatment of Connectionism," *Behavioural and Brain Sciences* 11 (1988), p. 1-74.

based on his distinction between conceptual level representations and sub-conceptual or lower level representations. Mental representations corresponding to commonsense concepts such as BACHELOR, CUP, etc. are treated as distributed over several microfeatures, which themselves have representational content. To put it in more technical terms, the higher or conceptual level units correspond to vectors in a sub-conceptual space of micro features, where "vector" means an ordered set of numbers. Thus, for example, the concept BACHELOR corresponds to a vector in a space of features like HUMAN, ADULT, MALE, MARRIED, etc. When the value (+) is assigned to the first three features and the value (–) to the last feature, the concept BACHELOR comes into being. The feature vector at sub-conceptual level is more precise than the high level concepts because all features of a concept are present only at the sub-conceptual level and cognitive activity is sensitive to these features. Since it is heavily context-dependent as to which feature vector corresponds to a particular concept, it can be said that the concept level representation does not play a significant role in the connectionist analysis of cognition.

Smolensky considers the connectionist system to be dynamical with a space of continuous states. The change of states in this continuum of space is continuous and not discrete. This can be contrasted with the symbolic paradigm, which assumes that the representational states as well as the elements that constitute representation are discrete in nature. The change in a connectionist system is said to occur according to the soft constraints in the system. A constraint is soft if it can be broken without collapsing the whole system. In fact, each connection can be viewed as a soft constraint as the activities in the network depend on the connections among the nodes. Though the activities of the system at lower or subconceptual level is continuous, at higher conceptual level discreteness emerges.

But the higher level is only an approximation because "a sub-conceptual connectionist dynamical system . . . does not admit a complete, formal and precise conceptual-level description."[14] Smolensky claims that cognitive processes such as perception, language use and the states and processes responsible for the production of behaviour can be adequately explained at the sub-conceptual level, which lies in between the neural and the conceptual levels. The conceptual level provides a vocabulary that is adequate to formulate generalizations roughly approximating to the facts about behavioural regularities. Thus there is a harmonic co-existence of both symbolic and subsymbolic levels in Smolensky's account. For him, symbolic level is not foundational, but emergent out of sub-symbolic processes. Since symbolic level is emergent out of the sub-symbolic, within Smolensky's account, there is no need to postulate a language of thought to account for the cognitive processes.

Fodor and Pylyshyn Challenge

Fodor and Pylyshyn challenge the connectionist claim that cognitive processes can be explained without positing a symbolic architecture.[15] The complexity of mental representation and structure sensitivity of processes are the defining features of the symbolic account of cognition and they are essential to capture systematicity and productivity of cognitive phenomena. In Fodor and Pylyshyn's opinion, a theory that fails to account for systematicity and productivity of cognitive mental phenomena cannot fare well as a theory of cognition, and connectionist networks are noteworthy precisely due to their failure to account for systematicity and productivity.

---

14. Paul Smolensky, "On the Proper Treatment of Connectionism" p. 7.

15. Jerry Fodor and Zenon Pylyshyn, "Connectionism and Cognitive Architecture: A Critical Analysis" *Cognition* 28 (1986), pp. 3-71.

The features of complexity and structure sensitivity attributed to mental representations within the classicist approach are absent in the connectionist account. It might appear that connectionism can accommodate complexity of mental representations as microfeatures or sub-conceptual level representations could be thought of as constituents of concepts. But this is far from being a satisfactory account of the complexity of the representations; a symbol is a constituent of another symbol in the classicist sense if and only if one is both syntactically and semantically part of the other. For example, the word "John" appears in "John loves Mary" in the same way it appears in "Mary loves John." The word "John" is a constituent of both the sentences. The systematic relation between the two sentences is explained by pointing out that they are both composed of the same constituents. However, the microfeatural analysis that connectionism adopts does not have the resources to account for systematicity. This is because, within the microfeatural analysis, the emergence of a particular concept depends on the values of a given set of microfeatures. In this sense, the relation between the concept and the microfeatures is causal. But to be a constituent of the concept, the components themselves have to be semantically evaluable, which is not the case with the micro-features that realize a concept.

One way of overcoming this objection is to argue that sentential representations themselves could be subjected to a microfeatural analysis by considering the words occurring in them as microfeatures. Thus, in the sentence "John loves Mary," the subject term "John" may be considered as one of the microfeatures to which the sentence can be analyzed. The same may be said about the other words occurring in the sentence. But the problem with this account is that it would lead to a kind of combinatorial explosion. Since there is no concept as such in a connectionist network, the sets of microfeatures for all the possible sentences will have to be specified, which is a daunting task for it is, in principle, possible for a language user to produce infinite number of sentences. Consequently, the set of microfeatures that realizes "John loves Mary" would be different from the set that realizes "Mary loves John," for the microfeatural analysis does not allow identity of concepts across representations. In other words, the set of microfeatures that realizes "John" in "John loves Mary" would be different from the set of features that realizes "John" in "Mary loves John." If sets of microfeatures for all possible sentences are to be specified, then the ease at which language is produced without compromising systematicity would not have been possible. But language users are capable of producing infinitely many sentences. So the connectionist analysis in terms of microfeatures fails to explain systematicity and productivity of cognitive phenomena.

A similar criticism is made with regard to the connectionist view of cognitive processes as well. In the classicist paradigm, cognitive processes are characterized by their sensitivity to the structure of the representations involved and the structure, in turn, is sensitive to the semantic aspects of the elements that make up the complex representation. An important consequence of this is that the formal or syntactic processes involved in cognition are able to preserve semantics. However, connectionists are unable to explain how cognitive processes can account for the preservation of content because for them the notion of syntactic structure that is sensitive to the semantic elements of the representation is unavailable. Thus, connectionism fails in explaining the preservation of semantics which is an ineliminable feature of cognitive processes.

Connectionists accept two sorts of cognitive processes, one for explaining learning and the other for reasoning. Learning takes place through the process of back propagation in which the connection strengths among the units undergo a change.

The back propagation takes place when the output is not satisfactory and the consequent change in the connection weight gradually results in the system learning the correct output. Reasoning, for them, is a matter of statistical inference where the connection strengths determine the changes in the activation level in accordance with the statistical knowledge stored in the system. Fodor and Pylyshyn point out that neither of them amounts to the structure sensitive process invoked in the classicist account of cognition. Thus, according to them, the connectionists fail to provide an adequate and comprehensive account of cognitive processes. At the most, it can only be considered as an account of the mere implementation level details of the classicist account.

Conclusion

Viewed from a very broad perspective, both classicism and connectionism fall within the ambit of the computational-representational theory of mind. Yet, there is a significant difference in the way classicism and connectionism treat cognitive phenomena. The account of cognition provided by each has its own merits and demerits. Though classicism can successfully explain the systematicity and productivity of the cognitive mental processes, it is unable to provide a complete and satisfactory account of many cognitive processes, particularly those that involve parallel constraints. On the contrary, connectionist models are good at tasks involving parallel processes but their track record in dealing with high level processes is far from satisfactory. It is said that the argument that the connectionist networks are unable to account for the systematicity of cognition is the result of viewing language as essentially systematic. But the question whether language is essentially systematic or not is a debatable issue which could be settled only on the basis of empirical research in linguistics.[16] The outcome of such a research will certainly have implications on the question of the ability of connectionist networks to explain language use.

An important issue on which connectionism and classicism would diverge is the status of folk psychological categories. As we have already noted, classicism is committed to the view that folk psychological states are real and that scientific psychology is an extension of folk psychology. Many thinkers like Stich, and the Churchlands, on the other hand, believe that connectionism is not compatible with a realistic approach to folk psychology. Folk psychology thrives at an autonomous psychological level oblivious to the physical one. But connectionism, by and large, cannot grant that autonomy. So, folk psychology has no place within the paradigm of connectionism. This is not to say that the future of folk psychology is doomed. The only thing that can be said with certainty is that if connectionism can explain cognitive processes satisfactorily, then folk psychological categories will not find a place in our ontology. Only empirical research can settle whether it is classicism drawing on the resources of folk psychology or connectionism with its eliminative stance towards folk psychology that adequately explains cognitive phenomena.

16. Ken Johnson, "On the Systematicity of Language and Thought," *Journal of Philosophy* 101 (2004), pp. 111-39.

5

Fodorian Understanding of Folk Psychology and Computational Theory of Mind

An Analysis

S.Panneerselvam

My philosophical project . . . has been to understand the relation between a venerable, old idea borrowed from what philosophers call "folk psychology," and a trendy new idea borrowed mainly from Alan Turing. The old idea is that mental states are characteristically intentional. . . . The new idea is that mental processes are characteristically computational. My problem lies in the apparent difficulty of getting these ideas to fit together.

Fodor, *The Elm and the Expert*, pp. 1-2

Within fifty to a hundred years, a new class of organisms is likely to emerge. These organisms will be artificial in the sense that they will originally be designed by humans. However, they will reproduce, and will "evolve" into something other than their original form; they will be "alive" under any reasonable definition of the word. These organisms will evolve in a fundamentally different manner. . . . The pace . . . will be extremely rapid. . . . The impact on humanity and the biosphere could be enormous, larger than the industrial revolution, nuclear weapons, or environmental pollution. We must take steps now to shape the emergence of artificial organisms.

Doyne Farmer and Alletta Belin, "Artifical Life: The Coming Evolution," in *Artificial Life II*, p. 815.

Understanding Fodorian Project

It is argued by Gregory McCulloch[1] that Fodor is an intrepid materialistic Cartesian who moves over the years from one horn to the other. For example, the notion of narrow content was supported by Fodor in *Psychosemantics*. He considered it as an important psychological notion. "Being both narrow and content, it is supposed to be environment-independent and yet directed at," says Gregory McCulloch.[2] In later work like, *The Elm and the Expert*, Fodor rejected narrow content view and supported externalism by claiming that semantics is not a part of psychology. He says: ". . . the content of your thought does not supervene on mental processes."[3] The above two strands should be seen in the light of his commitment to folk psychology and physicalism. His aim is to locate folk psychology within the physicalist framework. Folk psychology as a descriptive, predictive practice, is a basis to human life. This predictive practice is necessary whenever we interact with our fellow beings. The understanding of the external world is possible by this. Thus folk psychology is related to the idea how human beings engage in behaviour, influenced by our mental states. When X utters a sentence, "Fang is ferocious and if there is one thing that I don't like it's ferocious dog," it means the following:

(1) The person X believes that Fang is ferocious

(2) X wants to avoid Fang.

---

1. Gregory McCulloch, *The Life of the Mind*, London: Routledge, 2003.
2. *Ibid.*, p. 8.
3. J.A. Fodor, *The Elm and the Expert*, Cambridge, Mass: MIT Press, 1994, p. 38.

Here mental states are expressed by means of language. We are engaged in a behaviour with a view to influence the mental states and subsequent behaviour. What is important is that the mental states in the example given above, were beliefs and desires. Beliefs and desires along with intentions and expectations, hopes, fears, etc. belong to mental states, known as the intentional states. Thus folk psychology examines the existence of a wide range of mental states and events. For Fodor, intentional states have semantic properties. In other words, they have meaning and they talk about the object and about something, and are expressed by a language.

But the intentional states are not acceptable to the eliminativists. The eliminativists argue that there are no such things as beliefs or desires or hopes or thoughts. The claim here is that all the intentional states and processes are nothing but myths. Stephen P. Stich says, "if eliminativism is right, then as Jerry Fodor has suggested, it might well be "the greatest intellectual catastrophe in the history of our species."[4] If eliminativism is right then we have to reject folk psychology. Fodor says that if eliminativism is right then many cognitive psychologists ought to do their science in some other way. Can the eliminativists be right? Let us see their claims:[5]

(1) Belief, desire, and other familiar intentional-state expressions are among the theoretical terms of a commonsense theory of the mind, which is often called "folk psychology."

(2) Folk psychology is a serious mistaken theory. The claims and the presuppositions of these claims are false.

(3) Beliefs, desires, and the rest will not be a part of the ontology of a mature scientific psychology.

---

4. Stephen P. Stich, *Deconstructing the Mind*, Oxford: Oxford University Press, 1996, p. 115.

5. *Ibid.*, p. 116.

(4) The intentional states of commonsense psychology do not exist.

Though all the four claims made by the eliminativists are important, one can meet the eliminativists by asking the question, how do you say that the claims of the folk psychologists are false? Because first of all, the folk psychologists do not make any claims or presuppositions and hence the question of their claims being false does not arise at all. Stich lists the folk psychological generalizations or capacities as follows:

(1) Terms like "belief," "think," "want," "desire," etc. are used in order to describe or interpret each other and ourselves.

(2) We also use the descriptions to construct explanations of people's behaviour. We have a capacity to construct explanations, which is prevalent among all of us.

(3) We also predict how people will behave. These predictions are very much available in our life based on the belief, desires and other mental states.

(4) We have the capacity to anticipate other people's behaviour.

(5) There is also a wide range of generalizations about the mental states.

The distinction between internal and external accounts of folk psychology is maintained by philosophers. Stich argues that on internal accounts, folk psychology plays a major role in the explanation of our ability to predict and explain each other's behaviour.

Computational Theory of Mind

Fodor's computational theory of mind enables us to see how minds might fit into the material world, and how minds are related to brains. Minds' relation to brains is something like the way computer programmers are related to the hardware. Minds are not identifiable with or reducible to brains for just the reasons that programmes or computational operations are not identifiable with or reducible to the hardware on which they run. Brains realize minds, much as computing machines realize particular programmes. Just as, in describing the operation of a computing machine at the programme level, we are describing its causal structure in abstraction from its hardware. Hence in describing mental operations, we are describing the causal structure of intelligent agents in abstraction from their biological hardware.

Fodor is of the view that the computational theory of mind is a new version of the representational theory of mind which considers mind as a "semantic engine," that operates on purely formal and syntactic principles. Although mental operations are blind to the semantics of the symbols they manipulate, their manipulations are indistinguishable from those that might be performed by someone who understood the symbols. But it fails to explain the understanding procedures. No doubt, one understands what is written in a piece of paper. But the mechanisms responsible for our understanding is not understood so easily. The representational theory of mind fails to explain the mechanisms involved in understanding. How to account for understanding? Understanding is not so simple. Searle's thought experiment shows the difficulty of the above. His paper, "Minds, brains and programs"[6] refutes the strong artificial intelligence by considering the work of Roger Schank. Roger Schank makes two claims in the context of strong artificial intelligence according to which the programmed computer understands the stories and that the

6. Searle, "Minds, brains, and programs," in *Philosophy: Basic Writings*, Nigel Warburton, (ed.), London: Routledge, 1999, pp. 325-44.

programme in some sense explains human understanding. Both claims are refuted by Searle. He says that computer and its programme do not provide sufficient conditions of understanding.[7]

Now let us see how Searle faces the representationalists. He explains that the process of understanding is not that much simple as the representationalists think. Searle's Chinese room argument explains this. The above thought experiment of Searle can be interpreted in terms of "Turing Machine" proposed by the mathematician, A.M. Turing. The idea here is to say that the mind can be best understood in terms of the operations of a computer. The Turing machine has the following: (a) a tape divided into "squares" and unbounded in both directions, (b) a scanner-printer positioned at one of the squares of the tape at any given time, (c) a finite set of internal states and, (d) a finite alphabet consisting of symbols. Turing, who was interested in the question whether it is possible to build an intelligent machine, though failed in his attempt to define intelligence, succeeded in defining intelligence operationally. He was aiming at the operational definition of intelligence. Whatever passes this is considered intelligent. He develops an "imitation game." The imitation game is played by three people. In the game, the interrogator puts questions to two players, a man and a woman, and tries to guess what is what. Here one of these players must answer honestly, whereas the other tries to mislead the interrogator. To avoid inappropriate visual or auditory clues, the players are placed in a separate room and communicate with the interrogator by means of a teletype. By asking clever questions, the interrogator will sometimes win the game, and will sometimes lose as well. Let us imagine that the interrogator wins about 30 per cent of the time. Turing argues that suppose

---

7. *Ibid.*, p. 328.

we substitute for one of the players a computing machine and if a machine can fool a clever interrogator about as often as a human player can, then we should say that it passes the test, i.e., it is intelligent.[8] Searle's Chinese room argument and Turing's test share something common. The Chinese scientists who are assembled outside the room are taking the role of the interrogator in the imitation game of Turing. In Chinese room argument, you neither speak nor understand Chinese. Similarly, as because you operate just as a computing machine, we should not say that a computing machine that passes the Turing test is genuinely intelligent or that it understands the sentences it receives as inputs or produces as outputs. By using the Chinese room argument, Searle tries to say that the representational theory of mind is based on the idea that mind is a semantic engine: mental processes consist of operations over uninterpreted symbols, for example, sentences in the language of thought. Thus by using the Chinese room argument, Searle makes one thing clear. In a real cognitive system, the symbols have real semantic contents. Real semantic contents are necessary for understanding. Cognition is not a mere symbol interpretation. In his argument, Searle could show that even though a system inside a room can manipulate symbols, it cannot necessarily operate on the level of meaning. Understanding, thoughts, etc. have mental contents. This means that minds cannot be equated with programmes. In other words, the computers are mere formal symbol manipulators and they have their limitation with regard to understanding or thought. Human minds have mental contents but not the computers. But Churchland has questioned the above view of Searle. Churchland argues that it is the overall system that is appropriately compared to a programmed computer. He points out that Searle is not in a position to argue that rule-governed symbol manipulation can never

8. John Heil, *Philosophy of Mind*, London: Routledge, 1998, p. 110.

constitute semantic phenomena. Searle argues that there is a distinction between syntax and semantics. He points out the distinction between a formal symbol manipulation that is done by the computer and the mental contents biologically produced by the brain.

Classicism vs. Connectionism

Connectionism is a theory developed in 1980 as a reaction to the Classicism, a classical model of the computer theory of mind. Connectionism emerged as an alternative to the conception of mind based on the model of the modern digital computer. The reason for the emergence of connectionism or the artificial neural network is that we believe that human cognition is, too rich and flexible to be simulated by computer programmes. Cognition needs a language of thought, which is not programmable or computable. In the classical view of cognitive science, the cognition, what the classical computer does, is rule-governed symbol manipulation. Here human mind is imitated by a computer programme with data structures corresponding to mental states such as beliefs and desires. Connectionism promotes an alternative way of understanding how mentality could be physically embodied. Thus Connectionism presents a different way of understanding the mind. David Marr's *Vision* has made an attempt to understand the cognitivist approach to the mind. Fodor to some extent adopted this in his *The Modularity of Mind*. According to the vision theory, we have the capacity to know the facts concerning the world through the means of vision. For example, facts about shape, size, colour, etc. are known by this. Marr claims that this visual capacity is a computer or information-processing system in the brain. This is known as "vision module," Marr argues, that describes its working and in doing so explains our visual capacities. He explains this at three levels. At one extreme, the top level, is the abstract computational theory of the device, in which the performance of the device is characterized as a mapping from one kind of information to another, the abstract properties of this mapping are defined precisely, and its appropriateness and adequacy for the task are demonstrated. In the centre, is the choice of representation for the input and output and algorithm to transform one into the other. At the other extreme, are the details of how the algorithm and representation are realized physically — the detailed computer architecture, so to speak.[9]

Marr's three level typology for cognitive science is as follows:

1. the computational theory,
2. theory of representation and algorithm, and
3. theory of hardware implementation.

At the first level, the computational theory is based on the semantic and intentional details of the visual module's activity. Here one deals with the goal of the computation. Why is this function appropriate, and what is the logic of the strategy by which it can be computed? These are the two important questions that arise in this context. In the second level, we have questions such as: How can this computational theory be implemented? What is the representation for the input and output, and what is the algorithm for the transformation? In the third level, the question is this: How can the representations and algorithm be physically realized?

What is important in the above analysis is that the top level is concerned with systematic transitional connections among intentional state types. For a model or a cognitive system as a whole, these are "total cognitive states" (TCS), a single TCS sometimes comprising several individual cognitive states that can be instantiated simultaneously. This level

---

9. David Marr, *Vision*, San Francisco, Freeman, 1982, pp. 24-25.

delineates a "cognitive-transition function" (CTF) over TCSs. For all TCSs instantiable by the system, the CTF specifies the appropriate immediate successor TCSs. The CTF is the function to be computed by the system.

Where does Connectionism differ from Classicism? In Classicism, the behaviour of the whole system is controlled at the control processing unit (CPU) whereas in Connectionism, there is no such processing unit and there is no programme to control the operation of the system. The Classical view holds that the cognition is rule-governed symbol manipulation. Though Connectionism has not developed any conception of cognition, it shows different ways of doing things. It teaches that there are different ways of thinking about particular cognitive processes and abilities like language learning. Connectionism explains the view that thinking activity is a neural network. The neural network consists of a large number of very simple neuron-like processes, known as modes or units. But the question here is this: Can it replace the classical computational theory of mind? What are its fundamental assumptions? Should we give up Classicism's fundamental assumptions? The supporters of Connectionism argue that there is "multiple soft constraint satisfaction." But it is not true that Classical view rejects the softness of multiple constraints. The Connectionism is supported by Marr, Patrick Churchland, Paul Churchland, Sejnowsk and others and is criticized by Fodor and Zenon Pylyshyn. Fodor's charge is that Connectionism constitutes an unpromising step backwards in cognitive science. What exactly are we supposed to be gaining, in term of our abilities to model cognitive process? This question, according to Fodor, has not been answered by the Connectionists.

The Classical view is that cognition is realized by an algorithm over symbolic representations, i.e., by rule-governed symbol manipulation, which involves three basic assumptions:

1. Intelligent cognition employs structurally complex mental representations.
2. Cognitive processing is sensitive to the structure of these representations.
3. Cognitive processing conforms to precise, exceptionless rules, stable over the representations themselves and articulable in the format of a computer programme.

But the classical cognitive science is also not acceptable to Fodor. In *The Modularity of Mind,* he argues that certain problems in classical cognitive science look to be in-principle problems and hence that the prospects for understanding human cognitive processes such as belief fixation within the framework of classical cognitive science are not encouraging. He claims that the human cognitive system possesses a number of important systems that are modular: domain specific, mandatory, limited in their access to other parts of the larger cognitive system. Fodor says that there is good evidence that human output systems, including those that mediate speech perception, exhibit modularity. Further he says that Classicism has not made much progress in understanding central process. He says that the belief fixation, i.e., the generation of new beliefs on the basis of current input together with other beliefs is an example. Fodor remarks: "The problem is to get the structure of the entire belief system to bear on individual occasions of belief fixation. We have, to put it bluntly, no computational formalism that shows us how to do this, and we have no idea how such formalisms might be developed. . . . In this respect, cognitive science has not even started; we are literally no farther advanced than we were in the darkest days of behaviourism."[10]

---

10. J.A. Fodor, *The Modularity of Mind,* Cambridge, Mass: MIT Press, 1983, p. 129.

Fodor's Theory of intentional states and processes

Fodor constructs physicalist justification of folk psychology on the theory of intentional states and processes. For Fodor, the intentional states are computational relations to mental representations and intentional processes. They are the processes involving the manipulation of mental representations by means of computation. These mental representations belong to the language of thought. Thus the computational theory of mind is a new version of representational theory of mind. According to the representational theory, intentional states are relations to mental representations. For example, believing that Fang is ferocious involves standing in the belief relating to a mental representation that has the meaning Fang is ferocious. In other words, the mental representations are meaningful symbols similar to spoken and written words. According to Fodor, the mental representations involved in the tokening of intentional states are more like linguistic symbols like the words and sentence of a language. Further, the mental representations belong to non-natural language, otherwise known as the language of thought. It is different from the natural language. The language of thought is different from a natural language because Fodor thinks that having a non-natural language of thought is a necessary condition to learn a language. It is because of the reason that learning a natural language involves acquiring knowledge of the meanings of the words of that language. Fodor believes that non-natural language of thought is important for learning a natural language. Construction and confirming hypothesis is necessary for understanding the natural language. This means that in order to construct and confirm such hypothesis, one needs a "representation." Fodor says in *Language of Thought* that unless one conceives of language of thought, as being a non-natural language, then it is a complete mystery how human minds ever manage to learn their first natural language.

Further Fodor claims that intentional states have determinate contents whereas the natural language does not. There are sentences, which are ambiguous. For example, in the sentence, "Fang chased the runner with a stick" may mean either the Fang has the stick or the runner has the stick. This made Fodor to conclude that language of thought is not a natural language. He believes that though thought involves the use of a linguistic system, it is prior to and independent of natural language. In this context, he talks about two important elements, namely, a theory of intentional states and a theory of intentional processes.

Fodor says that intentional states are belief, desires and the like. In *Language of Thought* he explains this. According to him, intentional states are contents that are precise and specific and it is different from images. The intentional states are computational relations to mental representations. He is of the view that mind is a computer and mental mechanisms manipulate sentences of language of thought by means of computation. As a result of this, the functional role of a sentence-token of language of thought is a matter of its functional role within a computational system so that distinct species of intentional states as relations can be characterized as distinct species of computational relations. He explains the theory of intentional states in the following manner. To believe that P is to token a sentence of language of thought that has the content P and that is located in one's belief box. All the other species of intentional state relations are like this. The mind is a computer that is programmed to process sentences stored in the belief box in a manner characteristic of sentence stored in the belief box. This processing involves a computational mechanism taking a sentence of language of thought as input and generating a sentence of language of thought as output, a sentence that is placed in some box or other. This means a sentence of a given type that is stored in the belief box will be processed by the mechanisms that have access to it in a way that is different from that in which a sentence of the same type stored in the desire box would be processed by the mechanisms that have access to it. The intentional processes are the causal processes that intentional states come in. The intentional processes are computational processes. They are the processes involving the disciplined manipulation of sentence of language of thought by means of computation. The intentional processes are generally logically coherent because of the meaning of the sentences of language of thought and the rules that these mechanisms apply to those symbols.

New-Dualism and its implication on Fodor's Computational Theory of Mind

For Fodor, the computational theory of mind is similar to functionalism because he believes that intentional state relations are functional relations. The importance of functionalism is that it plays a role in cognitive science and psychology. It offers a perspective of the mind that suits the need of many empirical scientists, one that offers solutions to a host of long standing philosophical puzzles about minds and their relation to material bodies. Generally the theory means that mind or any given mental phenomenon is what it does or is to be defined in terms of how it functions. Shoemaker, in *Identity, Cause and Mind* contends that it is the view that mental states are definable in terms of their causal relations to sensory inputs, behavioural outputs and other mental states.[11] Functionalism explains our feeling that though mental phenomena ought to be closely tied to what goes on in the brain or central nervous system, what goes on there, in one sense, is irrelevant. Functionalism explains the variable realizability of mental states. The

---

11. S. Shoemaker, *Identity, Cause and Mind,* Cambridge, Cambridge University Press, 1984, p. 337.

uniqueness of Functionalism is that it is considered to be a sophisticated theory of mind, identifying the states of mind not with states of brain, but with functional roles. Functionalists hold the view that the states of mind are "multiply realizable." This means that to be in a particular mental state is to be in a state that has a certain characteristic role. Here the mind is a device capable of performing a particular sort of operation. States of mind resemble computational states, at least to the extent that they are sharable in principle, by any number of material systems.

No doubt, functionalism is at its best with desires and beliefs. Functionalism faces the common objection that even if cognitive capacity is explained they cannot cope up with the Cartesian mental — with consciousness, qualia, pains and they fail in Nagel's phrase to explain "what it is like to be" a sentient agent.[12] By an imaginative analysis of a bat's experience, he tries to show that the physicalist theories of mind could not explain the notion of consciousness. He says that we have at present no conception of what an explanation of the physical nature of a mental phenomenon would be. The question here is whether functionalism can capture the inner content of experience. Can functionalism distinguish the ordinary mental state of seeing something red without having any actual experience? Can it distinguish an ordinary human from a cleverly fashioned robot or a zombie? Can functionalism cater for the possibility that I might have the experience of seeing red in just those circumstances where you have the experience of seeing what I call green, and vice versa? McGinn says that we withdraw our hand from something hot because we are in pain, not as part of being so.[13] Further he argues that

12. T. Nagel, "What is it Like to be a Bat?" 1974, *Philosophical Review* 83, pp. 435-50.

13. C. McGinn, *The Character of Mind*, Oxford. Oxford University Press, 1982, p. 35.

functionalism, unlike behaviourism offers a conceptual, not an ontological, reduction of the mental. It does not try to eliminate mental entities, but only explains the need for special mental terms to describe them. It does not say that qualia does not exist but that they cannot exist without manifesting themselves in the cause-effect sequences. One can say that functionalism is reductionism. It is silent on the experiential properties of the mental.

A highly popular and prevalent version of functionalism is otherwise known as "new dualism." The new dualists believe that to reduce mental states to the states of the brain would be parochial and chauvinist. Such reductions, they believe, would draw attention away from what is truly interesting. Like all forms of functionalism, the new dualism also has some difficulties. First of all, it conflicts with the well irresistible intuition that the structure of the brain must have some considerable bearing upon the nature of the mental states it underpins. Secondly, the micro-structures (i.e., different hardware realization) of artificial intelligence and real or human intelligence differ. Artificial diamonds are not real diamonds. Like functionalism, the computational theory of mind rejects the philosophical behaviourism and type identity theory. The essence of the difference between beliefs that have different contents is a functional one. The computational theory helps one to explain first language acquisition. Without this language, knowing process can never be explained. It explains the functioning of the cognitive mind. According to Fodor, the concept learning, perception, decision making are possible only through the computational theory of mind. The theory of cognition and the theory of mind are related. This led to the theory of connectionism. The computational theory of mind shows the relation between the intentional states and intentional processes. For Fodor, this computational theory of mind alone can explain the relation. Though Fodor considers that computational theory of mind is a physicalist theory, which will explain our intentional states as well as processes to explain the folk psychology, the computational theory of mind cannot explain one aspect of intentional states. For example, intentional states have content and the computational theory of mind cannot account for the content of intentional states.

According to Fodor, language of thought is innate. He explains this by his "concept nativism." A concept means having a symbol in one's language of thought, which has the content. To have a concept MAN is a matter of having a symbol in one's language of thought which expresses the property of being a man. Thus concept nativism is the view that all or most of our concepts that we grasp and deploy in thought are innate. Though Fodor was initially supporting this concept nativism, later he rejected it. In *Concepts: Where Cognitive Science Went Wrong*, Fodor rejected the concept nativism, which he had maintained in 1970s and 1980s. Now he talks about concepts, which are neither natural nor logico-mathematical and says that these concepts are not innate. A concept like DOORKNOB is not innate. He asks the question: "If concepts are innate rather than learned, then why is it the case that we typically acquire them as a result of experiences of items that fall under them?" He further says: "What doorknobs have common qua doorknobs is being the kind of thing that our kinds of mind look to from experience with instances of the doorknob stereotype. What makes something a doorknob is just: being the kind of thing from experience with which our kind of mind readily acquires the concept DOORKNOB."[14] Fodor thus says that concept DOORKNOB is not innate. If this concept is acquired by means of hypothesis-testing and confirmation, then it follows that it is not innate. It is because

14. J.A. Fodor, *Concepts: Where Cognitive Science Went Wrong*, Oxford, Oxford University Press, 1998, p. 137.

one cannot frame the relevant hypothesis unless one already has the concept DOORKNOB.

Evaluating Fodor

Though the computational theory of mind is an important contribution in the field of philosophy of mind, there are some difficulties raised by thinkers like Davidson, Dennett, Searle and others. Also there are criticisms from Connectivism. Let us see some of these criticisms in the background of the computational theory of mind.

Davidson argues in favour of folk psychology as central to human life. We always attribute intentional states to others in order to make sense of and to explain their behaviour and episodes in their mental life. For him, attributing intentional states is one interpretation. Thus by attributing beliefs, desires, intention to a person, I interpret him or her on the basis of observable evidence concerning his or her behaviour. How do I interpret? Here the interpreter ascribes to attribute beliefs and desires, the possession of which makes the subject's actions rational. They are normative because they enjoin the interpreter's beliefs and desires that they ought to have and reveal their actions to be rational. What is also important is that intentional states are not on one-by-one basis relation. It is holistic in nature. Though like Fodor, Davidson rejects behaviourism, he differs from Fodor in some respects. First of all, Davidson makes a distinction between folk psychology and science. For Davidson, the nature of the intentional and the principles that govern the attribution of intentional states places a huge gap between folk psychology and physics. Davidson is of the view that Fodor is confused in viewing folk psychology as being akin to science. Secondly Davidson is committed to semantic holism whereas it is rejected by Fodor.

Dennett's theory of intentional states has some similarities with Davidson's understanding. One such similarity is that like Davidson, Dennett also considers the practice of attributing intentional states as involving considerations of rationality and as being governed by normative principles. The role of such considerations and principles are reflected in his understanding of what it is to have intentional states. But there are some differences also. One such distinction is that token identity theory is not acceptable to him. He argues that intentional state tokens cannot be identified with physical state tokens such as internal states of the brain. According to Dennett, there are different stances, which one may adopt while attempting to predict the behaviour of a particular physical system like a human being or a machine. Physical stance is one such stance. Accepting or following the physical stance involves predicting the behaviour of a system on the basis of knowledge or its internal physical states. Another stance is the intentional stance. Following the intentional stance towards a system involves attributing to it, the belief that it "ought to have, given its perceptual capacities, its epistemic needs, and its biography along with the desires that it "ought to have" given its biological needs and the most practicable means of satisfying them," says Dennett.[15] This means that following the intentional stance towards a system involves employing normative principles and attributing a modicum of rationality of the system. This intentional stance, according to Dennett is an instrument for the prediction of behaviour. A system has particular intentional states only in so far as the attribution of those states to it would facilitate the accurate and effective prediction of its behaviour. This Dennett calls "mild realism" for the reason that the intentional stance works

---

15. D. Dennett, "Three Kinds of Intentional Psychology," in *Reduction, Time and Reality*, R. Healy (ed.), Cambridge, Cambridge University Press, 1981, p. 49.

with respect to many systems and intentional states as real as centres of gravity and line of latitude. Folk psychology according to Dennett, is a rationalistic calculus of interpretation and prediction — an idealizing, abstract, instrumentalist interpretation method that has evolved because it works and works because it has evolved.[16] Thus the mild realist theory of intentional states is important for folk psychology. Dennett is of the view that human behaviour can be predicted by means of the adoption of the intentional stance and it proves that we have intentional states. This has a bearing on inner workings, which is responsible for our interaction with the external world. The differences among Fodor, Davidson and Dennett simply show that Fodor's understanding of folk psychology and computational theory of mind of mind is unique in spite of its limitations.

16. *Ibid.*, pp. 48-49.

6

Mind and Language
Their Inter-dependence

By P.R. Bhat

Introduction

The term "mind" is a familiar one which is used in both ordinary sense and as a technical term in philosophy. Similarly, the term "language" is used in ordinary sense as well as a technical sense. We shall explore these notions from the point of view of ordinary usage keeping in mind the philosophical significance of these notions. The methodology adopted here is not to reject the obvious for the sake of philosophical advantage, rather, try to modify philosophical perspectives in favour of the common sense.

We begin with what is a philosophical method. After concluding that all philosophies are *a priori*, we move on to the issue of philosophy of mind. We see the possibility of making the distinction among mental processes, mental states and mental acts. We then move on to discuss language. We notice that language consists of two types of rules, one regulative and the other constitutive. Regulative rules are grammatical in nature and constitutive rules are the ones which help us in sentence formation expressing certain meaning. We then notice that a word may have several rules for its use sometimes resulting in ambiguous sentence. A word has several rules for its use does not necessarily mean that the word is ambiguous. We apply this to understand the mechanism that we use in ascribing the truth to subjective experiences. We conclude that philosophers are unreasonable in showing dissatisfaction towards ascription of mental attributes to others.

A priori Philosophies

There are hosts of philosophical issues which are based on both mind and language. Among the issues, the issue of philosophical method, perhaps, is the most fundamental one. We, as students of philosophy are aware of the methodology used by other philosophers in doing philosophy. For instance, when we ask the question: What is mind? a philosopher proceeds in a certain way. He may first make a statement of the sort "*mind* is a substance," and then proceed to analyze the term "substance": What does it mean to say that something is a *substance*? In other words, a philosopher asks a question which is general in nature. That is to say, the question cannot be an empirical one and the answer that he expects in return too cannot be an empirical one. Thus, he expects general answers to his philosophical questions.

We speak of different methodologies in philosophy: speculative method, analytical method. In the speculative method, we speak of different sub-versions. Synthesizing two ideas and providing a new organic view could be one type of speculation; providing the ontological categories as the basis of our ethics or explaining the presuppositions of our epistemology could be another type of speculation. Similarly, there are sub-categories of the method of analysis: logical analysis, linguistic analysis, conceptual analysis, ordinary language analysis, and speech act analysis. These methods of analysis are not exclusive methods; one overlaps with the other, sometimes the distinction between the two analyses may not be very clear when one does philosophy. There are overlaps, for instance, while making the distinction between relation of ideas; one might use both the methods of conceptual analysis and ordinary language analysis. Sometimes, the analyses may be different and sometimes, they may appear similar to one another.

One might wonder as to what is the basis on which a philosopher proceeds offering his solution to the philosophical issues, say, the method of philosophy. We are aware of the method of empirical investigation and the method of rational investigation as two methods of acquiring knowledge. In doing philosophy, the manner in which they do, it appears that even the empiricists who refuse to believe in the rational method, seem to make use of rational method in developing their philosophy. Whether a method is speculative or that of analysis, ought to be considered rational in the broad sense of the term "rational." This is so because, even the conclusions arrived at speculative method are reasoned systematically such that they are intelligible to a philosopher.

The point that we do not make use of empirical mode of acquiring knowledge is clear in the case of speculative method. Speculations are generally going beyond experiences. That is to say, though we need some basis for speculations, the result of speculation is something more than what is observed through senses. For instance, answering the question: are there realities which are beyond space and time? would necessarily involve speculation. If the answer is in the positive, certainly one is speaking of realities which are not in space and time and hence cannot be experienced through senses. One may indicate the laws of nature, or the theorems in geometry as examples of this kind. Both laws of nature and theorems of geometry are universal and hence cannot be restricted by time and space. They are truths grasped by mind and not learned through sense experiences.

Another good example of application of speculative method is the result we obtain by invoking the distinction between *primary* and *secondary* qualities. By definition, primary qualities are the qualities which the objects possess independently of the observer, and in contrast, the secondary qualities are qualities that emerge in the interaction between the perceiver and the perceived through the senses. It is quite obvious that we cannot know the primary qualities using the senses. Primary qualities such as, solidity, extension, figure, motion or rest, etc. are not knowable through senses by definition. If they are known at all, that would be using speculative method.

Speculative philosophers have the habit of asserting something and then justifying it. For instance, there are only two types of realities: mind and matter. Or consider the example of pluralism of Nyaya philosophy: there are multiple realities, both material as well as spiritual. Having made the claim, one moves on to justify the claim. This is what applying the speculative method would be. We use speculative method to build grand metaphysical systems. Prakrti and its evolutes in Sāṁkhyā philosophy are conceived using speculative method. The same is the case with seven categories of Vaiśeṣika philosophy.

A philosophical method, any one of them, is *a priori*. We simply do not make use of empirical method of observation or that of experimentation in doing philosophy. This is not to deny the importance of our experience and knowledge both of language and reality in doing philosophy. We do make use of our knowledge about the use of words in offering ordinary language analysis; similarly, we do make use of our knowledge of the concepts in offering the conceptual analysis. In a sense, the knowledge that is made use of in offering different philosophical analyses is certainly not based on sense perception. We make use of examples in providing analyses, but that would not amount to deriving philosophical knowledge of one kind or the other from the empirical study.

Our understanding of philosophical method would be highly inadequate if we do not mention the role of philosophical intuitions that we often make use of in doing philosophy. We, for instance, claim that a stick must have two ends. Similarly, we take it for granted that everyone would agree that a nominal reality if it exists, cannot be a part of the phenomenal world. We make use of such intuitions in making philosophical points and no doubt these insights do help us to carry on the philosophical discussions.

It would be a mute point to claim that our philosophical intuitions are based on long experiences in life. Such a claim can only prove that philosophical maturity comes late in one's life. By clinging to such a view, one would not be in a position to prove that a philosophical method and its application are entirely derivable from sense experience. No doubt that wider and longer the experience, better is the chance of giving good examples in the philosophical analyses. Moreover, if wider is the experience in life, one is in a better position to assess the scope of a philosophical solution.

A philosophical theory, developed on the basis of speculative method or that of analytical method, is a result of activity which we may name as "philosophical" as opposed to empirical. As remarked earlier, even an empiricist does not follow empirical method in developing his philosophical thesis. For instance, he would begin by holding the general thesis that only sense experience would give a person knowledge of the things that are in the world. He does not sensually experience the truth of such a statement first, and then make such a claim. In fact, one can never know the truth of a general statement through sense experience. Thus, all philosophies are *a priori* philosophies.

Having said that all philosophies are *a priori* philosophies, we may now turn to the issues of mind and language using available philosophical methods. Both mind and language are very familiar concepts in philosophical discussions as well as in our day-to-day life. Since these concepts are not alien to us, we may make use of our prior knowledge about the concepts for philosophical treatment.

The Conception of Mind

What is mind? This question invites a metaphysician to assert something. When one thinks of asserting something, one is made to assert about the existence of something. Thus, the normal response that one may get to this question is: mind is a substance, or mind is a quality. On reflection, one may find that both the answers are unsatisfactory. For instance, if mind is a substance, then the question arises: where does it exist? We cannot indicate the space where it exists and thus are led to a difficult situation. Alternatively, we might opt for brain-mind identity. If we do so, since brain is totally governed by the causal laws of nature, we are compelled to believe that mind too is totally determined by the causal laws of nature. If we conceive causal laws operating in the realm of mind as well, it becomes enormously difficult to explain the human freedom. Alternatively, if we claim that mind is a quality, then we are obliged to give an account of its relationship with the substance, since a quality ought to be a quality of a substance. If we claim that this quality is the quality of the body, then we are obliged to answer the question: how does one make sense of ethical responsibility expressed in the judgement "I am responsible for what I did"? It is absurd to attribute responsibility to a quality of an object for an action.

Having said that absurdity ought to be avoided, we are back to the issue of the nature of mind. Neither of the solutions offered are acceptable for the reasons stated. We have the third alternative of speculating something else as the nature of mind. We have the option of calling mind as a form of energy. We need to explain then how one makes sense of different statements pertaining to mind.

Energy can be in the state of flow, or in the state of rest. We have the concept of energy that is stored in a battery. We also have the concept of energy flowing, for instance, water flows, wind blows, heat gets transferred and electrical energy can be transported from one place to another through wires and so on. Moreover, we also speak of enhancing the energy or curtailing the energy or spending them. Parallely, we speak of mental energy, spending of mental energy and storing of mental energy and so on. Thinking, imagining, hearing music etc. can be taken as mental processes: there is a sense of movement from one stage to another within a certain period. In contrast, expecting, intending, wishing, having certain attitude, holding certain values, etc. can be considered to be mental states like the battery which has the energy stored in it. We expect the rain tomorrow all the while and therefore, it is a state of the mind. Thus the distinction between mental processes and mental states makes sense and the distinction can be sustained philosophically.

The absurdity with reference to the consequences of holding the view that mind is a substance or it is a quality need not worry us now. But onus is on us to show how we make sense of the attribution of actions to individuals and show how the laws of nature do not eliminate our freedom. Moreover, we need to explain the nature of mental processes and mental states.

The term mental act is in currency. In addition to mental processes and states, one needs to explain the mental acts such as taking decisions, asserting something, questioning something, predicting something, promising something and so on. The most important mental act seems to be making rules and following them which is the basis of all languages.

Like any other event, mental act has time dimension. We claim that we have taken a decision at a point in time. "I decided to go to Hyderabad yesterday" is a sensible statement. Similarly, questioning, predicting something are all activities done with reference to some time or the other. Offering explanation, offering justification, providing evidence, proving something, arguing something, etc. are all mental acts done at a point in time. As the name itself would suggest, all speech acts are mental acts. Promising is a good example of speech act which is clearly a mental act.

Mind is capable of acting is the most central theme to the philosophy of mind. What is it to say that something is a mental act? Consider the example of evaluating a behaviour of a person as bad behaviour. What facts do I need to know about the behaviour in order to judge it as bad? Nothing more than the knowledge about the behaviour itself. Judging is a mental act, and that act can be performed without knowing anything more than the behaviour itself. However, I judge the action to be bad with respect to a norm. That is to say, I must have a norm, or a standard to judge the behaviour as bad. Similarly, what more do I need to decide something? No amount of information about the world can give me the decision. That is to say, "ought" cannot be derived from "is." I decide the moment I am ready to decide. Collecting information on certain aspects of decision making is only a process prior to taking the decision. The decision does not depend on facts, though facts are supporting factors in favour of a decision. When does one decide to undergo certain surgical operation? It all depends, may be immediately after the surgeon suggested. Or may be after second opinion is obtained by consulting another expert. Or may be after suffering from the pain for a certain period.

Predicting is a mental act. I predict heavy rain in the evening. This does not add any fact to the state of affairs. I am aware of the humidity level, the clouds and the wind that is blowing in a certain direction. My prediction of the rain, may turn out to be true or may fail. Again, prediction could be on the basis of some facts. It is the living being who predicts; predicts when one wants to predict.

All mental acts are generally characterized as intentional acts. That is to say, we hold ourselves responsible for our acts. For instance, if I take the decision to help someone, I take full responsibility for my decision. If someone charges me of helping the criminal, I need to answer this charge. Similarly, I am responsible for the explanation I offer as to why I did not do certain things. The same is true of other mental acts. We hold each one responsible for the mental acts that he performs.

Autonomy of the Mind

Mental acts on their own bring no change in the universe. Mental realm is one like super-structure: it is autonomous. The autonomy of the mind over the causal structure of the universe is clear from the point of view that no physical fact can determine the mental act, and *vice versa*. No amount of taking decision can automatically make the body act. The relationship between mind and body are contingent. One and the same physical condition need not result in the same mental act, and similar mental acts need not lead to comparable changes in the physical world. Yet, mind and body are related but contingently.

Mind has autonomy does not mean the body is not related to it. Autonomy simply indicates the freedom that mind can exercise, the voluntary nature it has which cannot be robbed by the physical conditions. For instance, making a rule does not add to the existing facts of the universe. Consider the decision to allow vehicles of odd numbers to ply on the road on every Monday. This decision adds no fact to the existing facts of the world, yet humans can follow this as a principle. Rule-making is an intentional act and performing such an intentional act does not happen to be part of the natural history of the universe. However, it is an event in the cultural history of mankind.

Evolution of language is part of cultural history of man. Humans are capable of formulating rules for themselves and capable of following them. Culture is full of conventions using symbols. Man has gained much from his mental acts. His civilized behaviour, his cultural norms are all possible because he can perform mental act of formulating rules and obeying them. He initiates a new convention by taking arbitrarily something as a symbol. For instance, he declares what is his signature and follows it consistently. It does not matter whether he spells his name properly or not; it does not matter whether it is readable or not. A signature is what it is by virtue of the person's act of declaring and adopting it.

A norm has been introduced the very moment a signature is accepted. Anything that is systematic and regular is a norm. Any deviation would not be accepted if one has adopted a certain signature. Banks for instance, will not honour your cheque if your signatures do not match. Similarly, any legal documents will not be respected if your signatures do not match.

Rules are said to be either constitutive or regulative. For instance, traffic rules are regulative. You are supposed to drive the car on your left in India and overtake a vehicle on the right. One is supposed to stop at the signal if it is red and supposed to proceed when it is green. Drivers are guided by these regulative traffic rules; that does not mean that no one can break these rules. One can drive the car without respecting the traffic rules. It is a different matter that one would risk one's life if one does not follow the traffic rules.

Syntactic rules are regulative in this sense. We are supposed to follow the syntactic rules, i.e., rules of grammar in formulating sentences. But one may not follow it knowingly or unknowingly. For instance, there may not be any agreement between the subject and the verb in a sentence: "I is coming" one might say. Or "There he come." In both these cases, there is no agreement between the subject and the verb. Those who know English grammar can edit the sentences and correct them in this manner:"I am coming" and "There he comes."

Rules could also be constitutive. A game like chess is possible because the rules of the movement of each piece in chess is defined in a certain way. For instance, the manner in which a horse moves is different from the manner in which an elephant moves in chess. What makes a horse on the chess board is the rule according to which the piece is to be moved. If you change the rule, it is no more horse of chess or chess game does not remain what it is. Similar is the case with all the rules that are there for the use of words. Wittgenstein has pointed out that we cannot say "It's cold here" and mean "It's warm here."[1]

When it is the matter of constitutive rule, we do not have much liberty but to obey the rule. This can be demonstrated in this way. After offering an operational definition of an infant as a child below three years, one cannot say that a two year old is not an infant. This is because, when we offer a definition whether it is operational or general, we are offering a constitutive rule for the use of the word. We cannot be inconsistent in our approach to the use of words. Regularity and systematicity is presupposed at least in that particular

---

1. Wittgenstein, L, *Philosophical Investigation,* tr., G.E.M. Anscombe, Basil Black Well, 1963, p. 510.

context. If in another study, if we want to alter the use of the term "infant" to cover children below four years, that could be done. But in that study, we cannot deny ascribing the child as infant if it is three years. This is the reason why Wittgenstein claims that rules are arbitrary but their applications are not.

If syntactic rules and the semantic rules are arbitrary and man-made, the issue of their being logical or illogical does not arise since everything would depend on convention. Syntactic rules are generally durable rules, they are not modified quite often. Whereas, the semantic rules keep changing. The use theory of meaning is basically talking about the semantic rules rather than the syntactic rules. Even in the syntactic rules, one notices the changes over long period of time. That is how we have old grammar and new grammar in the history of natural languages.

Meaning and Mind

Let us consider a least controversial thing: Philosophers have found ambiguity a philosophically troublesome issue. For instance, the term "bank" may be used in association with other terms to refer to money bank, blood bank, question bank, river bank, etc. Similarly, the term sharp can be used in the context of knives, blades, pencils, edges, minds, tongues etc. The term hand may be used in several ways such as under hand, hand over, high handed, upper hand, handi craft, helping hand, hired hand, handy and so on. But what factor makes us agree on the ambiguity of a term? The account of ambiguity of terms could be varied, but the view that a term is ambiguous may not be contested. Why is this so? A person may indicate that the term "table" is ambiguous. The other person may indicate that it is not the word that is ambiguous, but the use of the word in a sentence is. For instance, the sentence "The mathematics teacher was using table to explain basic concepts in mathematics" is ambiguous. This is so because, it is not clear whether the wooden table in the room was used or the mathematical table was used in explaining mathematical concepts. Ambiguity is grasped by one and all.

We have thus made our initial observation, that is, an ambiguous term or an ambiguous sentence can be identified by more individuals than one if we know the language adequately. When we explain to others that a term is ambiguous all that we do is to indicate two distinct contexts where the term can be used justifiably. But is it not questionable that just because a term is used in two distinct contexts the term is dubbed as ambiguous? Consider the term "dead." We call a tree dead, an animal dead, a PC dead, yet the meaning of the term may not be treated as ambiguous. Consider another case, the case of pet. A parrot, a squirrel, a cat, a dog may be a pet, but the term "pet" is not ambiguous. Similar is the case with the analysis of the term "game" by Wittgenstein. This term is general and not ambiguous. But the term "table" is not general, but is ambiguous. It is used in the context of mathematics in one sense, in the context of furniture in yet another sense.

But why do we consider the term "table" ambiguous why not the term "game"? Any answer in terms of context is inadequate is clear within the framework of *use theory* of meaning. Wittgenstein said that "don't think, but look"[2] there is nothing common to all games, implying thereby, meaning of a word is not an entity in the world. If use is supposed to give what we mean by a term, then when we extend the use of a word, the extended use of the word should become normal use over a period of time. Not that it never happens that way. For instance, the word "network" had certain meaning before computers were inter-connected. It retains old meaning along with this extended meaning and use. But why this does not

2. *Philosophical Investigation*, p. 66.

happen when we extend the use of the word "mouse" to cover a device in computer? The term is immediately sensed as ambiguous having two meanings: one in the sense of a computer device and another in the sense of an animal.

One might want to go into the ontological category of things to which the word is applied in order to find a more satisfactory answer. One suggestion may be that if a name is used to identify things that belong to two entirely different categories, then the word becomes ambiguous. Quite right. But what is not clear is that whether the discovery is that of the disease or of the cure. Are we calling the computer device and the mammal two different things because they are ontologically different or because the word "mouse" has different meanings and hence we consider the object they refer to as two different types of things ontologically?

It is amazing that we can create new and newer categories at our will. We can speak of the same human being as infant, child, adolescent, adult, old. Similarly, we can increase the categories of employees in an organization, starting with workers, junior supervisors, supervisors, junior officers, senior officers, deputy managers, managers, and so on. We can do the reverse as well, collapse several categories into one and have only three categories: workers, supervisors and officers. What this indicates is the human ability to conceptualize about the world in different ways. We can also have a very general term covering all these categories: an employee of the organization.

Aristotle spoke of ten categories and Kant specified four basic categories involving three sub-categories in each. Vaiśeṣika philosophers spoke of seven basic categories which are sub-divided further summing up to twenty four. The question is: are these categories ontological or conceptual? Take for instance the category, substance and attribute. This is one category which you find in all the three philosophers mentioned above. It is clear in Kant that the categories are not ontological since they are of judgements. But in both Aristotle and Vaiśeṣika philosophy, the categories are not epistemic; they are metaphysical and hence ontological.

Whether a category is metaphysical or epistemic, it does not matter when we consider meaning of terms. The terms which belong to the category of attributes cannot be merged with the category of substance. Even Rāmānuja who believes that one and the same thing can be viewed as substance and attribute from different perspectives, would not believe that the categories of substance and attribute can be at par. The world can be viewed as attribute from the point of view of *Saguṇa Brahman*, and the world can be viewed as substance from the point of view of its attributes such as colour and shape for instance. That is to say, the substance and attribute is a type of relation which can be viewed in different ways. We can speak of a whole as whole of a particular part, or we can equally speak of the part as the part of the whole. Thus, what is taken as qualifier and what is to be taken as qualified depends on the way we relate them. But the distinction between qualifier and qualified would always remain from the point of view of epistemology.

It may appear that we need not show so much of concern whether we speak of ontological categories first and then the recognition of these categories epistemically or *vice versa*. But what is important to note is that if there are words cutting across the boundaries of some of these fundamental categories, those terms would acquire multiple meanings. One can easily recognize these shades of meanings. Use-theory of meaning, even if granted as insightful, cannot be accepted unconditionally because what is "same" or "different" *use* cannot be explained without reference to some ontological distinctions. When do we consider the use same? For instance, the rule of addition applied to different numbers would be considered the same use. But if the rule of addition is applied to the context of substances, such as two heaps, then it is a different use of addition. That is to say, one plus one heap do not make two heaps, but only one bigger heap.

We have the concept of synonyms and antonyms. Synonyms are said to be terms with similar meanings and antonyms are said to be having meanings opposed to each other. It is interesting to note that we can recognize meaning as similar or dissimilar. How do we compare meanings? It is said that "kind," "considerate," "humane," "sympathetic," "empathetic," "friendly" have meanings akin to one another. In order to describe a situation appropriately we choose the right word from the list, for instance one might say that a government official was considerate, but not sympathetic. Consider this sentence "I thought he was my friend, but he turned out to be my enemy." We say that the antonym of the word "friend" is "enemy." It is obvious that one and the same person is being spoken as friend and enemy at the same time, and yet the meaning of these two terms are opposite. It is again an interesting thing to note that we recognize the meanings of these terms and call them opposites.

Another observation we need to make regarding meaning is the following: certain combination of words are permissible and certain other combination of words are not permissible at all. When an extended use of a word is made in a new context, one of the two things happens: either the word acquires a general sense or it becomes an ambiguous word. For instance, the word "memory" when it is extended to cover hard disks and magnetic tapes or compact disks in computers, the word acquires more general sense, whereas the word "mouse" when extended to cover a device in computers becomes ambiguous.

Why certain words become general and why certain other words become ambiguous when their uses are extended is to be seriously examined; whether ontological categories have forced our mind to think in that particular manner or *vice versa*. Even an empiricist like Quine is made to believe that there are natural kinds. Granting that there are natural kinds is another way of granting that categories of kinds are ontological.[3] One wonders whether the laws of thought are only laws of thought or whether they are laws of reality as well, especially the law of identity and the law of contradiction. Some have contested that the law of excluded middle is really a law of reality. If we say that the son of a barren woman is either alive or dead, the statement need not be true even though the law of excluded middle is applied here.

How are we to understand what is analytic and what is a tautology? Or ask the question as to how do we know what is *a priori*? Or ask the question: how do we know that a sentence is contingent? Knowledge of all these types can be had on the basis of philosophical definitions of them. That is to say, if someone offers a philosophical idea, we are able to grasp that idea. Similarly, I am able to grasp the idea as to what is *appearance* and what is *real*. I am able to get the notion of *real essence* of Locke for instance. We are able to talk about *thing in itself* of Kant and *Nirguṇa Brahman* of Advaita philosophy.

Autonomy of Language

Language is autonomous, that is the reason why we need not refer to any reality to speak of truth of certain sentences. All analytic sentences are true, so is the case with tautologies. Further, we know certain sentences cannot have truth values, since they cannot be actualized in the real world. For instance, there cannot be the son of a barren woman. Similarly, a hen cannot be born without an egg.

---

3. Please note that Quine would like to avoid admitting any ontological categories or universals. See "Universals" by W.V. Quine, in *Metaphysics* by Charles A. Baylis, New York: The MacMillan Company, 1965, pp. 78 ff.

The fact that we have several philosophies or perspectives on the same thing indicates that philosophical languages are autonomous: independent of each other. If language were not autonomous, we should have held the same view regarding, say, truth. The fact that we have several theories of truth, such as correspondence, coherence and pragmatic, is a proof that language stands in different relationship with reality.

However, language is not autonomous from the mind. Language is interconnected with mind. Mind makes language possible, and language helps the mind to evolve further or perform its acts judiciously and efficiently. Philosophical developments take place when the mind is capable of making required philosophical distinctions, synthesize certain ideas and so on. The credit goes to language along with good mind for all its philosophical achievements.

Mind may be limited by certain conceptual framework. What one thinks impossible need not be impossible. For instance, in 1928 majority of the scientists believed that no space craft could be sent to moon. The main argument was that any space craft required support to go up against the gravitational force. Air becomes thinner and thinner as we go up in the sky and therefore, air cannot support any space craft beyond three miles up in the air. Therefore, it was thought that no space craft could be built such that it could reach the moon. We now know that what was thought impossible is possible. If this can happen, one might argue that what is thought to be logically impossible today might turn out to be possible in future. Another example of this type is the cloning concept. Scientists earlier thought that one could have new form of life only through birth, whereas cloning has proven it wrong.

Different languages recognize different distinctions. For instance, there is only one word for snow for most of us, but for Eskimos, twelve words are there to refer to snow in place of our one word. For instance, there is no phonetic distinction between "Vinay" and "Binay" in Bengali. Both will be pronounced as "Binay." Whereas, this distinction exists in some other Indian languages, e.g. in Kannada. Kinship terms are different in different cultures. Certain distinctions are drawn in one culture and the same distinction may not be drawn in another culture.

We fail to make the distinction between two red billiard balls. Similarly, often we fail to distinguish our pens from others if they are of the same brand. We may not count the difference between my pen and the pen of other person. I need a pen and either of them serves the purpose equally. This is true of philosophical distinctions as well. Some make the distinction among a posteriori, contingent and synthetic statements whereas positivists did not find the need to make these distinctions.

A language is closely linked to a culture. Within a culture, there could be different languages. What is important to note is that within such languages, certain philosophical distinctions are made and defended. There is no surprise that these distinctions are not found in another civilization. A philosopher's language need not be taken as universal though in principle it has the potentiality of becoming one.

Assertability Condition

A word in a sentence may be justified if the use is in accordance with the semantic rules. For instance, one is justified in claiming snow is white if the snow is white. Similarly, one is justified in claiming that a car is an automobile since car is capable of moving on its own. There can be several criteria for the use of a term. If any one criterion is met, the use of the word may be said to be justified. For instance, one can claim to be a citizen of a country if one can produce the birth certificate indicating that he was born in the country. Alternatively, if one can produce passport that would be a proof enough to recognize someone as the citizen of the country. If one can show that he possesses a voter identity card, he has proved that he is a citizen of the country. Not necessarily a citizen has to produce all the proofs for claiming that he is the citizen of the country, any one would do equally. In other words, one can assert that the person in question is a citizen of the country if he is aware that he meets one of the criteria.

A rule is a sufficient rule, and if there are many rules each one of them taken individually suffice as a rule. In the above analysis, it is enough that one shows the passport to prove that one is a citizen of the country. Alternatively, voter's identity card would serve the same purpose. Essentialist demand that a rule for the use of word ought to be both *necessary* and *sufficient* does not apply to the semantic rules of words. This is the reason why Wittgenstein asks us to examine the use rather than believe *a priori* that there must be an essence of the concept of game.

It would be a gross mistake to believe that if a term has many criteria, it would have shades of meaning. The term citizen is an unequivocal term. It has one clear meaning and has several criteria for its use. The same is true of the term flower, it has several criteria yet one meaning. However, this can also happen that there can be multiple criteria for the use of a term and multiple meanings. We have noted earlier that the term "bank," "sharp" and "hand" have several criteria for their use and have several meanings. One cannot conclude whether a term is ambiguous or not only from the fact that a term has one criterion or multiple criteria for its use. However, what is clear is that if there is only one criterion, there can be only one meaning. A term like straight line is unambiguous given the definition that it is the shortest distance between any two points.

Should the criteria be necessarily public? Wittgenstein insisted that there cannot be any private criterion. His argument against private language is basically against the possibility of private criteria. The criteria used by an individual to know whether he has pain are not the same that the others would use to know whether a person is in pain. The word "pain" would have been useless and meaningless if there were only private criteria. But if there are both private and public criteria, then there should be no difficulty. A moment's reflection would be enough for a person to know that he has pain in the left leg. He may also adopt the method of pressing gently his left leg to check whether he has pain. This method could be adopted by the doctor to discover whether there is pain in the left leg of the patient. From the behaviour or verbal report of the patient, the doctor declares that the patient has pain in his left leg.

Private criteria is psychological associated with the public criteria. There cannot be private criteria which are constitutive of meaning. If that is the case words like "pain" will not have common meaning. The meaning of the term "pain" is constituted by public criteria, yet a person might make use of private criteria to use such a term. I know my pain by using internal criteria and I know the pain of others by using external criteria.

Not that one cannot imagine the situations where one can go wrong in making the judgements about the pain of others. However, when the criterion for ascribing pain to someone is met, one is linguistically justified in ascribing pain to him. If a person declares that he has pain following the inner criteria, and if another person declares that the person wounded is in pain, both are using different criteria yet mean the same thing. Remember our example of a citizen. Even if the criteria used are different, yet the meaning of the term can be the same.

The confusion and unreasonable demand is due to the belief that a statement is true if and only if it meets the criteria of truth condition. We need to draw the distinction between truth conditions and assertability conditions. One can claim that the patient knows the truth conditions of the statement that he is in pain, whereas, the doctor who judged that the patient is in pain has only assertability condition. In no way, the doctor's judgement is less justified linguistically since he is also following the rules of the language. But a philosopher who is interested in eliminating all possible errors in knowledge might demand that we ought to know the pain of another person exactly the way we know our pain. That is to say, we ought to have the experiences of pain of others in order to admit that others could be in pain. Such a philosopher could only be termed as unreasonable who wants to achieve something impossible.

In the realm of ethics, we make such statements: "You ought to have avoided doing such an unethical act." We cannot provide truth conditions here. We cannot, in fact, show conclusively, going by causal explanation, that someone was indeed free. But, if we can show that we have the right to ascribe intention to someone, we could show that the person could have avoided doing something even after he actually did something. This is ascribing intention to someone and holding him responsible.

If ascription is the method used in speaking about the intention of others, metaphysical claims too are in the same plane. To the question "What is the ultimate structure of the world?" one might answer by claiming that there are spirits and there are material objects. A metaphysician asserts something first and then shows how his assertion makes sense. He would then show how matter is different from mind and show how they combine to form an organism. He offers his criteria as to how to use the words "mind" and "matter."

If our understanding of language is correct, a metaphysician's language too can make sense. The language of metaphysics is not something that we fail to understand, but we cannot apply truth conditions to them. The philosophical justification if a metaphysician can offer to his metaphysical thesis, that should be intelligible to all of us and what we require is the assertability condition in a metaphysical framework and not the truth condition. One speaks of possible worlds in describing the metaphysical truths. The best possible world is asserted as actual world by Leibnitz.

Concluding Remarks

One might wonder whether the consequence of this essay is a form of relativism. As I understand, this need not be the conclusion. We have not maintained that anything and everything can go. All that we have maintained is that within absolutism, there is scope to make statements of different sorts. If a metaphysician starts with his metaphysical thesis and provides justification subsequently, an analytic philosopher might begin with his analysis of the central concept of his philosophy and unearth the metaphysical presuppositions of them. Both are equally acceptable in philosophy. To say this is not to say that anything goes.

7

Reason and Language
An Appraisal of Richard Rorty's Pragmatic-Post-modern Approach

N. Sreekumar

A non- or anti-foundationalist conception of language redefines the nature and role of the notion of reason in our intellectual endeavours. It often uncrowns reason by historicising it and relating it with a concept of language which emphasises a contextualist outlook — fixing it to the numerous contexts of life where language is employed. The contextualist position itself does not necessarily uphold a single version of dethroning reason, as it has representatives ranging from the Wittgenstenians, the post-modernists and to those who prefer to retain the spirit of modernism. For instance, Richard Rorty maintains a pragmatic-post-modern perspective — a thesis I would be elaborating in the following pages — that espouses decentering of perspectival force and consequently opposes the conception of ahistorical reason.[1] Habermas, on the other hand, visibly supports modernity and some claims that the concept of reason traditionally makes, yet deconstructs the latter with a critic of a subject-centered reason, linguistifies it

1. See Rorty, Richard, *Essays on Heidegger and Others, Philosophical Papers,* vol. 2 (henceforth *EHO*), Cambridge, Cambridge University Press, 1991, pp. 1-2. Rorty says that though he had earlier used the term "postmodern" to describe himself in a narrow sense defined by Lyotard as "distrust of metanarratives," now he prefers the term post-Nietzschean philosophy.

and replaces it with a communicative model and announces his commitment to contextualism. Communicative reason, for Habermas, still retains the power of unification and he urges to grasp reason, not in terms of subjectivity — as done by the epistemological tradition of enlightenment — but in terms of communicative intersubjectivity[2] The tension between the diverse positions on the nature and role of reason refers to the conceptual dilemma which we encounter as a result of denying the possibility of an interpretation-free access to reality/a representational line that connects the linguistic with the non-linguistic reality and also in our losing a firm ground on which we can cement the validity of our vocabularies. While Rorty follows the logical consequences of contextualism to its radical anti-foundational conclusions, Habermas attempts to preserve reason within the framework of a theory of language — the communicative paradigm — which nevertheless allows room for diversity and hence is not thoroughly foundationalist in nature.

Reason denotes many things and connotes differently for different thinkers. Many take it as a general human capacity which enables us to choose the most appropriate or effective means to achieve a desired goal, but for many like Rorty and Habermas, as we have seen, it is not so. For them as well as for John Rawls and Putnam, reason is not just matching means to an end.[3] Wolfgang Welsch, who develops a concept of transversal reason, argues that traditionally reason is conceived as the faculty capable of providing and guaranteeing first principles. According to him, two kinds of expectations were connected with reason — a substantial one and a formal one. While the former assumes reason to be giving us a

---

2. See Habermas, Jurgen, *The Philosophical Discourses of Modernity*, Cambridge, Mass, MIT Press, 1987, p. 48.
3. See Dews, Peter (ed.), *Habermas: A Critical Reader*, Oxford, Blackwell Publishers, p. 2.

comprehensive view of the world by establishing its fundamental structure, the latter associates it with the highest faculty of reflection.[4] Welsch recognizes that the substantial distinction of reason has been under attack by the postmodernists. We could see that an anti-foundationalist thesis also tries to dispense with this distinction of reason with its propagation of alternate vocabularies for understanding the world and coping up with it in various ways, as we normally do in our conversational practices.

This paper is largely expository in nature as it tries to bring out some features of the anti-foundationalist deconstruction of reason, especially as Richard Rorty advocated it. Rorty sees that this is an enterprise that involves the completion of a project that was undertaken by some of the first generation philosophers of language in analytic philosophy and the phenomenological and philosophical hermeneutics of Heidegger and Gadamer respectively, in the continental tradition. Rorty's status as a representative of the analytic tradition of philosophy who considers the American pragmatic outlook as vital for philosophical thinking and who conceptually contributes in bridging the gap between the analytic and continental divide in European thought gets reaffirmed in his analysis of the concept of reason.

We could see that Rorty seeks to take this project of antifoundationalist deconstruction of reason to its completion by showing how the idea of reason is rooted in a tendency to see the particular from the perspective of general principles with definite aims. In philosophy of language this tendency reappears with a repeated assertion of faith in a "general conception of language." Rorty's position eventually denies

---

4. See Welsche, Wolfgang, "Reason and Transition: On The Concept of Transversal Reason," downloaded from http://www2.uni-jena.de/welsch/Papers/reasTrans.html. p. 1

legitimacy to such a conception, as he argues that the explanation of language by means of the metaphor "mirror of nature" needs to be replaced. By his project Rorty envisages to free man from the "horror of finding oneself to be only a copy or replica" and thereby ensure self-overcoming.[5] For him this is secured by the assertion of contingency — contingency of both language and selfhood — as against the false certainty promised by reason. In his later writings Rorty further develops the basic arguments he initiated in his 1979 book, *Philosophy and the Mirror of Nature*. Thus the basic premises, which sounded Wittgensteinian in the beginning, turned out to be more radical and prominently pragmatic and sounded even post-modern. The emphasis on the contingency of language that fashions our selfhood was coupled with preserving a private domain for the assertion of individuality. This was further contrasted with the public domain, which according to Wittgenstein constituted the essential realm of all linguistic activity. Rorty's anti-representationalism takes insights from the American pragmatism of James and Dewey as well as from Nietzsche who in his *The Will to Power* considered the categories of reason as representing nothing more than the expediency of a certain race and species.[6]

Rorty's critique of reason tries to exhibit that this concept is basically ineffectual as human intellectual history can very well be accounted with alternate ways, without invoking faith in some mysterious entity like consciousness as different from nature and thereby avoid the problematic of epistemological binaries. Rorty, when commenting on the works of Heidegger

---

5. Rorty, Richard, "The Contingency of Selfhood," *Contingency , Irony and Solidarity* (henceforth *CIS*), Cambridge, Cambridge University Press, 1991, p. 29.

6. Quoted by Rorty in the Introduction titled "Pragmatism and Post-Nietzschean Philosophy," of *EHO*, p. 2, from Nietzsche, F: *The Will to Power*, tr. Kaufmann, New York, Random House, 1967, sec. 608.

and Derrida says that they fail to overcome the Diltheyan distinction between *geist* and *nature*. He claims that Heidegger has succumbed to the urge to make language a quasi divinity and expresses his unhappiness in the manner Rodlphe Gasche has portrayed Derrida as offering "conditions of possibility" for the use of language. According to Rorty, both these approaches attempt to make language a substitute for "God" or "Mind" and thereby making it mysterious, incapable of being described in the same terms in which we describe tables, trees and atoms.[7] Rorty thus seeks to make language look less mysterious by stressing on its contingency and this aspect has to be emphasized more in our attempt to understand him as a contextualist and anti-foundationalist philosopher of language. The position he adopts with regard to the nature and role of reason is based on the notion of truth he advocates — the idea that "truth is not out there" — a conception which makes Rorty a natural occupant of the post-modern territory and a successor of Nietzsche, who claimed that truth is a mobile army of metaphors. This has led to the accusation that Rorty is an advocate of relativism and irrationalism to which Rorty responded by arguing that, ". . .the distinction between absolutism and relativism, between rationality and irrationality, and between morality and expediency are obsolete and clumsy tools — remnants of a vocabulary we should try to replace."[8] In other words, he attempts to point out the limitations of the vocabularies that revolve around notions of truth, rationality and moral obligation on the basis of which the objections to his position are phrased, and replace them with those vocabularies that revolve around notions of metaphor and self-creation.[9]

---

7. *EHO.* p. 4.
8. Rorty, Richard, "The Contingency of a Liberal Community," in *CIS*, p. 44.
9. *Ibid.*

In the following three sections I will briefly examine the picture of language Rorty develops by getting rid of the above-mentioned vocabularies. He tries to show that it is possible to give an account of language from a pragmatic conception, which takes care of the possibility of all normal life projects getting carried out by the contextual use of language by the participants of a linguistic community. One basic feature of his arguments is the assertion of contingency at various levels. We find that he does away with the rational-irrational division by showing that often the notions of truth and rationality are very closely interlinked and to define one of them philosophers refer to the other and vice versa. Another point to be examined is Rorty's project of naturalizing reason, which counters Habermas' thesis of communicative rationality and Hilary Putnam's notion of internal realism. Rorty here says that Habermas is half way through in deconstructing reason when he linguistified the subject-centred reason of the traditional epistemological thought. But this process of linguistifying reason, reminds Rorty, will necessarily link it with the network of needs and necessities of other human beings with whom we interact. Rorty sees the entry of pragmatism here. Finally I will try to show that it was the idea of contingency that underlies all the basic arguments Rorty advances against the concept of reason.

The first section examines the way in which the vocabulary of reason appears in our cultural and intellectual history and how Rorty analyses it by showing that it is nothing more than a contingent European project. We will see how Rorty naturalises reason by showing its genesis in language and the way we encounter others and our environment in language — more precisely, the way others suggest a language for us to speak. The major conceptual block in conceiving the possibility of naturalizing reason is the traditional epistemological ideal, which operates within the subject-object framework. Rorty tackles this by examining the assumptions of the deep within of the self — the idea of an essential human nature and the world out there — the permanent world of facts. The process of linguistifying and naturalizing reason will do away with the myths of "deep within" and "out there" by dispensing with the notion of "medium," a metaphor widely used to understand the essential nature and function of language in traditional thought.

The Vocabulary of Reason

With a close look on the intellectual history of Europe, Rorty tries to answer the questions, "what brings such an idea of "reason" to our vocabulary?," and "what makes reason such a concept, which the present culture considers as extremely indispensable with?"

He points to the temptation to construe an illuminated state of consciousness, which enables one to arrive at true beliefs by obeying mechanical procedures and simply ticking off the way things are.[10] It is the result of a temptation of a tradition to see things from a perspective which is beyond the contingencies of human historicity. A society which encountered diverse "other" ways of legitimizing social life and conceiving belief and knowledge systems, found it necessary to assert its own "ways" of thinking and understanding reality as the "correct" ones, so as to escape from the fear of being contingent and possibly fallacious — a temptation to assert that the basic beliefs and desires one's community thinks to be legitimate are "justifiably" so. In other words, the attempt was to idealise the contingent and historically conditioned beliefs and desires of one particular community and assert their universal validity, ignoring the

---

10. Rorty, Richard, "Pragmatism, Relativism and Irrationalism," in *Consequences of Pragmatism,* (henceforth *CP*), New York, Harvester Wheatsheaf, 1991, p. 164.

fact that most human communities remain exclusivist.[11] In that sense, it was a contingent historical period in European life that brought the vocabulary of reason to human civilization. But, for the traditional philosophical thinking the task of exploring the possibility of grounding the European form of life and showing it to be more than a contingent European project was central.[12] The enlightenment reassertion of the belief in universal criteria and the identification of knowledge with science further cemented the vocabulary of reason in the intellectual life of the Western world. With the invasion of other continents and territories, the project of universalizing reason acquired new dimensions.

Moreover, the present cultural environment makes irrationalism a vital issue to be aggressively countered in the European world, which enforces the repeated assertion of faith in the enlightenment ideals and subsequently hope that, ". . . by formulating the right conceptions of reason, of science, of thought, of knowledge, of morality, the conceptions which express their essence, we shall have a shield against irrationalist resentment and hatred."[13] The possibility of having beliefs and desires common to all human beings, irrespective of the exclusivist character of communities, assures the possibility of "democratic politics," the term Rorty uses for referring to the attempt to bring a planet-wide inclusivist community. This concept sounds very important as the other possibility, the totalitarian politics, has to be well countered due to obvious reasons and for this purpose we might tempt to demonstrate that somehow democratic politics is "better" than totalitarian

---

11. See Rorty, Richard, "Universality and Truth," in Brandom, Robert B (Ed): *Rorty and his Critics*, (henceforth, RC), Oxford, Blackwell Publishing, 2000, p. 2.
12. See *CP.*, p. 172.
13. *Ibid.*, p. 171.

politics, as it is more rational. In short, the rational-irrational division is paramount even to the present culture.

But the two factors cited above explain only why our culture considers the possibility of reason as indispensable and not how we can prove its very possibility as such. We do not have any neutral grounds to stand on when we defend democratic politics against totalitarian politics,[14] argues Rorty. He again says that the notion of unconditionality associated with reason is neither indispensable, nor useful and urges to focus on the relation between the organisms and their environment to understand the nature of reason — and hence naturalise reason — rather than focusing on a relation between human beings and something like Truth or Reality.[15] This presupposes a paradigm shift. We may have to start thinking that the question that our fellow human beings think is more pivotal than the question what the world really is. The second question is not just unimportant but nonsensical, with its metaphysical attire. This is the crucial juncture where Rorty makes his pragmatic turn.

Rorty finds yet another way in which the vocabulary of reason has found circulation in our civilization; as a principle that asserts the fundamental premises about truth, viz. the universal human agreement on the supreme desirability of truth, truth is correspondence to reality, and finally, reality has an intrinsic nature.[16] It is also linked with the notion of an essential human nature, from which the idea of an illuminated state of consciousness is being construed. Rorty exposes the inconsistency in these arguments by showing that the first claim involves a tautology as the very use of the word reason

---

14. See Rorty, Richard, "Universality and Truth," in *RC*, p. 2.
15. See Rorty, Richard, "Response to Jurgen Habermas," in *RC.*, p. 62.
16. See Rorty, Richard, "Universality and Truth," in *Ibid.* p.1.

is often explained with reference to the three premises about truth cited above. The notion of essential human nature also loses its value with the recognition of contingency.

Corresponding to and sometimes often prior to the use of the vocabulary of reason, there is a notion of irrationality. But the rational-irrational division itself presupposes a criterion, which paradoxically has to be rational. The anti-foundationalist thus reaches a point where the replacing of the criterion of reason becomes unavoidable. But from the very outset, it has to be clarified that replacing the set of vocabulary of universal reason does not consist in substituting it with another set of vocabulary with claim for universality, as that would never replace reason per se, but only one version of it and retains the idea that there exists a criterion for adjudicating conflicting claims. It would deny the value of one set by showing that there is another set which is "better" than the former. Such substitution involves self-referential inconsistency as it asserts to know what it claims cannot be known.[17] A strict form of anti-foundationalism will do away with the notion of universal criteria as such. Rorty sees this temptation to look for criterion as a species of a more general temptation to think of the world or human self as possessing an intrinsic nature[18] and by disposing of the latter he envisages to show how we can go beyond the idea of any criterion that aims at fundamental grounding. The doing away with the two assumptions involves a redescription of European intellectual history, as the former were the indispensable tools of the tradition for its self-understanding. Rorty tries to show that the intellectual history and progress of the West can be described with other tools, without making a claim that these tools are in any way better and hence "rational" than the older ones, but they are simply more suitable for the present purpose.

---

17. See Rorty, Richard, "The Contingency of Language," *CIS.* p. 8f.
18. *Ibid.* p. 6.

At least for now, and hence contingently, they seem to have more scope and hence sound more attractive.

The foundationalist conception is cemented on the traditional epistemological dual of the subject and the object, where the self which possesses certain essential attributes stands at one end and the reality with its permanent structures at the other end. The substitution of mind with language never solved the problem as the notion of medium — here language functions as a medium between self and reality — is retained without any major alteration. This view of language assumes that there is a "correct" way of talking, over and above the numerous ways we talk in our day-to-day life. Rorty rebukes the realism — anti-realism controversy in the contemporary philosophy of language, as it debates on the issue whether thought determines reality (anti-realism) or reality determines thought (realism). Both these claims, he asserts, are entirely empty and pseudo-explanations and well remain within the representationalist framework of thought.[19] Though this debate overcomes many of the unwarranted prejudices of the epistemological tradition, it retains the basic assumptions. Rorty attempts to do away with two most important assumptions — the metaphors of the "deep within" and the "out there." These two basic assumptions, he argues, legitimizes the very possibility of reason as such and once they become unfounded, reason itself becomes a shaky assumption.

The Myth of the "Deep Within of the Self" and the "World Out There"

Rorty traces what he thinks is the central doctrine of pragmatism and presents them as three sloganistic

19. See Rorty, Richard, the Introduction titled "Antirepresentationalism, Ethnocentrism and Liberalism" in *Objectivity, Relativism and Truth: Philosophical Papers vol. 1*, Cambridge, Cambridge University Press, 1991, p. 5.

characterizations. For him they constitute an anti-essentialism applied to the notions of truth, knowledge, language, morality, etc. doing away with the fundamental distinctions between facts and values as well as science and morality and finally asserting that our sole constraints are from our fellow social beings and not from the nature of objects.[20] He further highlights the third characterization, as here a fundamental contingency has been recognized and no attempts are being made to overcome the same. This in other words is, ". . . to accept our inheritance from, and our conversation with, our fellow-humans as our only source of guidance."[21] Such a position apparently refutes the possibility of an infallible criterion like reason or essential underlying linguistic structures, which can make validity claims with cosmic extension. Rorty asserts that we need to *socialise* and *linguistify* the notion of reason by viewing it communicatively — as Habermas does — and further by *naturalising* it.[22] Reason has to be necessarily founded in the conversational practices. This is to say that it has to be unfounded or uprooted from any fictitious permanent structures that are transcendental in nature. And further, this will take away from the concept of reason two most important and distinctive features that have been associated with it traditionally; the unconditionality and universality.

But does this process of relating it with the conversational practices of a community may also allow the entry of a monitoring faculty like reason? It can be argued that any conversation may necessarily aim at agreement and at rational consensus.[23] Rorty diagnoses that this tendency to conceive

---

20. Rorty, Richard, "Pragmatism, Relativism and Irrationalism" in *CP*, pp. 162-65.
21. *Ibid.* p. 166.
22. See Rorty, Richard, "Universality and Truth," in *RC.*, p. 2.
23. *Ibid.* p. 170.

our conversations possessing a natural goal emanates from the assumption that there is something deep within us, a permanent self, which is the starting point of all our thoughts. Like the Platonic self who recollects when it knows something, here we recognize the vocabulary in which our conversations are best formulated once we hear it. But even after we do away with the Platonic universalism and stick to linguistic provincialism we may still be searching for a common ground, at least within that limited community where conversations take place. Accepting the possibility of such an element will, instead of replacing reason, substitute it with another version of rationality, which has scope of application within a limited sphere of activity. Rorty rebukes the criticism that, in the absence of something common or permanent the conversation becomes goalless and an empty exercise, by arguing that this criticism is the result of confusing course of an activity with the end of the activity.

The temptation to locate universal conditions for human existence appears in a variety of forms in the history of thought. The Greeks and the Catholic Church had their versions, and later the epistemological tradition of modern Europe and the idealists, all conceiving the presence of something which is ahistorical and permanent. This deep within makes the contingencies of the periphery irrelevant and also suggests an ultimate goal for human understanding; as consisting in the realization of the full potential of universal conditions that is within. Rorty's contention is that the notion of "knowing the truth which is out there" has its origin in this idea of universal context of human life. In Rorty's language, this universal context enabled the pre-Nietzschean philosophers to assert the essential worthlessness of the particular contingencies of individual lives. By emphasizing on the "universal" the knowability of the imperishable truth also is warranted, as here we visibly go beyond the status of an animal. It is the search for an eternal within from the midst of contingent perspectives and historicities.

Rorty reinstalls perspectivism to counter the vocabulary of universal reason. In the process of replacing this vocabulary with the vocabularies that make the notions of metaphor and self-creation pivotal, the Nietzschean perspectivism plays a vital role. His condemnation of truth and the rejection of representationalism, and a subsequent search for the cause of our being in the "will to power" prompted to conceive self-knowledge, which consists in knowing the basic impulsive nature of man, as constituting self-creation. In this sense, knowing oneself is to be aware of one's contingency, as there is nothing permanent to be known apart from the contingencies. Rorty sees the Nietzschean revolution as a shift from the "will to truth" to "will to self-overcoming" or ". . . thinking of redemption as "making contact with something larger and more enduring than oneself" and redemption as "recreating all "it was" into a "thus I willed it.""[24] The important point of Nietzsche's departure consists not in devising another way to overcome human contingency, by revealing one more profound truth about the world, but in emphasizing the vitality of finding new descriptions of human contingencies different from the familiar inherited ones. The point here is not that Nietzsche was right — as he himself was not free from thinking that there is something deep within us determining our essential nature — but he proposes a different vocabulary which is not familiar to the Platonic and Kantian philosophy. Rorty says that Freud also does propose a set of new vocabulary by dedivinising conscience. "Freud thus helps

---

24. See Rorty, Richard., "The Contingency of Selfhood," in *CIS*., p. 29.

us take seriously the possibility that there is no central faculty, no central self, called "reason" — and thus to take Nietzschean pragmatism and perspectivism seriously,"[25] adds Rorty. Freud's revelation that the so called conscious goals are in no way less idiosyncratic and less contingent than the unconscious passions provided additional force of legitimacy to a new set of vocabularies which can explain human life without bringing in concepts like the universal conditions of human existence.

The possibility of "constituting a different world" by different people, in spite of having the same intuitions, had sharpened its scope and widened its dimensions ever since Kant revealed the active faculty of mind vis-a-vis the passive faculty and brought to the forefront the notion of "alternative framework." But so long as a passive faculty, which apparently receives intuitions from an external source remains, the myth of the given and therefore, the conception that "truth is out there" survives. This will also make the necessary-contingent division legitimate and consequently validates the concept of unconditional criteria. In order to counter this Rorty points to Quine's attack on the concept of meaning and shows how the latter has blurred this necessary-contingent distinction, by showing that the difference between *a priori* and empirical truth is *de facto* a distinction between the relatively difficult to give up and relatively easy, and hence the distinction between questions about alternative theories and questions about alternative frameworks also sound worthless.[26]

The faith in the world out there is a metaphysical one and its denial involves an equally metaphysical standpoint. Rorty's analysis thus deviates from the attempts which aim at explicitly

---

25. *Ibid.* p. 33.

26. See Quine, W.V, "On Carnap's View on Ontology," in *The Ways of Paradox,* New York, Random House, 1966, pp. 126-34, quoted by Rorty in "The World Well Lost," in *CP.*, p. 5.

denying the interpretation-free, independent factual world. The basis of this belief, as he sees, is the assumption that the world is a creation of a being who had a language of his own.[27] This non-human language and the conceptual environment from where such a notion emanates are responsible for construing a belief in a world that has systematically divided into facts. Rorty writes:

> If we cease to attempt to make sense of the idea of such a non-human language, we shall not be tempted to confuse that platitude that the world may cause us to be justified in believing a sentence true with the claim that the world splits itself up, on its own initiative, into sentence-shaped chunks called "facts." But if one clings to the notion of self-subsistent facts, it is easy to start capitalizing the word "truth" and treating it as something identical with God or with the world as God's project. Then one will say, for example, that truth is great, and will prevail.[28]

Rorty's way out is Wittgenstenian in style and content. He draws our attention from facts-representing single sentences to vocabularies which stand for forms of life, and which by their very nature calls for alternate language games. This essentially pluralistic conception makes the idea of a criterion — like the world — deciding between the alternate forms of life sounds farce. Rorty draws his Nietzschean conclusion from these premises and argues that we find it impossible to find which vocabulary is "better" on the basis of any ultimate grounds like the "world out there" other than mere expediency. Vocabularies, unlike single sentences — which represent a fact and hence whose truth can be verified with reference to the latter — are definitely not a matter of our

---

27. See, Rorty, Richard, "The Contingency of Language," in *CIS*, p. 5.

28. *Ibid.*

discovery, rather they are our creations, creation of human communities in praxis. The ". . . fact that Newtons vocabulary lets us predict the world more easily than Aristotle's does not mean that the world speaks Newtonian."[29] It only suggests that now the Newtonian vocabulary suits our purposes more than the Aristotelian one, and also implies that but our purposes are contingent and do not represent any eternal human project.

Rorty sees that the Wittgenstenian framework of language games opens the route to a pragmatic conception of self-creation, where it is not the world, which is permanent and has a rational universal structure that proposes us to speak a language, but other human beings do so. Our identity as humans owes not to anything like an essential human nature but depend on how we use language and define our own being and create ourselves. It also depends on the way other human beings propose us to speak a language and hence contingency is built into the very structure of our beinghood. The metaphors of the inner and outer spaces — the two essential entities in the epistemological dual — are dropped from our philosophical lexicon or are replaced with better ones — better not in terms of universal rational grounds, but because they are more appealing for the time being and may not be so tomorrow. Rorty writes:

> Conforming to my own percepts, I am not going to offer arguments against the vocabulary I want to replace. Instead, I am going to try to make the vocabulary I favour look attractive by showing how it may be used to describe a variety of topics.[30]

What Rorty aims at here is to show that in the absence of something "intrinsic," which is eternal and permanent, which would explain the essential nature of the self and something

---

29. *Ibid.*, p. 6.

30. *Ibid.*, p. 9.

which is "out there" with a predesigned structure, there remains nothing for us to "discover" or unravel. Hence we find ourselves in a position with no other option but to recognize and accept the contingency of our language and our selfhood. It also places us in the midst of various conversational practices where we take suggestions from others and eventually are limited to a set of conventions. This pragmatic approach understands the story of intellectual and moral progress as a history of increasingly useful metaphors rather than of increasing understanding how things really are.[31] Before we examine how a notion like reason, a universal criterion, is dissolved in the contingencies described above, we shall see how the epistemological dual of representing subject and represented object further get deconstructed with a refutation of the conception of language as a medium.

The Metaphor of Medium

Wittgenstein shows how different language games can coexist without contradicting each other. He made this coexistence possible by disposing of the idea of a special language game, which has an elevated status so that it can mediate between the rest. The notion of a self with intrinsic nature becomes shaky in the absence of such a language which the self speaks when it correctly depicts reality. On the other side, the idea of a reality that gets represented in the language spoken by the self also sounds extremely dubious as it becomes impossible to conceive a self for us, alienated from the various forms of life which form our being and the numerous language games we are engaged in. Wittgenstein argues that language is part of man's natural history as walking, eating, drinking and playing.[32] Wittgenstein's language-game theory places the

---

31. *Ibid.*

32. See Wittgenstein, Ludwig, *Philosophical Investigations,* Trans. G.E.M. Anscombe, Oxford, Blackwell Publishing, 25.

concepts of self and reality — the epistemological dual of subject and object — in the framework of an entirely different form of relationship by linguistifying the whole process to its totality. Language is conceived not just as a medium situated externally and connecting two entities with different attributes, but as architectonic as both the self and the world are constituted in the linguistic praxis. This picture inaugurates the deconstruction of the metaphor of language as the medium between the self and reality by going beyond the mere substitution of language for mind or consciousness. Rorty seeks to do away with this notion of medium conclusively as he realises that this will not take us beyond the subject-object picture and hence limit us within the conceptual domain of all those issues with which the consciousness-centered epistemological philosophy had concerned itself with. The metaphor of medium retains the basic epistemological assumptions, as a medium is always either a medium of expression — of a deep within, the self — or of representation — of the out there, the world.

Rorty clarifies the fading picture of "language as a medium" that intervening between self and reality by referring to Davidson who asserts that, the idea of a clearly defined shared structure which language users master and apply to cases has to be given up.[33] With this elimination the anti-foundationalist conception develops a different version of human life and intellectual history which posit the centrality of conversational practices and therefore of language use. The way Davidson, like Wittgenstein conceives alternate vocabularies as alternate tools exemplifies the correct attitude for Rorty, as here both reductionism as well as expansionism

---

33. Davidson, Donald, "A Nice Derangement of Epitaphs," in Lepore, Ernest ed., *Truth and Interpretations: Perspectives on the Philosophy of Donald Davidson*, Oxford, Blackwell, 1984, p. 446, quoted by Rorty in "The Contingency of Language" in *CIS*, p. 15.

are avoided. New vocabularies replace the older ones, not when new discoveries are made about reality but when we realise that two or more vocabularies are interfering with each other and it becomes necessary to invent a new one to replace both,[34] like the invention of a new tool taking the place of old tools.

It has been argued that the anti-foundationalist would be envisaging the possibility of a conversation that is ongoing, which has no goal external to it. Even the idea of arriving at agreements does not constitute a fundamental objective of conversational practices. Once the status of language as a medium is forfeited it appears to be goalless. But this is not to say that we recognize the ultimate worthlessness of our conversational practices. We only cease to think that our engagements in them ought to take us out of them — out of language to the world out there. The world on its part is nothing but a world created by us and our fellow humans, by the various contextual uses of language, which are bound to be contingent. Rorty points to the pragmatists who see that the European intellectual's form of life takes the continuance of conversation as a moral duty, though it has no epistemological or metaphysical guarantee of success. Even "*. . . we do not know what "success" would mean except simply "continuance."* We are not conversing because we have a goal, but because Socratic conversation is an activity which is its own end."[35] Attempts to envisage a goal lying external to this conversation represent endeavours to overcome the necessary contingency of our language and self. The same predilection is reflected in the efforts to ground the European form of life by showing it human in general.

---

34. See Rorty, "The Contingency of Language," in *CIS*, p. 12.

35. "Pragmatism, Relativism and Irrationalism" in *CP*, p. 172.

We come to a point where we can draw certain conclusions about Rorty's pragmatic-post-modern position as far as the question of reason is concerned. We must acknowledge that a notion like reason cannot be upheld so long as we conceive contingency as part of our very life and being, something which Rorty emphatically does. Recognizing this essential contingency Rorty tries to give an account of human intellectual history as a history of metaphors. This will overthrow the traditional philosophical and religious conception which assumes that human cultural history has a *telos,* which manifests in the various intellectual and other endeavours to discover truth.[36] The history of culture he tries to reveal sees language as evolving with reality and life, whereas Rorty says ". . . new forms of life constantly killing off old forms — not to accomplish any higher purpose, but blindly."[37] The contributions of great scientists like Galileo and Newton are seen not as discoveries of "words which were needed to fit the world properly," which their predecessors missed, but as hitting upon tools which happened to work better for certain purposes than any previous tools.[38] Here the benchmark is not the world with a permanent structure, but the environment, which includes other human beings as well.

I call this Rortian position pragmatic-post-modern, owing to two reasons. On the one hand he himself explicitly acknowledges the influence of pragmatism in developing his position. Replacing the "universal" and "permanent" structures of thought and language with a notion of language that our fellow humans suggest us to speak is the most accurate pragmatic contention about reason. On the other hand, his views about the nature and role of reason — as he not only

---

36. See Rorty, "The Contingency of Language," in *CIS*, p. 17.

37. *Ibid.*, p. 19.

38. *Ibid.*

linguistifies reason but also naturalises it — sound too radical so as to fit the post-modern assumption, which amounts to the denial of reason, as it was conceived by the enlightenment era. Rorty sees contingency as central and draws this conclusion from the essential linguisticality of human life and reality. The thesis of linguisticality is further extended not only to show the inconsistency in positing the notion of reason but also to expose the worthlessness of such a concept. Human cultural as well as the intellectual history can be satisfactorily explained by revealing the process of new metaphors replacing older ones, a process which does not involve any rational choice, but takes place blindly. Rorty tries to show how human life is worth living, not because it has to aspire for something higher — like the Christian heaven or the universal truth of the philosophers or the enfranchisement of any sort, but by making genuine attempts to attain novelty with recognition of contingency. Novelty and genuineness, not by surpassing the contingency which comes with our linguisticality, but by a process of self-creation that takes place within language, but differ drastically from others by virtue of tools which enable to do things differently, without just imitating others. Contingency, and not reason, germinates genuineness. Metaphors, and not truth that define human progress.

8

Naturalizing Intentionality

A Searlean Critique

Ranjan K. Panda

Introduction

Intentionality is a distinguishing feature of the mind differentiating the mental phenomena from the physical phenomena.[1] It exhibits *directedness, about-ness* or *of-ness* of thoughts and expressions. Mental phenomena like thoughts, experiences, imagination, etc. are characterized by intentionality because it unfolds their intentional structures in which they are represented. The involvement of intentionality in thinking is a necessary involvement. Intentionality shares an intrinsic relationship with consciousness. As a result, it discloses the intentional relationship of the mind with various types of experiences. Thinking and experiencing are not two different forms of intentional activities. Rather these activities are characterized

---

1. Intentionality as the mark of the mental or a distinguished feature of the mental phenomenon is related to the very "act of presentation." See, Franz Brentano, "The Distinction between Mental and Physical Phenomena," *Philosophy of Mind: Classical and Contemporary Readings*, ed. David J. Chalmers, New York: Oxford University Press, 2002, p. 479 Also see, Tim Crane, "Intentionality as the Mark of the Mental," Supplement of *Philosophy*, **43**, *Current Issues in Philosophy of the Mind*, ed. Anthony O' Hear, Oxford, Cambridge University Press, 1998, p. 229.

by intentionality. Thought as representation shows its content refers to something beyond itself. Similarly, the experience of representation unfolds the intentionality involved in the content of representation. The content of representation and experiencing the content are same — share the same form of intentionality, because intentionality not only reveals the directedness of thought but also unifies various forms of thoughts and experiences. The unifying features of intentionality shows that consciousness or the mind is not a discrete phenomenon, rather a unifying principle of thoughts and experiences, and relates to the reality *from a point of view* — it is perspectival.[2] This paper brings out the naturalist controversy regarding the nature of intentionality as an *intrinsic* feature of representation. In general the naturalistic world-view locates intentionality in the causal framework of nature. The causal explanation of intentionality denies the *intrinsic* relationship between the intentionality and the mind. As a result, the mind that loses its *intrinsic* relationship with intentionality becomes epiphenomena. On the contrary, the Searlean position has been different. Searle accepts that intentionality is intrinsic to the mind and it can be placed in nature, which entails dualism or panpsychism. The paper defends John Searle's notion of intrinsic intentionality while juxtaposing his biological naturalism with the physicalists' notion of intentionality advocated by Daniel Dennett, Fred Dretske, Jerry Fodor and many others who favour scientific explanation of the mind. All naturalists locate intentionality along with the bodily features rather than locating it in the domain of conscious experience. In this regard, the paper delves into the naturalist controversy about the ontology of intentionality. If intentionality is an intrinsic feature of the

---

2. John R. Searle, *The Rediscovery of the Mind*, The MIT Press, Massachusetts, 1992, p. 131. Also see, William Lyons, *Approaches to Intentionality*, Oxford, Clarendon Press, 1995, p. 1.

mind then its ontology must be beyond the world-view of naturalism. Thus the paper is a critique of naturalistic theorization of intentionality.

Searle's Linguistic Perspective of Intentionality

Intentionality, according to Searle, is an intrinsic feature of the mind, i.e., it is a property inhering in consciousness. Intentionality is one of the essential properties of consciousness. As an essential property, it defines the nature of mental states and processes. Over and above, intentionality is embedded in the very form of thoughts and experiences. Thinking and experiencing are mental activities entangled in intentionality. Intentionality relates various forms of thoughts to experience, though experience itself is intentional and presupposes intentionality. In this regard, there are not two different forms of intentionality; rather intentionality has the unifying characteristics to connect all types of thoughts. Thoughts are concatenation of various mental states and events that represent something. The representational feature shows the directedness of mental states, i.e., they are being directed *at* something or being *about* something which suffices forming and unfolding the intentional relationship between the mind and the reality. For Searle, all mental states are not intentional. He writes, "Intentionality is a feature of certain mental states and events that consists in their (in a special sense of these words) being directed at, being about, being of or representing certain other entities and states of affairs."[3] The inherence of intentionality in thought does not show that all mental states are intentional. Though every mental state emerges and involves intentionality still some of them fail to represent the reality with specific reference. Intentionality involved in the mental states lacks the ability to develop the form of

---

3. John R. Searle, "Intentionality and Its Place in Nature," *Synthese*, vol. 61, 1984, p. 4.

representation. For instance, the feeling of sudden elation, joys, and fears, etc. is not considered as full-fledged intentional state. It so happens that in one fine morning I feel very delighted and have a sense of joy in me in doing things. We may not have any specific reason for my feeling of joy. In that case, particularly intentionality fails to have a specific reference. On the other hand, mental states like belief, desire and intention are completely intentional states as they express the form of *direction of fit* as well as *condition of satisfaction*.[4] The direction of fit and condition of satisfaction involve the *double levels* of intentionality that completes the intentional structure of experience of the representation. Representations at one level have the directedness from the *mind-to-the world,* and at another level, from the *world-to-the mind*. So far as the first level is concerned the direction of fit is determined by the *psychological mode* of the speaker. Whereas in the second level the prepositional content results in the condition of satisfaction. For example, when I ask someone to "bring me a glass of water," it is an expression of my desire of having water. The expression of desire gets satisfied if the hearer properly understands the *content* of the expression and brings to me a glass of water. The *content* of the expression determines the condition of satisfaction and the psychological mode characterize its modality of reaching at the world. In both the cases, intentionality is involved. The mode of reaching to the hearer is preliminary condition of communication, whereas, the condition of satisfaction is the second level intentionality and it results in showing the effectiveness of the first level intentionality. The action of the hearer either makes me happy or makes me unhappy. In both the cases, the intentionality signifies different ends of the reference and reveals the *self-*

---

4. John Searle, *Intentionality: An Essay in Philosophy of Mind*, Cambridge, Cambridge University Press, 1983, pp. 14-15, (Henceforth, in short *Intentionality*).

referential feature of intentionality in experiencing and understanding the intention of representation and communication.

Understanding the content of the expression and performing the action accomplishes the intention of communication. According to Searle, representational state or intentional state is essentially a part of communicative intention. However, the content of representation as a mental phenomenon is realized in connection with the other representational states or intentional states. The representational states are intentional states. The totality of the intentional states forms *the network* by connecting one another through intentionality. Intentionality as connecting principle not only links one mental state to another mental state, but also has the potency to link an unconscious mental state and bring that to conscious experience. Thus intentionality works as an underlying principle with its unifying characteristic and ultimately defining the functional relationship of the mental states. In this regard, Searle emphasizes that representation, as intentional states have to be characterized in terms of intentionality so that we don't lose the "sight of *intrinsic* intentionality."[5]

The content of representational states appears at two levels: mental and linguistic. At the level of *thought*, representation is known as mental, whereas at the level of *expression* of thoughts and feelings, it is known as linguistic. The content of representation is *isomorphic* to thought and expression. The structural isomorphism between the mental representation and the linguistic representation is drawn by the content of intentionality, rather than by the structure. The content of representation is revealed in different modes of intentionality working simultaneously, such as seeing and experiencing,

5. *Intentionality*, p. 16.

believing, desiring, hoping, etc. They are logically correlated with each other. When I wish to do better in the game, I must believe in myself, my performance and I must have desire to learn how to do well, and finally to learn from mistakes, etc. This tiny expression involves so many intentional states. Their co-relation is based on intentionality and the experience of various levels of intentionality. Intentionality working as conscious mode of representation is about the experience of the *content* of representation rather than the *object* of representation.[6] Experience of thought is a mental phenomenon directed toward the object or state of affairs. So the representation of thought involves the experience of the content of thought in which the object is represented.

According to Searle, intentionality as a representational feature is biologically more primitive,[7] so far as the expression of the representational states is concerned. He writes, "By explaining intentionality in terms of language I don't mean simply that intentionality is essentially and necessarily linguistic. On the contrary it seems obvious that infants and many animals do not in any ordinary sense have a language or perform a speech act; nevertheless they have intentional mental states. "Language is derived from intentionality and not conversely. The direction of pedagogy is to explain intentionality in terms of language; the direction of logical analysis is in terms of intentionality."[8] Intentionality of linguistic representation is derived from the intentionality of mental representation. As we have mentioned earlier they

---

6 *Intentionality*, p. 18.

7. For Searle, consciousness is biologically evolved and intentionality as one of the intrinsic properties of consciousness is also understood as an evolutionary phenomenon, See, John Searle, *The Rediscovery of the Mind*, 1992 (Introduction).

8. See, *Intentionality*, p. 5.

are not two different forms of intentionality, rather one follows the other. The experiential form of intentionality is prior to the expressional form of intentionality. And since experience of thoughts is prior to its expression, Searle characterizes it as the primitive form of intentionality that makes the experience possible. The brain processes cause the emergence of intentionality. Brain processes are causing intentional states though intentional states have logically distinct functions for the realization of the content. Although the biological root of the human is celebrated in the Searlean world-view, still intentionality is treated as an independent feature of conscious mental states. The representational feature of the intentionality is not causally reduced to its biological origin, rather maintains its functional autonomy at the realm of the network of the mental states. Thus, the mental states are biologically primitive but so far as the linguistic representation is concerned representational states stand in continuation with the linguistic counterpart. The semantic rules and the socio-cultural background construe meaning of representation. So far as the linguistic activities are concerned, semantic rules determine the very function of the performative expressions. Whereas, the language use in general is embedded in the socio-cultural background of the human beings. Intentionality works in both the levels connecting the constitutive and regulative feature of speech acts and forming as well as developing the socio-cultural etiquettes. In this regard, intentionality helps in explicating different levels of relationship from the biological to the mental and from the mental to the social. Nevertheless, it is important to note that the derivation of intentionality from the content of representation discloses the continuity of semantic relationship between thought and expression, in which intentionality is presupposed.

Physicalists' Perspective of Linguistic Intentionality

A physicalistic perspective gives a different interpretation to the linguistic form of intentionality. It aims at giving an extensional explanation of intentionality along with its linguistic characteristics. The intentional element of the *language of thought* is explicated in terms of the extensional features of the mental representation. The explanation of mental representation based on the intentional feature of the mind leads to circularity. That is, the content of representation is by nature intentional and explains the nature of representation through intentionality, though its overall explication does not break the circularity of explanation. Hence, intentionality and intentional states are to be explained in non-intentional terms. In this regard, a viable notion of intentionality along with its semantic feature demands *extensional* theorization.

The extensional thesis ascribes content of representation to the functional feature of the brain states and events. The neurophysiological function of the brain causes *propositional attitudes* states like beliefs and intentions, forms the symbolic representation of *thoughts* and experiences. The symbolic representation of thought contains the semantic content — is a syntactic representation of thought. The syntactic representation causally manipulates its representational states to evaluate its content. The causal manipulation operates in the system of conglomeration of symbols related to one another in a crisscrossing pattern to the content.[9] Symbols stand in a causal relationship with stimulus and responses, and are ultimately operated by the causal function of the neural states and processes. The process of transmitting the content of representation from the physical states to the syntactic states and *vice versa* reduces the *semanticity* of the content to the causal

9. See, Jerry Fodor, *Psychosemantics: Problem of Meaning in Philosophy of Mind*, Massachusetts, The MIT Press, 1987.

neurophysiological function. Thus, in brief, it naturalizes content of representation with causal explanation. For instance, the causal transmission of content is analogous to the computational model of information processing, in which a program is involved in encoding and decoding information. The mind is conceived as a modular system performing certain mechanical action by processing information and producing effect. The input-output relationship is causally linked in the system of representation. No doubt, the computational model of processing the content involves intentionality, based on an algorithm — the language of the machine. For the physicalists, the intentionality drawn in algorithm displays the causal function of the representation, and is not the *derived form* of intentionality as Searle interprets. On the contrary, the physicalists' understanding of linguistic intentionality is a part of the program. And it indicates fairly the *original* form of intentionality shown in the behaviour of the physical properties of a system. The program of the system is self developed or not installed as it is done in the cases of computers, then the system is causally efficacious to explain the intentional attitude of expression.[10]

The extensional explanation of the ontology of intentional content is based on the neurophysiological functions of the brain. Dennett writes, "So, one can ascribe content to a neural event, state or structure when it is a link in a demonstrably appropriate chain between the afferent and efferent. The content one ascribes to an event, state or structure is not, then, an extra feature that one *discovers* in it, a feature which, along with its other, extensionally characterized features allow one to make predictions. Rather, the relations between intentional descriptions of events, states or structures (as signals that carry

---

10. Daniel C. Dennett, *Intentional Stance*, Massachusetts, The MIT Press, 1987, p. 48.

certain messages or memory trances with certain contents) and extensional descriptions of them is one of *further interpretation*. If we relegate vitalist and interactions hypotheses to the limbo of last, desperate resorts, and proceed on the assumption that human and animal behavioural control systems are only very complicated denizens of the physical universe it follows that events within them characterize extensionally in terms of physics to physiology should be susceptible to explain and prediction without any recourse to content, meaning and intentionality."[11] The Dennettian interpretation maintains the extensional explanation of content and its relationship with intentionality and meaning. Intentionality is an effect of the function of the brain or the physical system. Since there is nothing phenomenal about it, there is no *surplus* to intentionality as such. Rather the neural networks of functions causally explain its phenomenal features. The extensional theorization is the explanation of the physical and neural properties of the brain. It shows the significance of the downward trajectory for explaining the reality in terms of the microphysical structures and functions. Dennett calls this as sub-personal levels of explanation. The micro level of the brain initiates the function and regulates the processes. Once the process goes on in certain way — a normal operation persists to have the interaction with the environment. Moreover, the very function that it facilitates to carry on certain operations shows initial plasticity of the brain. It is the initial function of the brain that generates and develops its pattern of processing the afferent and producing the efferent. It unfolds the "ability of the physical system to discriminate its input and produces its output according to the environmental significance."[12]

---

11. Daniel Dennett, *Content and Consciousness*, London, Routledge and Kegan Paul, 1969, p. 78.

12. See, the chapter "Evolution in the Brain," *Ibid.*, pp. 47-48.

The brain's ability to build up a functional pattern is an intrinsic physical characteristic. The functional pattern further develops its *design stance*. The design stance thereby is related to the physical stance. The configuration of various sub-systems to develop the design stance is analogous to the Searlean schema of naturalizing the mind. As in Searle, the brain processes cause the mind; the brain process is ontologically primary. The primacy of the functional aspects of the design stance is conceived irrespective of its physical constitution. The belief states as cognitive states contain intentionality, but the intentional stance is dependent on the design stance. Intentional stance can be contrasted with the functional co-relationship with the design stance, which ultimately succeeds in "making wonderful shortcut."[13] For example, the alarm clock when produces sound, one can make prediction about the mechanism of clock knowing fairly well that the mechanism is responsible for making wake-up call. There is no doubt about the functional physical laws that operate to run the mechanism. Doubting the functional capacities of the alarm clock is something analogous to doubting the function of the robots. Robots' behaviour is indeed complicated and it functions according to the programs; by certain goals and sub-goals. But fixing up the goal and the mechanism of processing it is a task performed at several levels of abstraction by the strategy generators and consequence-testers, multipliers and dividers, or transistors and switches,[14] etc. In this regard, the design stance is important rather than its physical stance. Design stance therefore is essential for stressing out the intentional features and their extensional counterparts. Intentional features having the causal relationship with the extensional-functional features refer to

13. Daniel Dennett, *The Kinds of Minds: Origin of Consciousness*, London, Phoenix, 2001, p. 38.

14. See, Dennett's "Intentional Systems," *Brainstorms*, p. 4.

the physical ontology — the ontology of neurophysiology. The extensional explanation maintains that the *design stance* of a physical system produces *intentional stance*. The design aspect is necessary and biologically speaking the system evolves certain independent features in constant interactions with the environment.[15]

A biologically evolved system adopts the intentional stance. As Dennett further argues, "If rationality is the mother of intention, we still mean intentional systems form the criteria that give them life, and set them up to their own. Less figuratively, if we are to make use of the concept intentional system in particular instances, at some point we must cease testing the assumption of the system's rationality, adopt the intentional stance and grant without further ado that the system is qualified for beliefs and desires."[16] Rationality is a common source of explanation and prediction. And it is expected that every normal human being is a rational being. Our communication and judgments are based on the rational ability of processing the information. Adequate inferential rules and set of beliefs may help us concluding something viable. The design stance is an attribute of the functionally developed system of making rational choice and the capacity of developing its own strategy of interpreting behaviours. The system, therefore, adequately makes representation by realizing its *stance*. In other words, the system exercises beliefs and desires in making "choice of action" — the system acts *as if* like a *rational agent*.[17]

---

15. See, Dennett explains this in the chapter "Evolution, Error and Intentionality," *Intentional Stance*, p. 269.
16. See, Daniel Dennett, *Brainstorms*, Massachusetts, The MIT Press, 1986, p. 19.
17. For Dennett, a system whether biological or artificial with a proper designed stance can fairly "adopt the intentional stance." →

Bodily Intentionality: Intentionality in the natural world

There are two conceptions of intentionality that appear from a reading of the above two sections. One, the intentionality is intrinsic to thought and experience advocated by Searle. Two, intentionality is a functional feature of the design stance of a physical system argued by Dennett. Both have reference to the physical reality; as the Searlean theorization of intentionality ultimately reaches to the biological naturalism, and the Dennettian conception of intentionality leads to the idea of a functional system of a physical organism with a proper design stance to process information. Here, I would like to explicate more on the second type of intentionality argued by the physicalists. If the human brain has evolved in the process of constant interaction with the environment then the evolutionary features are related with the features of the physical universe. Dennett and many other physicalists challenge the Searlean interpretation of intentionality. In the physicalists' world-view, intentionality is based on the extensional functional features of the matter. Matter whether it is living or non-living; the intentional stance is determined by the *physical stance*. For instance, the physical body of virus is composed in such a way that its "atomic level works in mindless ways," and unlike virus, the robot is a non-living body constituted of different types of *macromolecules* — "the huge crystals from the point of view of chemistry, may be tiny in size but they build up *macro*molecular *nano*technology. They are in effect natural robots."[18] The structural features of each and every part of the robots are important to explain the *homunculus*[19] that makes the function intentional. The

→ He explains this in the chapter "Intentionality and Intentional Systems." See his book *The Kinds of Minds: Origin of Consciousness*, pp. 35-36.

18. *Ibid.*, p. 26.

19. Dennett's homunculus argument justifies that each sub-systems →

homunculus represents that as if there is a *little man* residing in each sub-system of robots. The operation of sub-system is about processing the data at a sub-personal level. There is no Cartesian notion of centrality involved in the Dennettian framework. Dennett refutes to accept the notion of rationality and intelligence as an attribute at the personal level, which refers to the person as unity of consciousness. The sub-personal level, which gives an extensional explanation of thought process, refers to each sub-systems working and making discrete analysis of mental phenomena. As it happens in the case of robots, each sub-system in it is self-regulatory and performs in their own way to fix the goal. This is an indication of producing intentionality at different levels of system feature working towards realizing goals.

A proper explanation of the *intentional stance* of a system *eliminates* the abstraction embedded in the explanation of intentionality *per se*. Following this spirit of the thesis Dretske rightly points out: "Here we are trying to understand, after all, not intentionality *per se*, but the mind. Thought may be intentional, but that is not the property we are seeking a recipe to understand. As long as intentionality we use is not itself mental, then we are as free to use intentionality in our recipe for making a mind as we are in using electrical conductors in building an amplifier or gumdrops in making cookies."[20]

→ of a system have intentional stance which are syntactically definable. It is like each unit of the brain has got a mind — as if there are little men inside the brains and each of them functions optimally determines certain goal or they are strategically aware of "how to do it." See, the chapter on "Instrumentalism" in *Intentional Stance, op. cit*, pp. 72-74, where Dennett argues against Searle's semantic characterization of the mind.

20. Fred Dretske, "A Recipe of Thought," *Philosophy of Mind: Classical and Contemporary Readings*, ed. David Chalmers, *op. cit.* p. 492. This paper was originally published as "If you cannot make one, →

Dretske is exactly putting forward his view in Dennettian framework that while understanding intentionality we need to explicate the microelements of the mental phenomena, rather than just associating it with the features of consciousness. The microanalysis focuses on the real constituents of the mental phenomena, as gumdrops have significance with reference to the making of cookies, or the amplification of sounds is produced and regulated by the electrical conductors. Dretske is indifferent to both notion of taste generated from the microelements of cookies and about the softness of sound waves regulated by the amplifier. While explaining everything in the language of physics and chemistry, we often leave out the essential element of the *semantic content* of these processes. It is because semantic content as an emerging property for brain function is not causally efficacious to make any significant effect. Nevertheless, the content is causally reducible to its micro constituents. The micro constituents are essentially related with the sub-systems of the brain. Therefore, the brain system constituted of neurons, thalamus, hypothalamus, amygdala, pituitary gland, hippocampus, pons, cerebellum, the cerebral cortex, motor cortex, sensory cortex and corpus callosum, etc. are responsible for explaining mental states or experiences. There are two things important here, one is the difference in *micro level* properties of each sub-system working cohesively, and the second is the interrelationship among the different sub-systems causing entirely a different system feature giving an impression that *as if* their behaviours are goal directed. For instance, human brain system constituted of neurons of the brain; the hypothalamus, the cortex, etc. have different functions than antibody, hemoglobin molecules and vestibule-reflexive machinery, etc. Nevertheless they all are important to fulfil

→ you don't know how it works," eds. T Vekling and H. Wettstein, *Midwest Studies in Philosophy*, vol. 19, 1994, pp. 468-82.

some function and they act together. This indicates that their behaviours are goal directed — as if they act intentionally to fulfil certain goal, defined as *bodily intentionality*.[21] It characterizes the functional capacities with relation to the dispositional features of the body, e.g., the optical lobe at the back is concerned with the visual processes whereas the parietal lobes cause the three dimensional representation of spatial layout of physical objects. Similarly, if we take the totality of brains function at various levels then *bodily intentionality* does succeed in relating the body with the environment — the natural world. Each microelement works with relation to other. It eventually refers to the causal relationship that holds the micro and the macro level functions of the world. At the macro level the body is sensitive to the temperature, the oxygen level; ethereal conditions are defined as intentional mode of causal co-existence with the world. Thus, in the physicalists' framework, there is no gap between the micro level and the macro level functions.

However, the notion of causal co-existence can be discussed with relation to the concept of extensional regularities of the bodily functions developing intentional *stance.* The bodily function could be also treated as *dispositional*[22] properties of the physical system. Since the functional regularities of a system are based on the causal efficacies of its sub-systems

---

21. See, Corbin Collins, "Bodily Intentionality," *Inquiry*, vol. 31, 1998.
22. Collin argues that the regularity of the functional relationship between the body and the environment is "felicitous dispositional fit" in which the skill develops. See, *Ibid.*, p. 508. Also see Stephen Mumford, (Discussions) "Intentionality and the Physical: A new theory of Disposition Ascription," *The Philosophical Quarterly*, vol. 49, no. 195, 1999. It is followed by Place's response. Mumford in his discussion rejects U.T. Place's idea that "Intentionality is a dispositional feature of the physical." Cf. U. T. Place, "Intentionality as the Mark of the Dispositional," *Dialectica*, vol. 50, 1996, pp. 91-120.

and units, which facilitate conditional functions. The function of the stimulus and manifestations, is one of the instances of conditional function of processing sensation. The very function of the body *acts* as if it *aims at* or *strives to* realise certain goal. The extensional having an *animistic* way of explaining intentionality gives an impression that every part of the body is spatio-temporally conditioned and oriented towards certain kinds of possible events. In the micro level, a single neuron can make multiple contacts — most probably, one thousand to ten thousand contacts a neuron establishes with other neurons while processing stimulus and producing responses. So the stimulations carried out by neurons and the synapses show a conditional relationship that persists in the brain system. One can imagine the function of a well-programmed satellite that moves around the earth and transmit information. The physicalists earnestly believe that the satellites work with their *original* intentionality. May be in a similar way the functions of the eruptions of lava or the digestive system of a biological organism would imply having original intentionality. But in reality it only exhibits their inherent dispositions. This sort of *ascription of intentionality* to the physical and biological phenomena does lead to panpsychism. Panpsychism believes that all physical body possess has some degree of sensitivity. The structure of the system is important to realize and produce the sensory effects. The emergence of consciousness unfolds the development of sentient beings to conscious beings. The emergence of sentient features from the physical constituents of the body reveals the dispositional features of the body. Moreover, we must note that "all dispositional characterizations of properties are functional characterizations, but not vice versa."[23] Even if dispositions are functionally construed there is a need to specify the causal properties of dispositions, which would explain further the manifestation

---

23. See, Mumford, *op. cit.*, p. 223.

of intentionality. Disposition itself is not an explanation of the teleological function of the body; rather "an additional programme is needed for reinforcing the concept of intentionality, that would exclude the notion of bodily intentionality and favour the mental representational form of intentionality."[24] While transmitting the information the satellites neither interpret nor understand the significance of the message and the concern for the security the information they bear. They only perform their activity that is programmed and by doing that they serve the goal of someone who requires the information. In this regard, an extra "programming" is necessary to understand the performed activities of any physical organism. Similar is the case with gumdrops; lava and digestive system only possess certain dispositional properties, which exhibit the mechanical actions of the body. The mechanical force embedded in the body to produce dispositional features is not sufficient to hold realization condition.

Since the physicalists treat intentionality like any other physical phenomena, it can be placed in the natural world. The causal law that operates in nature also operates in defining bodily functions. The bodily functions can be determined by inducing certain devices. The mode of the activities of the devices gives the impression of "intentionality of the device." The mechanical performance of the devices acts differently, than the "intentionality of purposes, attitudes and knowledge of its user." For example, "the navigator compass acts as a reliable instrument to indicate *north* and being a reliable indicator it does not depend on us."[25] This may be true for

24. Mumford observes this notion initiated by C.B. Martin and K. Pfeifer "Intentionality and the Non-Psychological," *Philosophy and Phenomenological Research*, vol. 46, 1986. Cf. Mumford, *op. cit.* p. 224.

25. See, Fred Dretske, "A Recipe of Thought," *Philosophy of Mind: Classical and Contemporary Readings*, *op. cit.* p. 493.

the programmed robot, which makes the satellite function, or a robot that helps in doing little bits of household work. The goal-oriented function of these systems vindicates *a pre-intentional form of teleology*. The pre-intentional form of teleology is a mark of bodily intentionality. In that case, "there is no need to naturalize intentionality. It has already become a natural phenomenon; a pervasive feature of our physical world."[26]

The Searlean notion of naturalizing intentionality agrees with the basic idea that *intentionality is a biological* phenomenon and part of the natural world. Searle's biological naturalism comprised "atomic theory of matter and evolutionary biology."[27] It reflects upon the causal explanation of the microstructure of the physical as well as the evolutionary behaviour of the biological. Since the mental is evolved in the biological processes, he further introduces the micro and the macro levels of explanation for the brain functions causing conscious mental states and the mental states causing representation of thoughts and actions respectively. The micro level function "builds up the inclusive fitness" by its different traits of causal mechanism and its relationship with the environment. This involves the notion of survival of the species as well as causal relations with nature. Biologically the body evolves its own immune capacities for our survival and that shows its causal relationship with the environment as well as its own internal system function. However, Searle writes, "Furthermore, this is the crucial point, some extremely complex nervous system are capable of causing and sustaining conscious states and processes."[28] Intentionality is the intrinsic

26. *Ibid.*

27. John Searle, "Consciousness and Its Place in Nature," *The Rediscovery of the Mind*, p. 86.

28. *Ibid.*, p. 89.

property of consciousness caused by the brain processes but is not fully sustained by the causal powers of the brain processes. This is indeed an important aspect of the Searlean naturalism where the brain is accepted as a vital part of human physiology. Consciousness and intentionality are treated as independent features of the brain function. Although brain function causes consciousness, but logically speaking "consciousness is squirted and has its own life"[29] implies a different notion of emergence, in which the mental is not reduced to the physical. Rather it builds up the background conditions for the functions and realization of the network of intentional states. Thus the emergence of consciousness as a non-reducible property of the mental causes the *gap* between the intentionality *per se* and the brain processes.

Thus, in the over all naturalists' agenda intentionality remains a system feature — a feature caused by the brain/ bodily functions. But bodily functions are not enough to suggest that intentionality is a part of the dispositional states or the functional features of the body. The animistic characteristic of the body exhibits sensitivity as reflexive mode of action, rather than an intentional action. On the other hand, the intentional features of action involve experience of thoughts, feelings, sensations, etc. As Gillett remarks, "consciousness paradigmatically or essentially is a matter of the capacity for directed and flexible sensitivity toward the environment. It implies that consciousness involves ability which are also central in the grasp of concepts and therefore

29. Consciousness could cause things that could not be explained by the causal behaviours of neurons. The naïve idea here is that consciousness gets squirted out by the behaviours of the neurons in the brain, but once it has been squirted out it has life of its own. Searle explains it while describing the notion of emergence of consciousness, See, Searle, "Reductionism and Irreducibility of Consciousness" in *The Rediscovery of the Mind*, p. 112.

elucidates the link with language."[30] That precisely brings back the notion of representation into the discourse of intentionality. In the discourse of intentionality the person would have manifolds of experience of his personality, memory, desires, beliefs, intentional actions, social interactions, thoughts, feeling, sentience, etc. Moreover, if we ascribe intentionality only to the sentient feature then "there is a danger of committing panpsychism — a suggestion to inanimate objects having purposes and performing actions. It would undermine the excellent form of intentionality shown in the representations of beliefs and desires. They are the intentional notion par excellence."

Over and above, there cannot be teleology without intentionality. The teleology of the bodily states and events exists in the pre-intentional form, rather than in principle intentional. The pre-intentional form of intentionality is the physical states and processes. For instance, the capacities of neural states and processes involved in seeing and experiencing things reduce the phenomenal properties of experiences to the micro-levels physical analysis. For a physicalist, as brain functions explain the intentional activity then the language of mind is not different from the language of the brain. And so is the case with understanding the *content* of expressions. The content is realized not only in the syntactic level, the level of unconscious mental states, but also explained with relation to the functional features of neural states and processes — the neurons and synaptic relations. The phenomenal features of semantic content no more retain its intentionality; rather is considered as epiphenomenal. Only the physical properties have effectiveness and can cause something.

---

30. See Grant Gillett, "Consciousness, the Brain and What Matters," *Bioethics*, vol. 4, no. 3, July 1990, p. 183. He also discusses it in detail in his earlier paper, "The Generality Constraint and Conscious Thoughts, *Analysis*, vol. 47, 1987, pp. 20-4.

Intentional Causation: Intentionality to the world and beyond

In the naturalists' schema causality as a universal physical law pervasively involves the psychological laws. The psychological properties and functions are causally determined by the close proximity with laws of biophysics and biochemistry. As a result, psychology and cognitive science as special sciences can be reduced to the physical sciences through *bridge law*[31] — a connecting principle between the law of special sciences and the law of the physical sciences. It suffices a transitive relationship between the physical and the psychological with the help of introducing certain additional formula that discloses the symmetric relationship between the neurophysiological properties of the brains and the mental representational states. Thus, the causal relationship holds a causal identity theory between the mind and the brain.

Searle is an exception to the naturalists' camp. The Searlean biological naturalism follows a middle path. It goes for the scientific explanation of the mind but denies reductionism — the identity relationship between the brain and the mind. The micro realities of the brain function though *cause* consciousness, still consciousness or mental features are neither causally *identical* nor causally *reducible to* the physical brain properties. This is indeed a radical position of the Searlean scientific world-view. According to him, the micro level constituents of the reality differ from its macro level features though the former is *causing* the latter. Hence, the mind and the brain need two levels of explanation. The micro level realities are different from the macro level realities. They are different because of their respective properties and features. Nevertheless, the micro and macro levels hold "distinct forms of regularities of

31. See, Jerry Fodor, "Special Sciences," in *Representations: A philosophical foundation to cognitive science*, Sussex, Harvester Press, 1981, p. 131.

their functions, require logically independent descriptions and hence the concept of identity between them itself is a contingent truth."[32] The difference of description about the mental phenomena is based on intentionality of the mind, whereas the functions of physico-chemical processes of the brain are regulated by causal principles. The causality and intentionality have two distinct levels of function, the micro and the macro level respectively. At the micro level neural properties are causally linked with various levels of brain systems, whereas at the macro level the intentional states are intentionally related and realized. However, if the micro-level function is causing the macro level phenomena then, for Searle, there is no strict or permanent causal relationship. The relationship is contingent. The contingent relationship denies the independent function of the mind; rather it is always dependent on the brain processes. Intentionality being intrinsic to consciousness is explicated differently along with other features, such as, subjectivity, self-referentiality, unity, and aspectuality, free will, etc. The extensional causal nexus between the brain functions and mental representation is not necessarily found. But Searle does not deny the *causal relations* of the body with the natural laws. For instance, the brain function *causing* conscious intentional states is different from the gravitational power operating in nature.[33] In both the cases, law of causality is involved. Besides that he suggests, causality as a universal law correlates the natural events in a distinct order than the notion of "universal regularity" that we draw in the case of "agent's causation." Searle writes, "It seems to me quite unlikely that there are any relevant purely psychological laws: suppose all the psychological factors were repeated exactly (whatever that means), suppose I have some

32. See, *Intentionality, op. cit.* p. 114.

33. *Intentionality*, p. 116.

degrees of thirst, water has same degree of availability, etc. Does my original claim commit me to the view that in an exactly similar situation I would behave similarly."[34] The psychological factors are regulated by intentionality, rationality, emotion and freedom, etc. A person is free to act differently implies that justification to such generalization is not conclusive. Therefore, the regularity of action does not confirm the universal regularity or a law like regularity. Rather a person's intention to act differently and more interestingly *willing* to act freely presupposes intentionality which could never be captured by any form of causal law.

According to Searle, the language use is based on intentionality of the mind. Intentionality defines the relationship among the mental states and explicates the internal relationship between the *content* of mental representation and condition of satisfaction. The relationship is *asymmetrical*.[35] The asymmetry relation lies between the cause of mental representation and the condition of satisfaction. Though brain functions cause mental representations still mental representations are not causally defined by the brain states. The asymmetry between the mental and the physical operations is evident. One can relate this with the notion of contingent relationship between the mind and the brain. Does contingency imply the asymmetrical relationship between the micro level and the macro level? They may be sharing some relations with reference to their respective dual functions. I am not concerned with the problem of dualism here. My interest is rather to bring intentionality into the heart of discourse where the issue of dualism can be minimized. Nevertheless, the asymmetry relationship in Searle's intentionality thesis brings the *experience of causation* as well as

---

34. *Intentionality*, p. 118.

35. *Intentionality*, p. 121.

condition of satisfaction into discussion. The experience of causation shows the *performance* of double level of intentionality connecting the *mind to the world* and followed by the *world to the mind* directions of *fit*. While feeling thirsty, I may intend to quench my thirst immediately by having a glass of water. Having the desire to have water and drinking a glass of water are mainly about the macro level explanation experiencing things and realizing satisfaction. Does one need to refer to the brain states there? The proper scientific answer to this may look for the physiological or neurophysiological states cause thirst. Of course, we know that my body needs water for survival, and we drink water whenever we feel thirsty. Apart from the causal explanation there are two things important. Firstly, the realization is that having some drinks can quench thirst. The causal nexus of the feeling is realized by the intentional mind. So, intentionality is a precondition to explain the causal relationship. Secondly, apart from quenching thirst we do get tremendous relief, and satisfaction extends the semantics of human survival. The realization of this relationship as a mental phenomenon presupposes the role of an intentional agent. And the agency is not bound by the function of the causal operation of the brain — the biological engine. It is because a mere causal explanation is not sufficient to explain the significance of a person's desire for something and having it — unfolds the levels of intentionality of experience. But if the explanation of having drunk is about processing the liquid stuff into energy then we only succeed in providing neurophysiological explanation.

The ontology of experience of mental states would give impression of experiencing content. The *content* is not an *object* of observation rather it is experienced in intentional mode of consciousness. While seeing a flower, my experience of the flower unfolds me being conscious of the content of the object of visualization; the content is formed in the visual experience.

So, the content is visualized. Similarly, experiencing the intention of doing an action, Searle takes away the causal relations between intention and behaviour. For Searle, "that part of the actual phenomena of action is the experience of causation. In these cases, there is not any problem about how we get the form of the experience of causation, the experience itself does the causing; where successful it causes what it is directed at."[36] Thus intentionality unfolds the *form* of the content in experience. In an intentional mode of experience the internal relationship between the cause and effect is realized. As he cites the example of "raising the hand up," satisfies the performance of action of passing information, which involves the person's intention to do it and realize by seeing its effect on my fellow friends. In both the cases intentionality involves self-referentiality, is the part of the content of representation and not the object. As he puts it, "Now the peculiarity of intentional causation is that we directly experience this relationship in many cases where we make something happen to us."[37] Thus, intentionality reflects upon the experiential features of the content in order to show that content can be realized in an intentional mode of experience.

The Searlean notion of intentional causation is not free from the dispute. As Mohanty remarks, "that [Searle's] intentionality is never totally disconnected from causality that a physical, really efficacious nature, is intruding into intentional life and preventing the latter from being an autonomous domain of pure consciousness."[38] If the brain process *causing* consciousness and intentionality is an *intrinsic* feature of

36. *Intentionality*, p. 125.

37. *Intentionality*, p. 123.

38. See, J.N. Mohanty, "Intentionality, Causality and Holism," *The Possibility of Transcendental Phenomenology*, Dordrecht, Martinus Nijhoof Publishers, 1985, p. 70.

consciousness then intentionality is not free from the causal link of the physical. As a result, it becomes problematic to consider a causally non-free intentionality as the mark of mental. Searle's response to this is problematic so far as his naturalistic world-view is concerned. The contingent link between the brain and the mind and vice versa, for me, is something not just leading us to naïve dualism or property dualism. Rather needs deeper level analysis and it is discussed elsewhere.[39] However, here I would like to put metaphorically as someone else would say that the *causal power* of the brain to a great extent *drains away*[40] with the emergence of consciousness along with its other intrinsic co-features like intentionality, subjectivity and rationality. My preference to take on this metaphor here is to relate Searlean conception of intentionality with a non-causal explanation of the mind. If for Searle, mind is emerging out of brain process and the emergent feature gives the mental a new life then the mind is certainly not bound by the causal principles. These cited features are not only unique to human mind, "rather they are peculiar with their logical properties."[41] The semantic features of the mind define the logical properties of intentionality, in which intentionality is intrinsically involved in the exercise of

---

39. I have discussed it in the section; "Searle's Cartesian Legacy" in the concluding chapter of thesis *Mind, Language and Intentionality: with special reference to John R. Searle,* submitted to the University of Hyderabad, Hyderabad, March 2000.

40. Searle may not agree with Block and Kim who make some interesting illustrations regarding the concept of *mental causation* and its relationship with the micro level causal properties. See, Ned Block "Do Causal Powers Drain Away?" and Jaegwon Kim's "Blocking Causal Drainage and Other Maintenance Chores with Mental Causation" *Philosophy and Phenomenological Research,* vol. LXVII, no. 1, July 2003.

41. See, *Intentionality, op. cit.,* p. 160.

meaning, understanding, experiencing, etc. which are different from all other forms of biological properties. If intentionality maintains its central role by being irreducible to the physical brain process then it is due to its logical properties like intentionality, subjectivity, aspectuality, etc. that form the intentional states. Thus, the logical properties having distinct functional features entail the ontology of intentionality different from the ontology of the physical. And the mental is to be located in all forms of intentional modes of conscious-experiences. As Searle writes, "All of my conscious forms of intentionality that give me information about the world independent of myself are always from a special point of view. The world itself has no point of view but my access to the world through my conscious states is always from my point of view."[42] In the intentional mode of experience we realize the intentionality of mental states. Mental states are not only directed to the world from a point of view but also perspectival in its experience of the representation. Intentionality is presupposed in both the cases.

All forms of consciousness are unified by intentionality — it's a thread that has woven into a form called *subjectivity*. My subjectivity represents my point of view — the way *I* experience the world. The representation of the world is always from the *first person point of view*. The experience unfolds the first person point of view of representation in which the world is given to my intentionality. And in a similar way my body is given to my intentionality. As an embodied being, I *feel* my body — my *bodily subjectivity* is experienced in an intentional mode of consciousness. The shift from the experience of *my* bodily subjectivity, to the subjectivity of world and from my own representations discloses the *act* of

42. *Intentionality*, p. 63.

the intentionality of consciousness.[43] Thus the ontology of intentionality *per se* is located in the very form of experience.

Conclusion

The physicalists' motif of naturalizing intentionality lies in the scientific explanation of the mind, to which the Searlean naturalism has some bearing. The Searlean naturalism significantly differs from the physicalists' metaphysics of mind, as the physicalists reduce intentionality along with other mental properties to the physical properties of the brain or any artificial system. The reductionistic approach in general is a tendency to avoid dualism and advocate physicalism, i.e., the mental as an effect of the physical is causally explainable by the physical. Moreover, a stronger version of reductionism is put forward to deny dualism and more specifically to deny the ontology of the mind. Hence, intentionality in the physicalist schema restricted to the causal explanation of the functions of the physical configurations of the material bodies. The human as an embodied being possessing consciousness is treated as an epiphenomenon intrinsic to the bodily activities. The intrinsic relationship of the intentionality with the body naturalizes intentionality and thereby naturalizes the mind making it further causally linked with the natural world. The naturalized intentionality has no autonomy, because it is causally inefficacious. The causal inefficacies of the ontology of the mental nullify its reality. On the other hand, if someone argues that the mind as part of the bodily system works as dispositional features then the dispositional form of the mental is also intrinsic to a deterministic world-view, i.e., the ontology of the pre-intentional teleology of the physical. To say that the pre-intentional features of the body are embodied with different types of *homunculi*, then the functions no more become

43. John Searle, *Mind, Language and Society*, London, Phoenix, 1999, p. 81.

syntactically or causally explainable. Any form of syntactic or causal explanation would simply take away their *subjectivity*. The subjectivity of *homunculi* is not bound by causal function, as they own their individuality — the freedom of establishing their own function. No amount of multiplicity of neural pattern can logically determine the notion of freedom — the principle of freedom and determinism logically oppose each other. On the other hand, the intentionality of the homunculi is causally determined. The physicalists' ascription of radical or unlimited form of intentionality to the instrumental or bodily behaviours deconstructs the nature of mind with a deterministic world-view of science. The deconstruction develops a new metaphysics of the mind based on silicon chips, transducers, and algorithms eliminating the ontology of the mind.

Searlean biological naturalism holds intentionality is one of the logical properties irreducible to the causal functions of neural states and processes. But it does not disown the causal relationship that brain shares with the mind in connection with the emergence of mental life. The intricacy that biological naturalism brings to the readers is its naturalistic interpretation, which disowns the ontological status of the mind. The Searlean naturalism would fail only if the macro level explanation is real and the mind is explainable with its own logical properties. These properties do not deny the micro properties of the brain. Rather if both micro and macro constituents are real, then dualism is inevitable which Searle admits as a naïve phenomenon. On the contrary, if the mind as an effect is logically different with its unique logical properties like intentionality, consciousness, subjectivity, aspectuality, etc. then from that perspective at least the Searlean dualism does not remain naïve as Searle considers it to be. Rather it allows widening the scope of the mind to intervene in the physical or in the world as discussed in the fourth section. Thus, in this regard, the paper is an attempt towards capturing the logical relations of the intentional involvement of the mind and the world in which the form of experience itself is sufficient to unfold the metaphysical foundation of intentionality as the hallmark of the mental.[44]

---

44. This paper was presented in the national seminar on *Language and Mind* organized by the Deptt. of Philosophy, University of Hyderabad, during 16-18 November 2004. I am deeply indebted to Professor R.C. Pradhan for inviting me to present the paper. My special thanks to the commentator of my paper, Professor P.R. Bhat, whose valuable suggestions and comments immensely helped me to improve the paper. During the discussion session of the paper observations and comments made by Professor Bijoy Boruah, Professor Prajit Basu and Professor S.G. Kulkarni did benefit me to visualize the problem in a better perspective. I am thankful to all of them.

9

Fodor on Meaning Holism
Why Narrow Contents do not Hold Promise for a Meaning Theory

R.C. Pradhan

In this paper I will attempt to defend meaning holism against Fodor's attack. I will show that the divide between wide and narrow contents is not necessary for meaning holism. Fodor's espousal of the theory of narrow contents is not admittedly an adequate ground for refuting meaning holism. Meaning holism holds good on semantic grounds and not on the psychological nature of the contents. Contents are the necessary correlates of meaning and are not the same as the latter. While maintaining meaning holism one could retain content holism; even one could remain neutral on content holism while holding meaning holism.

My strategy is twofold: first, to refute Fodor's arguments against meaning holism by showing that failure of content holism does not entail failure of meaning holism and second, to argue that meaning holism is a semantic thesis and does not depend on the psychological theory of contents.

My argument against Fodor's narrow content is based on his account of it in his *Psychosemantics*.[1] Fodor himself has

---

1. See Jerry A. Fodor, *Psychosemantics: The Problem of Meaning in the Philosophy of Mind* (Cambridge, Mass., The MIT Press, 1987).

revised his views on narrow content in his *The Elm and the Expert*[2] which I have not taken into consideration in the main body of the paper. Though the broad contents are now acceptable to Fodor, he does not yield any ground to meaning holism.

Meaning Holism: Fodor's Taxonomy

Fodor's[3] account of meaning holism is based on the threefold route to meaning holism, viz. (A) from the confirmation holism to meaning holism, (B) from psychofunctionalism to meaning holism, and (C) from functional-role semantics to meaning holism. These three routes are, according to Fodor, fraught with difficulties and hence cannot be relied upon to prove meaning holism.

Confirmation holism attributed to Quine[4] runs on the well-known line that sentences are not confirmed in isolation but as part of the corporate body of sentences. The sentences function as part of a complex web of sentences and so they need mutual support for their confirmation. This thesis is, according to Fodor, an epistemic thesis in the sense that it requires that the sentences and the beliefs have epistemic liaisons with other sentences and beliefs. Fodor writes:

> Confirmation Holism is of interest to us here only because it is often taken to suggest a corresponding holistic treatment of semantics. It's not, after all, a long step from the doctrine that the belief system is *the minimal unit of confirmation to the*

2. Cf. Jerry Fodor, *The Elm and the Expert* (Cambridge, Mass., The MIT Press, 1994).
3. Fodor, *Psychosemantics: The Problem of Meaning in the Philosophy of Mind.*
4. W.V. Quine, "Two Dogmas of Empiricism," in *From a Logical Point of View* (Cambridge, Mass.,The Harvard University Press, 1953; Second Revised Edition, 1980).

> doctrine that the belief system is *the minimal unit of intentional content*[5] (italics are original).

The holistic implications are drawn by virtue of the fact that just as beliefs are intricately involved with one another, so are the contents of the beliefs. Meaning holism and content holism thus follow from the semantics of the beliefs and the propositions expressing them.

Fodor points out that semantic holism does not follow as a matter of necessity from the epistemic or confirmation holism because what is true of the method of confirmation does not affect the meaning and contents of the beliefs concerned. The point of disagreement between Fodor and the meaning holists is that the beliefs may be in liaison, however complicated, but the contents themselves which are intentional do not follow suit in getting liaisoned with other contents. So Fodor argues that "beliefs have contents, but their contents are not determined by their systematic connections; specifically, the contents of a belief are not determined by its epistemic liaisons."[6] Thus a wedge is inserted between contents on the one hand and the confirmation relations on the other; while the former is psychological and intentional, the latter is a matter of how we relate the sentences to experiences.

Fodor refutes attribution of meaning holism to Quine in "Two Dogmas" as he thinks that Quine is holding no meaning thesis there and that he is a meaning nihilist.[7] All that Quine is taken as holding is confirmation holism. "Quine's tactic is to infer Confirmation Holism from the refutation of semantic localism, and *not the other way round*."[8] Therefore there is no

---

5. Fodor, *Psychosemantics,* p. 63.
6. *Ibid.*
7. *Ibid.,* p. 67.
8. *Ibid.,* p. 66.

way we can prove semantic holism from the refutation of semantic localism. Fodor argues further:

> Putnam's Quine rejects Semantic Localism because he thinks meaning is global. But Quine's Quine rejects Semantic Localism because he thinks meaning is nonsense. But if so, he must, in all conscience, reject Semantic Holism too.[9]

If Quine's Quine rejects semantic localism because meaning does not exist, then semantic holism also falls prey to the same nihilism. But is it true? Putnam thinks otherwise as he thinks positivism was satisfied with semantic localism keeping room for unrevisable or analytic truths. Quine wanted to dispense with the analytic truths by adopting semantic holism and not confirmation holism alone. Confirmation holism cannot do away with analytic truths and so Quine opted for semantic holism which is well suited to do it. Therefore we cannot conclude that semantic holism was not Quine's aim at all. Fodor's account of Quine does not take into account Quine's rejection of beliefs and contents which is one of the reasons why he relied on semantic holism and not on content-holism for understanding language and its functions. Mere confirmation holism is not enough to meet the Quinean requirements.

Holism does not depend on the size of the "the unit of empirical significance"[10] as Fodor rightly points out, but the size does matter in the sense that the whole of language is considered to be the unit of significance by the holist. But if that is so, there is no reason to believe that meaning holism has no stake in the size of the unit of meaningfulness.

The second route to meaning holism is admittedly psychofunctionalism which demands that beliefs and their

---

9. *Ibid.*, p. 65.

10. *Ibid.*, p. 66.

contents are functionally dependent on the causal network of inputs and outputs. That is, the liaisons of beliefs are established on the functionalist grounds such that beliefs are networked together; hence, "if Psychofunctionalism says that mental states are individuated by their relations, then Psychofunctionalism implies that believing P is individuated by its relations; hence, presumably, by its relations to its epistemic liaisons."[11] What is contended by the meaning holist, according to Fodor, is that these liaisons constitute the holistic network of the belief-relations in a belief system.

Fodor's objection to the meaning holist is that the belief liaisons do not amount to meaning holism via content holism. It is because even if beliefs are inextricably related to other beliefs, it does not follow that the contents of beliefs are also similarly related. Fodor writes:

> What you don't need . . . is the much stronger claim that being the belief *that P,* being a belief that has a certain *content,* is a matter of having the right connections to inputs, outputs, and other mental states.[12]

The point of contention here is whether the contents of beliefs are liaisoned like the beliefs themselves. Beliefs form a system, no doubt, but not the contents. That seems to be the argument of Fodor. "But it's only Psychofunctionalism about *content* that offers a route to Meaning Holism; functionalism about *believing* (as opposed to believing-that-P) isn't a semantical doctrine at all."[13] That is, belief holism is not meaning holism as the former is not a semantic thesis. Thus Fodor holds that meaning holism does not follow from belief holism.

---

11. *Ibid.*
12. *Ibid.*, p. 69.
13. *Ibid.*, p. 69.

Fodor's argument against semantic holism is not strong enough because it identifies meaning holism with content holism. For him, since content holism does not follow from belief holism, so there is no meaning holism. But why are these two to be identified? Meaning and content are not the same, because while the contents are the constituents of the beliefs, meaning is not a constituent of the beliefs. Meaning holism issues from the fact that an account of meaning needs the whole system of semantic relations of the propositions. There is, however, no *a priori* argument against the possibility of belief and content holism. In that case, meaning holism is independent of holism of belief and content. Beliefs and their contents have the same logical behaviour as both are subservient to meaning and other semantic rules.

The third route to meaning holism is functional-role semantics which promises to lead to meaning holism via the functional-role of the beliefs in the belief system. Beliefs have a functional-role in the system as they determine the semantic role of the beliefs. For example, Oedipus's beliefs "I will marry Jocasta" and "I will marry my mother" are not the same because they have two different functional-roles in semantics. They express two different thoughts, though they refer to the same woman. The functional-role semantics holds that thoughts are interconnected to other thoughts and so are identifiable through these interconnections. Fodor's objection to this argument is that meaning holism does not follow from the functional role of the beliefs because we have to depend on the singular beliefs and their contents for identifying them and not the system itself. Oedipus's case shows that each belief has its peculiar satisfaction conditions and does not depend on other beliefs; hence the beliefs have a non-holistic functional role which is grafted on the belief's singular reference to the world. Fodor writes:

> I think it is probably true that some aspects of functional role have semantic force. What I hold (to put it very roughly) is that functional role is a marginal — a not very important — determinant of meaning. And, in particular, that since the contribution of functional role to the determination of meaning is marginal and not very important, you can get from functional role everything that semantics demands without opening the floodgates to Meaning Holism.[14]

Fodor's contention is that functional role only marginally contributes to the determination of meaning and so meaning should not be linked with the functional role. Meaning is independent of functional role and thus there is no passage from functional-role semantics to semantic holism. But the question is, why can we not treat meaning holism as presupposed by functional-role semantics and not as entailed by it? The case may be that meaning holism is more fundamental than functional-role semantics. The latter is more a case of how the concepts and beliefs function in a system than how they constitute meaning. Beliefs and concepts do not contribute to the formation of meaning but presuppose it in the sense that concepts must be already meaningful in order to have a functional role. Fodor writes:

> The implied conclusion will be that it's no good offering functional-role semantics in support of Meaning Holism because functional-role semantics (a) doesn't work and (b) isn't needed.[15]

That is, for Fodor, functional-role semantics itself is not needed because it does not work and therefore it cannot entail meaning holism. This is true but it does not answer the question why functional-role semantics should entail meaning holism rather

14. *Ibid.*, p. 71.

15. *Ibid.*, p. 72.

than presuppose it. Meaning in any case is prior to the functional-role of the concepts and beliefs.

Breakdown of the Individualistic Strategy

Fodor builds up an individualistic strategy to counter holism by raising the question of individual contents and their identification. The individual contents are psychologically intentional and are located in the specific beliefs as their contents. Hence the only strategy available for understanding the contents is to posit them as the "narrow" or individual contents.[16] These contents are such that they have a place in the individual psychology by virtue of their being the intentional contents. The question of making them part of a larger whole does not arise because they are located in the specific psychology of the individual.

Fodor rejects the externalist strategy of Putnam and Burge by playing down the "wide contents" as they are supposed to be dependent on the external world. These contents, as Putnam's Twin Earth and Burge's Oscar examples[17] suggest, are externally determined because they are concerning the external world. Fodor believes that this strategy does not work because it takes us away from the realm of the intentional contents to the external world. Meanings are not determined by the external world as the externalists believe. They are in the human mind and its intentional realm. Fodor writes:

> The Burge and Putnam stories show that the commonsense way of individuating the attitudes violates supervenience; by contrast, the psychologist individuates the attitudes nonrelationally ("narrowly," as one sometimes says), thereby preserving supervenience but at the cost of requiring

16. *Ibid.*, p. 77.

17. Cf. *Ibid.*, Chapter 2.

> an individualistic ("nonrelational"/"narrow") notion of content.[18]

The argument against the commonsense taxonomy depends on the fact that in the psychological taxonomy contents are non-relationally individuated and thus they preserve supervenience. While the externalists rely on the relational account of the beliefs and contents, the internalists depend on the non-relational individuation. What makes it a different strategy is that contents are taken back into their original home, that is, the domain of the intentional contents.

The individualists have the assumption that contents have a unique function of being the objects of beliefs and that they can be evaluated as either true or false beliefs on their own terms. This does not rule out the fact that beliefs are about the world. But their being "about" the world is taken care of by the beliefs themselves. Here the internalist has the option of saying that the narrow contents are so embedded in the beliefs that they do not have to look beyond the beliefs. This is a psychological move to argue for the autonomy of the psychological states against the externalist demands to take the beliefs as responses to external world.

Fodor is of the opinion that the mental contents have an existence of their own which is intentional in character.[19] He is a realist about the intentional contents in view of the fact that contents exist even if there is no external object corresponding to them. Thus Fodor argues that contents have to be individuated non-relationally by virtue of their own structure. What is important to their structure is their syntax and not their semantic properties. Syntax relates the narrow contents to other narrow contents in terms of their formal relationships. Besides, the mental contents being supervenient on the

18. *Ibid.*

19. *Ibid.*, p. 31.

physiological features of the brain, the narrow contents bear a fat syntax. So, in the words of Stich, "fat syntax supervenes on physiology."[20]

The internalist strategy breaks down where the "fat syntax" becomes too fat and eats up semantics altogether. This situation arises when the syntactic properties become too much confined to the narrow contents themselves and lose touch with the external world. In such a situation, the syntactic properties of the mental states cannot be semantically evaluated, as it has been pointed out by Stich.[21] Therefore the narrow contents will remain outside the bounds of semantic evaluation and thus will have no meaning. Stich writes:

> . . . as I see it, the real problem with narrow content is not that it fails to be "semantically evaluable" (whatever that might come out) but that it fails to match up with the syntactic taxonomy of a computational psychology.[22]

This shows that the narrow contents themselves do not automatically have a fat syntax and that they may fail to be completely syntactic in character. The possibility of semantic evaluation itself guarantees that the syntax of the narrow contents is not enough.

The Intentional Contents: The Externalist Strategy

The externalists argue that the mental contents which are intentional in character are about the world and therefore are to be evaluated in accordance with the requirement of truth and reference. The semantics of the contents must be such

---

20. Stephen P. Stich, "Narrow Contents Meet Fat Syntax" in *Mind and Cognition: An Anthology*, ed. William G. Lycan, (Mass., USA and Oxford, UK, Blackwell Publishers, Ltd., 1990; Second Edition, 1999), p. 313.

21. *Ibid.*

22. *Ibid.*, p. 315.

that the contents are considered widely, that is, truth-conditionally in reference to the world. Hence Putnam calls these contents "wide contents"[23] as distinguished from the "narrow contents." These contents are wide for the reason that they have to be placed with reference to the world. This strategy is to break the internalist apparatus of taking the contents in themselves by their internal role. The internal role is not enough, according to Putnam, to know what semantic value they have.

Contents have to be evaluated semantically, though they are psychological in nature and are intrinsically intentional. Fodor thinks that they are not semantically evaluable within the sphere of the propositional attitudes and their causal properties. They are the narrow contents because they are not related to or anchored in the world. These causal properties are to be syntactically decided and hence there is no reason to adopt the externalist mechanism prescribed by Putnam. Fodor recommends an intenalist narrow psychology[24] in his *Psychosemantics* to solve all problems of narrow contents. He writes:

> Narrow content is radically inexpressible, because it's only content *potentially*; it's what gets to *be* content when — and only when — it gets to be anchored. We can't — to put it in a nutshell — *say* what Twin thoughts have in common. This is because what can be said is *ipso facto* semantically evaluable; and what Twin-thoughts have in common is *ipso facto* not.[25] (italics original)

---

23. H. Putnam, *Representation and Reality* (Cambridge, Mass., The MIT Press, 1988).
24. Fodor, *Psychosemantics,* Chapter 2.
25. Fodor, "Individualism and Supervenience" in *Mind and Cognition,* ed. William G. Lycan, p. 363.

Thus Fodor opts for a narrow psychology just to make room for contents as mental states which are supervenient on the physical states of the brain independent of their relation to the world. This leads the narrow contents to gather more syntax about them as they are semantically cut off from the world. In the words of Fodor:

> The "broad content" of a thought, by contrast, is what you can semantically evaluate; it's what you get when you specify a narrow content and *fix a context*.[26]

But the question arises, how can we have semantic evaluation without reference to the world? The externalist emphasizes reference as a method of relating mind to the world because it is believed that without reference the mental contents can collapse into mere syntax.[27] The narrow contents themselves cannot have semantic evaluation unlike the broad contents and thus can hardly be candidates for meaning.

The internalist has to explain how contents can have their intentional character if they can be syntactically explained and therefore can be made free of reference to the world. Fodor describes the following scenario for evaluation:

> In short: Given RTM, the intentionality of the attitudes reduces to the content of mental representations. Given a truth definition, the content of mental representations is determined by the interpretation of their primitive non-logical vocabulary. So it's the interpretation of the primitive non-logical vocabulary of Mentalese that is at the bottom of the pile according to the present view.[28]

---

26. *Ibid.*, p. 362.

27. See Michael Devitt, "Why Fodor Can't Have It Both Ways" in *Meaning in Mind: Fodor and His Critics*, eds. Barry Loewer and Georges Rey (Oxford, and Cambridge, MA, Blackwell, 1991), pp. 95-118.

28. Fodor, *Psychosemantics*, p. 98.

Thus RTM-based account can forgo the element of reference and yet manage with the interpretation of the mental representations. This gives rise to the suspicion that in this perspective syntax is enough to take care of the mental representations.

Putnam argues that the narrow psychology and the narrow content view do not fit in with the way we relate our beliefs to the world. Our beliefs are the mental representations which are either true or false. Thus reference of the mental representations to the world is a must, whether it is causal or social in character. That is, the reference to the world must embed our beliefs about the world. Putnam's Twin Earth example shows the role of world-reference in the determination of meaning of the language in which the beliefs are expressed. Though myself on the earth and my Twin-Earth counterpart entertain the same thought "water," we refer to two different things, H_2O on Earth and XYZ on the Twin Earth. This shows that thought does not determine meaning; it is the reference that decides what we mean by a word. Thus externalism supports the view that beliefs with their contents are all representations of the world and are semantically decidable on the basis of their reference to the world. For Putnam reference is not causal but social because it is the community of the speakers and its experts which decides what is referred to by the terms such as "gold," "water," etc.[29]

Putnam is a defender of the wide contents because he believes that the mental contents are semantically evaluable on the basis of their truth-conditions. Truth-conditions matter to the semantic status of the mental representations and their

29. See Putnam, *Representation and Reality,* Chapter 2. See also his "The Meaning of "Meaning"" in *Mind, Language and Reality* (Cambridge University Press, Cambridge, 1975), pp. 215-71.

contents. Their psychological autonomy does not rule out the possibility of their being true or false. Semantics must intervene in the process of the mental representations so that we are assured of their intentional character. The syntax of the RTM is not enough to account for the meaning of the mental representations. RTM itself needs revision to accommodate wide contents. Fodor has attempted to do this in his *The Elm and the Expert* in which he argues that the computational theory of mind can very well go along with broad or wide contents.[30]

Akeel Bilgrami[31] suggests a radical revision in the externalist strategy by ruling out the Burge-Putnam argument for externalism based on reference. He argues that mental contents are world-directed without being wide in Putnam's sense because the contents are neither narrow nor wide as they are "united," that is, are part of a whole, being holistic in character. The so-called narrow contents are not narrow since they remain fixed on the world; they are semantic in character and are bound up with the truth-conditions. The distinction between wide and narrow contents does not arise because contents are embedded in our language which is public and not merely social in character.[32] Bilgrami writes:

> My thesis, by contrast, states simply that contents are externally determined but it is these same contents which go into the commonsense psychological explanation or rationalization of behaviour. There is no need for a second internal (or, for that matter, a second external) notion of content to explain behaviour. It is thus a unified notion of content.[33]

---

30. See Jerry Fodor, *The Elm and the Expert, op. cit.*
31. See Akeel Bilgrami, *Belief and Meaning* (Oxford, UK and Cambridge, MA., Blackwell, 1992).
32. *Ibid.*
33. *Ibid.*, p. 3.

The suggestion here is that the internal-external distinction regarding contents does not hold good if we keep in view the fact that contents are in any case determined by the external world even if they are psychological in character and are "in the head." Bilgrami writes:

> Externalism makes the publicness of thought and meaning possible, but this need not be founded on the views of reference of terms due to Kripke, Putnam, Burge, etc.[34]

To establish this kind of externalism, Bilgrami puts forward a constraint (C) which runs as follows:

> When fixing an externally determined concept of an agent, one must do so by looking to indexically formulated utterances of the agent which express indexical contents containing that concept and then *picking that external determinant for the concept which is in consonance with other contents that have been fixed for the agent.*[35] (italics original)

The constraint (C) spells out the necessity of the external determinant of the concepts intact while, at the same time, keeping the contents together without bifurcating them into the narrow and wide contents. That is, externalism does not demand the postulation of a wide content for determining the extension of the concepts because the concepts are in any case determined by the external world. Thus there is no reason to believe that there are narrow contents which are distinguished from the wide contents because the distinction itself is based on the assumption that contents can be cut off from the world. For Bilgrami, the contents are unified in the sense that they are about the world in a holistic fashion. So it makes no sense to talk of the internal and external account of the contents. In the words of Bilgrami:

---

34. *Ibid.*, p. 4.

35. *Ibid.*, p. 5.

> Since the "unity thesis" is based on the rejection of a whole way of thinking which leads to certain basic distinctions about intentional content, and the "locality thesis" dissolves the very idea of content composed of context-invariant concepts, this account of intentionality is genuinely radical.[36]

Are Meanings "In the Head?"

It has been debated among philosophers as to whether meanings or contents are "in the head."[37] This question pertains to the idea whether meanings are mental entities or are determined by the world. In their enthusiasm many philosophers, notably Searle, have argued that meanings are mental in character and are therefore in the head.[38] But opposed to this view is the view of Putnam, Burge and many others that meanings are not mental and are based on the facts regarding the world, that is, are determined by the external world. While the former view is called internalism, the latter is called externalism. These two views dominate the discussion on meaning and contents.

The internalist argument is that meanings and the contents are part of the inner processes of the belief-desire psychology which is deeply intentional and so is embedded in the inner structure of the mind. Searle.[39] for example, argues that meanings are the same as the intentional contents which are embedded in the natural function of mind and language. These contents are the defining features of the intentional mental

---

36. *Ibid.*, p. 12.
37. See Putnam, "The Meaning of "Meaning"" in *Mind, Language and Reality* (Cambridge University Press, 1975), pp. 215-71. See also John R.Searle, *Intentionality: An Essay in the Philosophy of Mind* (Cambridge University Press, 1983), Chapter 1.
38. *Ibid.*
39. John R. Searle, *Intentionality*, Chapter 8.

acts like belief, desire, thinking, perceiving, etc. The propositions embedded in these acts bear the contents as their intentional meanings and thus they are part of the psychology of the individual human beings. Searle argues against Putnam that the intentional contents in our head determine the extension of the words like "water" both on the Earth and the Twin Earth. He writes:

> For the traditional cluster-of-concepts Intentional content, Putnam has substituted an indexical Intentional content. In each case it is a meaning in the head that determines extension.[40]

The argument for the mentalistic theory of meaning has been refuted by many philosophers like Wittgenstein[41] for the reason that meaning itself is not a mental entity because it cannot be part of the inner processes of the mind, not only because the mental processes themselves are metaphysically suspect, but also because the semantic properties like meaningfulness are not psychological properties. The mental processes themselves presuppose meaning rather than constitute it. Meaning is semantically distinct from those that are meaningful, e.g. symbols in language. It will be a category mistake if we reduce meaning to the mental processes.

It is absurd to say that meanings are in the head in the purely subjective psychological sense, because meanings always are expressed in language and are therefore public in character. If meanings were mental and therefore subjective in the Cartesian fashion, then there will be difficulty regarding how we can express meaning and communicate them to others. Meaning is public and not private[42] in Wittgenstein's sense.

---

40. *Ibid.*, p. 204.

41. See Wittgenstein, *Philosophical Investigations*, trans. G.E.M. Anscombe (Oxford, Blackwell, 1953).

42. *Ibid.*

Fodor's argument that there is a mental language[43] that embeds meanings does not cut much ice with those who refuse to believe that meanings are in the head. First of all, such a language of thought does not exist in addition to our natural language and that it is a fictitious entity for the purpose of explanation of the mental phenomena. Even if it is conceded that the language of thought hypothesis works well in explaining the mental phenomena, it does not follow that meaning itself is a mental phenomenon cut off from the rest of the linguistic community and the world at large. Language even in its mental form must be communicable and hence be part of the linguistic community. Language alone is the carrier of meanings and so is the vehicle of thought and communication.

Putnam argues against the internalist theory of meaning by showing that meaning is bound up with reference and truth such that the external world plays a significant role in the fixing of meaning of the words.[44] According to him, the words carry their reference to the objects in such a way that the community comes into the picture for deciding the objects of reference. The Twin Earth example shows that the objects of reference have to be decided by the community by appealing to the expert opinion.[45] This way of fixing meaning has a social perspective which imposes the norms of the society on the linguistic reference. Meaning cannot be detached from the community of speakers and their linguistic conventions and norms.

Meaning Holism

With the collapse of individualism and mentalism regarding

43. See Fodor, *The Language of Thought* (New York, Thomas Y. Cromwell, 1975).

44. See Putnam, *Representation and Reality.*

45. *Ibid.*

meaning and content, there is necessity of opting for meaning holism at least to get out of the difficulties encountered in meaning theory. This option is open for the reason that beliefs and their contents do not come in except in a related and integrated fashion. This point is the one that is emphasized by many philosophers among the externalists. The argument for holism is that both meanings and contents are interlocked with other meanings and contents in language.

Meaning holism is not the same as content holism because while contents could be viewed non-relationally as in Fodor, meaning cannot be so viewed because meanings come in clusters. Contents are the intentional objects of the prepositional attitudes and so are specific to the prepositional attitudes. A content is always dependent on the mental representations of which it is the content. This is not the case with the linguistic representations which are the correlates of the mental representations. The linguistic representations have meanings which are the semantic features intrinsic to the former. The meaning theorists have the option to advert to the semantics of truth-conditions to explain meaning of the linguistic representations. Therefore there is a point in the externalist argument that truth-conditions alone account for meaning of the sentences about the world, while the contents of the corresponding beliefs can remain neutral on this issue.

The proponents of the truth-conditional meaning theory, like Davidson,[46] seek to situate meaning in the network of sentences expressing beliefs. For them, meaning does not arise except in the network of sentences which account for why beliefs are interlocked together. Meaning is not a substitute for belief and so has to be distinguished from the belief-contents. Davidson makes a clear distinction between what the beliefs contain as their contents and how they express

46. See Donald Davidson, "Belief and the Basis of Meaning" in *Inquiry into Truth and Interpretation* (Clarendon Press, Oxford, 1984).

meaning. The latter is due to the way sentences expressing beliefs are truth-conditionally related to the world.[47] Meaning is a presupposition of the beliefs and their contents and so has to be semantically distinguished from the psychology of contents. Davidson espouses meaning holism because truth-conditions cannot be accounted for in isolation and have to be interlocked to the truth-conditions of other sentences. Davidson writes:

> A final suggestion along these lines is that we can interpret a particular sentence provided we know a correct theory of truth that deals with the language of the sentence. For then we know not only the T-sentence to be interpreted, but we also "know" the T-sentences for all other sentences; and of course, all the proofs. Then we would see the place of the sentence in the language as a whole, we would know the role of each significant part of the sentence, and we would know about the logical connections between this sentence and others.[48]

Davidson is well aware of the fact that the sentences in a language are interlocked in a logical space and that all of them are truth-characterizable in a holistic fashion. That is, the theory of truth available for one sentence is also available for the whole language in which the sentence is placed. Both the theory of truth and theory of interpretation constitute one holistic theory so that sentences are held to be true in a common agreed-to framework and that they are interpreted as such within the same semantic horizon. Truth being the overriding concern in this framework, it is through truth-connections that sentences are interpreted as meaningful. Meaning holism is inevitable keeping in view the fact that truth-theoretical semantics itself is holistic in character. Davidson writes:

47. *Ibid.*

48. Davidson, "Radical Interpretation" in *Inquiry into Truth and Interpretation,* pp. 138-39.

> Each interpretation and attribution of attitude is a move within a holistic theory, a theory necessarily governed by concern for consistency and general coherence with the truth, and it is this that sets these theories forever apart from those that describe mindless objects, or describe objects as mindless.[49]

Thus Davidson's truth-theoretic semantics tends to hold language and meaning in a holistic system not allowing molecularity[50] as a serious threat to the coherence of language, belief and meaning. Semantic holism is not after all an epistemic thesis geared to account for piecemeal language acquisition and language learning.

The opponents of meaning holism have not taken kindly to the fact that language operates in an interlocking fashion, either because they have no such conception of language as with the logical positivists, or because they do not have any theory of language except of a language of thought as in Fodor. The logical positivists viewed meaning wrongly by dissecting it into pieces; Fodor and his followers have no theory of natural language, hence reduce meaning to the narrow contents of the individualist psychology. The narrow psychology, as Devitt[51] points out, does not save meaning in any case. Meaning is denied by converting the narrow contents into syntax. Fodor's anti-holism is based on his bias for syntax in the matters of psychology. Even the intentional contents are syntactically explained.

The Holistic Semantics of Beliefs and Contents

The first step towards a sound semantics of beliefs and their

---

49. Davidson, "Belief and the Basis of Meaning," p. 154.

50. See Michael Dummett, "What is a Theory of Meaning?" in *Mind and Language*, ed. S. Guttenplan (Oxford, Clarendon Press, 1975), pp. 97-138.

51. Devitt, *op. cit.*

contents is to have a theory of meaning that reconciles the holistic and anti-holistic tendencies in semantics. The prepositional attitudes which dominate the discussion on the nature of mind are such that they are caused by the mind and are stored in the belief box. They carry the intentionality attributed to the mental processes. Fodor believes that semantics of the prepositional attitudes revolves round the concept of the psychological contents and has to be understood only in terms of the causal properties which they embody. Fodor thus admits Intentional Realism on the one hand and on the other accepts that the intentional contents are causally supervenient on the computational states of the brain. This brings him closer to the computationalist account of the mental states which leads him to propound the computational representational theory of mind (CRTM). This makes him accept only narrow contents as the basic stuff of his belief-desire psychology. Many find this position riddled with difficulties because it combines computationalism with intentionalism.[52] Fodor himself has realized the fact that the narrow contents can be sacrificed for the wide contents which can go very well along with the computational view of mind.[53]

Fodor's position on meaning is most tenuous because it appears he does not need meaning at all because he thinks that meanings are collapsible to the contents of beliefs. For him syntax is enough and does not need anything other than the causal properties of the mental states or representations. The whole process of coding and decoding the representations in the language of thought is a mechanical affair which can be accomplished by the computational psychology. This seems to be an inadequate procedure because the semantics of beliefs needs a theory of broad contents which brings in the semantic notion of truth-conditions. Broad contents are those that

---

52. Cf. Fodor, *Psychosemantics.*

53. See Fodor, *The Elm and the Expert.*

demand a truth-conditional base and are directed at the world. This is overlooked by Fodor in his *Psychosemantics* where he espouses a computational view of mind, though he revises this view in his *The Elm and the Expert*.[54]

Holism takes care of the broad contents within a broad sweep of the functioning of the mind. Mind does not work only in the computational way; it also works in unifying the mental process. The process of unification is a creative act and results in the holistic account of the mental processes. The unification of the contents, as suggested by Bilgrami,[55] is also act of the mind that acts holistically. There is no basic gap between the narrow and the broad contents because they are under the operational purview of the mind. Thus to raise the bogey of individualism at the cost of holism is to read the mind one-sidedly. This is what Fodor does. Bilgrami writes:

> My externalist position imposes a constraint upon the description of the external causes that fix the concepts of an agent, a constraint which brings into consideration the other beliefs which one has attributed to the agent. This just is holism, in one clear and accepted sense of the term.[56]

Holism goes well with externalism and perhaps can go well with internalism provided the barriers between the two are broken.

Can Computationalism Solve the Problem of Meaning?

Fodor's changed strategy to admit broad contents in the company of computationalism and informational semantics in his *The Elm and the Expert* leaves the problem of meaning unsolved. The changed strategy is to make allowance for broad contents in the framework of computational and intentional

54. *Ibid.*
55. Bilgrami, *op. cit.*
56. *Ibid.*, p. 142.

psychology associated with informational semantics. Fodor writes:

> In fact, I'm increasingly inclined to think that semantic theories ought to be externalist and informational and broad, so I'm in trouble if any of these clash with other doctrines in my bundle.[57]

The three theories which co-exist in Fodor's bundle of doctrines are (a) that the mental representations are intentional, (b) that the mental representations are syntactic and that the mental processes are computational, and (c) that the mental representations are informational in character. Thus there is a presumed harmony among the psychological theory of intentionalism, computationalism and informational semantics. Fodor reconciles the apparently irreconcilable doctrines like intentionalism and computationalsim.

Fodor's argument for the reconciliation of intentionality of psychological laws and the computationality of the psychological processes is that there is no point on which they conflict and that they complement each other in explaining the nature of mind and meaning. Fodor writes:

> The old idea is that mental states are characteristically intentional; or at least that those mental states involved in cognition characteristically are. The new idea is that mental processes are characteristically computational. My problem lies in the apparent difficulty of getting these fit together.[58]

Thus Fodor's effort is to make these two ideas, namely, the idea of intentionality and computationality fit together. There is, however, the legitimate apprehension that they may not go together unless a drastic revision is made regarding the very idea of the cognitive mind.

---

57. See Fodor, *The Elm and the Expert*, p. 7.

58. *Ibid.*, p. 2.

Fodor's main contention is that psychological processes are best explained as computational in character because they are basically syntactic as having formal properties. Computationality is thus an operational notion and has to be viewed as contributing to the systematic character of the mental representations like belief, desires, etc. There can be no quarrel on this as some mental states like thoughts have logical properties which can be captured in logical syntax. But can all the mental states be computational in this sense? Are there not non-computational mental processes as well? If there are, then computational theory of mind cannot be the final answer to all questions regarding mind.

Now, as regards intentionality, it may be said that mental states are intentional intrinsically and, as Searle[59] would say, naturally and biologically. But that only shows that the mental states are forward looking towards the world as the representations of the world. In this sense, they fulfil the externalist conditions of being true or false depending on what the world actually is. From this it does not follow that mental processes are mechanical in nature, or that the human mind functions like a Turing machine. If the mental processes are mechanical, then they cease to be intentional in the sense we generally use the word. Of course, they are intentional being about the world, even if they are mechanical. Fodor uses the idea of information to bridge the gap between the mechanical processes and the intentionality of those processes.[60] Intentionality accrues to those processes because of the informational nature of the mental processes themselves.

However, even if we accept the informational nature of the mental processes, it is not necessary to accept that the mental processes are mechanical in character. The mental

---

59. Cf. John Searle, *Intentionality: An Essay on the Philosophy of Mind*, Chapter 1.

60. Fodor, *The Elm and the Expert*, p. 6.

representations like the thoughts which are about the world and so have broad contents are not necessarily computational. They can be explicated formally and syntactically and so a computational framework can be imposed on them. But they are not intrinsically computational. To be computational is to be mechanically representable, but this is not to say that the mental representations are constituted of mechanical laws. The whole idea of computation is a formal device and it has no metaphysical implications regarding the status of mental contents. Mental contents like the mental representations are independent of how they are presented in a language. They are the core psychological concepts which need an autonomous treatment. Intentionality is a core concept which has autonomy of its own. Computationality is imposed on it for reasons that are extrinsic to the nature of mind.

Informational semantics, for Fodor, bridges the gap between the intentional psychological processes and their computationality by virtue of making the processes sensitive to the world. They are sensitive to the world by virtue of being about the world. Computationality is added in order to facilitate the mind-world relation being truth-preserving. He writes:

> . . . computation is by definition syntactic, and information is by definition etiological, and mental representations can mediate between behaviour and the world because their syntactic structure carries information about their (actual or possible) causal histories.[61]

Thus computation enters into the business of mind as a facilitator and not as a constitutive element of the psychological processes. There is no reason to believe that without being computational, mental processes will not be about the world or the mental contents will not be broad. The mental processes

61. *Ibid.*, p. 86.

will be information-centric without being computational. Fodor therefore must recognize that computation is not a *sine qua non* of the mental representations.

So far as the problem of meaning is concerned, it goes without saying that for Fodor meaning is the same as information and is collapsible into the broad contents. This is itself a very unsatisfactory solution of the problem because meaning has been given a short shrift being denied an independent status as a semantic category. If meaning is the information content, then the question is what is the meaning of the information content? Can information content be a substitute for meaning? If so, why should we need semantics at all with all its normative demands? Fodor in his search for the computational underpinning of semantics forgets the fact that meaning is a separate category to be dealt with independently of the contents of the mental representations. Besides, he believes that since information semantics is necessarily atomistic, meaning must also be atomistic.[62]

But the question is, why should information semantic be atomistic? Because we know that information is never piecemeal and that it always comes in a cluster. Information is always embedded in the belief-system and so cannot claim to be independent. In this sense we cannot say that meaning is atomistic because information is atomistic. Like information, meaning can also go holistic provided we recognize that meaning is associated with language and information as their pre-condition rather than as their consequence. Meaning is inherently holistic and pre-theoretical being given as the constitutive conditions of language and information. Hence it cannot be the case that meaning is a matter of informational contents, either narrow or broad. It is not only not identical either with narrow or broad content, but also it is independent

---

62. *Ibid.*

of the idea of content as such. Meaning is presupposed by the contents.

The Mind Doesn't Work That Way

Fodor has come round in his *The Mind Doesn't Work That Way*[63] to the view that computationalism does not work. The projected CTM goes too far in equating mind with the Turing machine and thus invites objections from the non-computationalist quarters. Fodor's well argued belief that mind is after all a Turing machine has never been universally accepted.[64] The reason is that mind has many functions which cannot be computationally mapped. The computational mapping is a peculiarity of the machine-functions which are performed by well-designed machines like the computers. This is not true of the human mind with its many-sided functions which include the non-cognitive functions like willing and feeling.

The standard understanding of the human mind as a cognitive system which is peculiar to cognitive science is only half true for the reason that there are many functions of the mind which are not covered by the idea of a cognitive system. The rationalist bias that mind is a system of thoughts and that it is basically a system of mental representations is rooted in the Western conception of mind since Descartes. But it is only a partial picture of the mind which has dominated the contemporary cognitive science. The full picture of the mind will include the non-cognitive and non-computational functions of mind as well.

---

63. Jerry Fodor, *The Mind Does Not Work That Way* (Cambridge, Mass., The MIT Press, 2001).

64. See John Searle, *The Rediscovery of the Mind* (Cambridge, Mass., The MIT Press, 1994).

Fodor is well aware of the fact that Turing machines have limited availability in tracking down the syntactic properties of the mental processes. He is of the view that even if some functions of the mind are syntax-driven, all functions of the mind cannot be so characterized. This is evidenced by the fact that the idea of a computing machine is of limited use only in the context of the syntactic structure of the mental representations. This is because, "the logical form of a thought supervenes on the syntactic form of the corresponding mental representation, and that mental processes are computational in a proprietary sense of "computation" that turns on the notion of a syntactically driven causal relation."[65] But all these devolve on the *a priori* notion that the mental processes are computational in character. That is, "the idea that mental representations have syntactic properties is at the heart of the nexus between rationalist psychology and the computational theory of mind."[66] Rationalist psychology itself suffers from the computationalist bias which needs to be grappled with before we can see through the limitations of the computationalist approach.

Fodor enumerates the principles which underlie the "merger between rationalist psychology and Turing's account of computation"[67] These principles are as follows:

1. Thoughts have logical form by means of which they have a causal role in the system of mental representations.
2. The logical form of thoughts supervenes on the syntax of the corresponding mental representations.
3. The mental processes are computations, that is, "they are operations defined on the syntax of mental

65. Fodor, *The Mind Does Not Work That Way*, p. 22.
66. *Ibid.*, p. 20.
67. *Ibid.*, p. 18.

> representations, and they are reliably truth-preserving in indefinitely many cases."[68]

These principles together constitute the very bedrock of the Computational Theory of Mind (= a rationalist psychology implemented by syntactic processes) which holds that all mental processes are computational by nature. To sum up, in Fodor's words: "So we can now (maybe) explain how thinking could be both rational and mechanical. Thinking can be rational because syntactically specified operations can be truth-preserving insofar as they reconstruct relations of logical form; thinking can be mechanical because Turing machines are machines."[69]

Fodor's account of CTM as delineated above is not a simple doctrine because of its complex maze of principles which are committed to a complex notion of computations. These principles are so interconnected that one cannot detach one from the other. For example, the idea of computation is connected with the syntax of the mental representations. The latter are connected with the logical form of thoughts which are expressed in a language of thought. The Principles E (CTM) and M (CTM) are two supporting principles which do specify the essential properties of mental representations and their supervenience on some syntax or other bring out the minimum ground of the CTM.[70]

The Computational Theory of Mind, however, comes to grief on the definition of the computation itself. If computation itself is definable only on the basis of syntax, then we need to define the syntactic properties of the mental representations which are derivable only from the assumption that there is a language of thought. Thus rationalist psychology is *a priori*

---

68. *Ibid.*, p. 19.

69. *Ibid.*, p. 19.

70. Cf. *Ibid.*, pp. 24-29.

committed to a language of thought innately built into the mind of the human beings. These are metaphysical assumptions which need independent proof. Even if they are sound in themselves, these notions need empirical grounding in the actual functioning of mind. Fodor follows this rationalist bias to a great extent in his computationalist approach to mind. But the limitations of this approach can be evident if we look beyond the computational cognitive processes. The non-cognitive processes are by no means unknown to the psychologists and philosophers.

The non-cognitive processes of the mind are invariably linked with those mental processes which are not modular and which fall outside the domain of thought. There are emotional and volitional responses of the mind to the external stimuli which need not be placed within the modular[71] structure of the mind. These processes therefore cannot be called computational the way the cognitive processes are called. The mind must have space for these functions which need no algorithm for their operation. There are no known modules which can account for feeling and willing which take place in the mind. Fodor realizes this when he says:

> In fact, what our cognitive science has done so far is mostly to throw some light on how much dark there is. So far, what our cognitive science has found about the mind is mostly that we don't know how it works.[72]

This is to recognize the limitations of the CTM which is crucial to cognitive science itself which centrally locates the mind of man in the model of the Turing machine.

Concluding Remarks

What is of utmost importance to be noted is that computational

71. *Ibid.*, Chapter 4.

72. *Ibid.*, p. 100.

psychology is very limited in its methods and goals. This psychology has exploited the Turing machine model of mind to explain every aspect of human mind much to the distortion of the nature of the mental functions and abilities. It has been shown by John Searle,[73] Roger Penrose[74] and others that the computational conception of mind is inadequate and limited and that the mind cannot be taken as a machine in any case. The creative nature of the mind is not fully captured by the computational model of the mind.

Fodor has done well to recognize the fact that there are many areas of the human mind which do not have a modular structure[75] and that therefore classical computationalism does not hold good in these cases. This opens up the possibility of a non-computational approach to mind which can include the much-needed semantics of truth, understanding and meaning. Fodor has admitted semantics as indispensable to any understanding of mind because it keeps the mind connected with the world.[76] This ensures a triumphant return of meaning into the fold of a theory of mind in order to show that meaning and truth are as much needed for understanding mind as the syntactic structures of the mental representations. Computations themselves are not enough to explain meaning.[77]

---

73. See Searle, *The Rediscovery of the Mind,* Chapter 9.
74. See Roger Penrose, *Shadows of the Mind: A Search for the Missing Science of Consciousness* (Vintage, 1995; First Published Oxford: Oxford University Press, 1994), Preface.
75. Cf. Fodor, *The Mind Does Not Work That Way,* p. 99.
76. Cf. Fodor, *The Elm and the Expert,* Chapter 4.
77. I am grateful to Professor Paneerselvam, University of Madras for pointing out the changes Fodor has made in his views on narrow contents in his book *The Elm and the Expert.* I am thankful to all those who had participated in the discussion on the earlier version of the paper which was presented in the National Seminar (under UGC-DSA) on "Language and Mind" at the University of Hyderabad.

10

Meaning and Mental Mechanism

A Critique

Amitabha Dasgupta

The Central Thread of the Argument

The main thrust of the paper is to provide a critique of the mentalistic conception of meaning. The claim that meaning is essentially a product of certain mechanisms of the mind seeks its justification from certain model of scientific theorizing regarding cognitive functions of the mind. Language being regarded as one of such functions an explanation of it thus requires a new framework developed in the recent approaches to mind, such as, cognitive psychology, generative linguistics and artificial intelligence.

However, the conception of meaning and the conception of mind that a mentalistic theme offers irrespective of its scientific claim seems to be wrong both in terms of its approach and its content. The goal that a mentalistic theory sets as a part of its scientific methodology is to discover the underlying mechanism that defines the essential reality of meaning. This has led to the assumption that meaning has a common structure behind its multiplicity of uses. But, ironically, such a conception of meaning becomes inevitably reductionistic. This follows from the very procedure on which the idea of mechanism is built. The possibility of mechanism depends on a set of conditions that have a direct bearing on the reductionistic move in semantics. Such a theory cannot be tenable primarily on the ground that meaning does not function in that way. Meaning is essentially non-reductionistic because it is not governed by any mechanism be it mental or otherwise. The three predominant features that characterize meaning as holistic, normative and autonomous refute the idea that meaning can be reduced to some from of mechanism. They show that there is no scientifically describable property which all instances of meaning must possess. The picture that the mechanistic theory offers about meaning and its place in the mind does not work. Its claim about the nature of meaning and the nature of mind is more of a speculative than scientific or empirical in nature.

In view of the problematics stated above the argument structure of the paper has been conceived in terms of the following sections. The first section introduces the problem by giving an overview of the contemporary perspective on language/mind interface. The basic thrust of the second section is on the nature of mind. It explains the idea of mental mechanism — its nature and structural composition inherent to it. The discussion will be carried out by giving a brief sketch of the functionalist/cognitivist model of the mind since it is within this model the notion of meaning gets a new interpretation — a new explanation offered in terms of the mechanisms of the mind. The functionalist/cognitivist model of the mind thus truly forms the background assumption of the paper. The objective of the third section, on the other hand, is devoted to explaining the nature of meaning as conceived within the framework of mental mechanism. In this respect the works of Jarry Fodor, particularly, his language of thought hypothesis will be specially highlighted to bring out the significance of the mechanistic theory of meaning developed within the functionalist/cognitivist model of the mind. The thrust of the next three remaining sections will be to critically examine the conceptual viability of the position held by the mechanistic theory with respect to both mind and meaning. Accordingly, the major focus of the fourth section will be to construct a critique of Fodor, particularly his project of naturalization of semantics and his theory of concept acquisition. The fifth section will address the question why mind be conceived as information processing system in the same way as computers are conceived? This has a serious implication since mentalistic theory of meaning has been formulated at the background of this conception. The final section argues that meaning cannot be conceived within the model of mental mechanism. This section will offer an alternative conception on meaning in the light of Wittgenstein's idea that meaning is normative, holistic and autonomous.

I

Language/Mind Interface

The relationship between language and mind has always been a constant source of philosophical perplexity. Philosophers belonging to different persuasions are thus found to be engaged in working out the exact nature of this relationship. To work out this relationship is by no means an easy task. Depending on one's understanding there are different ways that this relationship has been conceived. The traditional response to this problem was by and large speculative. It became inevitably speculative because of the unfathomable mystery that shrouded the mind. The contemporary response to this problem, on the other hand, was rather negative because it was influenced by the scientific study of the mind initiated by the behaviourist psychology. It is apparent that the greatest obstacle to define the relationship between language and mind has been posed by the mind itself. The mind remains a mystery without allowing any access to its internal mechanism.

This ambivalent negative situation did not exist for long. The whole approach to mind has been radically changed due to the emergence of functionalist theory of mind. The mind is viewed as a machine and accordingly the best way to explain it will be in terms of the functions that it performs. Just like a machine consists of machine states, the human mind similarly consists of various mental states. These mental states are thus viewed as analogous to machine states and the former functions in the same way as the latter. The machine picture of the mind acquires a strong scientific foundation with the rise of cognitive sciences. The brain which is a neurophysiological machine is now compared with a computer. Mental activities are performed according to a set of algorithms laid down by the computer model of the brain. Our various mental/psychological states, such as, believing, desiring, etc. are interpreted as computational states of the brain. To use Hilary Putnam's analogy, brain can be best qualified as digital computer whereas our psychology constitutes "the software of this computer."[1]

The cognitive/functional theory of the mind offers a clear formulation of how does mind function. For cognitive theory of mind the substantive issue to be explained is the notion of intelligent behaviour. It is said, while fulfilling this objective, that intelligent behaviour can be explained only by appealing to internal cognitive processes or mechanism. Explication of these processes will provide justification for intelligent behaviour. Explication in the functionalist vocabulary implies giving an account of the software that govern the operation of these mechanisms of the mind. The mind, so conceived, is thus characterized by J. Haugeland[2] as information processing system. Accordingly, the various human abilities or

---

1. Putnam, H. *Representation and Reality*, Cambridge, Mass, MIT Press, 1959, p. 73.

2. Haugeland, J. *Mind Design*, Cambridge, Mass., MIT Press, 1981.

competence, such as, memory, perception, language use, reasoning etc., are given a new interpretation involving postulation of mental/cognitive mechanism.

In the new picture, the relationship between language and mind is not viewed as problematic because by defining language as a mental organ it does not allow any place for controversy. It is not language but linguistic competence being mentally represented by speakers that becomes the object of explanation. This constitutes the psychological reality of language. Further, mentalistic language is also viewed as central to the semantic organization of the mind. The various mental states, such as, belief, desire, etc. have a propositional structure which implies that they possess meaning or content. This speaks for the inseparability of language and mind. Thoughts and the ideas of the mind and linguistic expressions become one and the same. The idea that mind has a linguistic organization provides a new dimension to the relationship between language and mind. However, this has been possible because the whole approach to language is shifted from the external to the internal perspective, from the social to the mental. Language is now essentially seen as a mental/cognitive enterprise which forms the basis of the scientific study of language.

It is evident from the contemporary philosophical and psychological studies on the mind that acceptance of mentionalism has been defended on a scientific ground. Its postulation becomes theoretically necessary on the ground that otherwise cognitive phenomena cannot be amenable to explanation offered in terms of underlying structures or mechanisms. Mentalistic explanation thus becomes synonymous with scientific explanation. It is widely felt that there is no mystery behind mentalism once we see it in terms of certain unobservable structures or mechanisms. Linguistic behaviour too, as has been pointed out earlier, is subjected to the same mentalistic explanation. It is a behaviour which is caused by the internal mechanisms of the mind.

In view of this new perspective on language and mind there is an influential view in the current philosophy of language which proposes what may be called mechanistic theory of meaning. It holds that meaning is the product of certain internal mechanisms operating in the mind. Such a conception of meaning finds its justification from the general methodological guidelines normally observed in scientific practices. Meaning conceived in terms of mental mechanism is indeed a scientific practice and its scientificity can be defended on the three following grounds. First, in order to discover what constitutes the real essence in semantics, it is necessary to discover those elements which are more fundamental than what is observed in the day-to-day semantic practice. Second, behind the linguistic/semantic multiplicities and diversities there is an inner unobservable core which is causally responsible for the emergence of the former. Finally, the mechanistic theory of meaning reveals that the ultimate account of meaning must be given in terms of mental mechanism since the latter reveals the ultimate nature of the former. Meaning and mental mechanism is thus a scientifically viable semantic project.

The two important versions of the mechanistic theory of meaning which have been advanced are by Jerry Fodor and Daniel Dennett. In Fodor's version of the theory, it is the nervous system which provides the ultimate justification for semantics because he considers nervous system to be analogous to a "semantic engine." His idea of language of thought as a biologically fixed code is same as the machine code built into a computing machine. Dennett, on the other hand, constructs a mechanistic theory which is alternative to the version proposed by Fodor. It does not involve sub-personal meaning-mechanism because meaning belongs to personal level.

However, Dennett does not delink the personal from the sub-personal which is constituted by a system of mechanism. Meaning in some way thus emerges out of this sub-personal mechanism. The present paper, of course, will be dealing only with Fodor's version of mental meaning.

II

The Idea of Mechanism and the Functionalist/Cognitivist Model of the Mind

It has been said in the earlier section that functionalism provides a new perspective in our understanding of the mind. This new understanding was further enhanced with the rise and development of cognitive science. These two approaches together give rise to a conception of the human mind and the nature of mental phenomena. It is a standpoint constituting the three following theses: First, mental phenomena are intentional. Second, they establish the causal link between sensory stimulation and behaviour. And third, though they are neurophysiologically realized they cannot be reduced to the neural or physical level. This shared conception of the human mind constitutes what may be roughly described as the functionalist/cognitivist model of the mind.

One may wonder, how is this shared conception of the human mind developed among the theorists of different disciplines? What explains this development? The development of this view has been possible largely due to the development of computer. The pioneering work in the theory of computability initiated by such figures as Alan Turing and the subsequent development of the digital computer led to the view that mental phenomena were analogous to computational phenomena. This was the view which became the basis of a common conception of the mind. To explain the meaning of the analogy between a computer and the mind, structurally a computer is an input-output device construed mechanically whose primary function is to manipulate symbols on the basis of certain rules. Accordingly, a computer in its operation takes one set of symbols as inputs and with the help of symbol manipulating rules produces another set of symbols known as its output. The important notion involved here is the process of symbol manipulation because it is a process which resembles the information processing capacity of the mind. This requires that the symbols which a computer manipulates must be given appropriate interpretation. Now if this can be done then a computer can be shown to have the same kind of reasoning and problem-solving capacities that a human mind is equipped with. In this way, mental phenomena are found to be analogous to computational phenomena. Equally important in this connection is to note the role that language plays in the computer conception of the mind. A computer is equipped with a language — a formalized language which is built into the system. Such a language which may be thus viewed as innate becomes central to the functional organization that a computer represents. It sets the preconditions essential for computational operation. It constitutes the medium through which the process of computation is carried out. But computation cannot be carried out without the system of representation. Hence, the built-in language of a computer works as a medium for both computation and representation.

The human mind since it works in the same way as a computer does must have the same linguistic organization with a built-in language at the centre. The picture of a mind that emerges, as Putnam[3] points out, is that of a Cryptographer having a language possessed secretly. The mind, so conceived, has its own internal language known as the language of thoughts through which it thinks. A natural language is viewed

---

3. Putnam, H. *Representation and Reality*, P. 78.

as a medium through which the speaker transmits his thought to the hearer. The hearer too has a Cryptographer in his head and on the virtue of this capacity is able to decode the speaker's message. The idea of mind having a built-in language is a part of the mental mechanism that functionalism proposes.

On the basis of these initial remarks clarifying the meaning of the computer metaphor of the mind, we can now give a few details highlighting some of the important aspects of mental mechanism and the way it operates. In this respect, our discussion will be guided by the three following questions: First, how is the mechanical concept of the mind conceived in functionalism? Second, how does it operate? and, Third, how does it provide a foundation for language and meaning?

In our earlier remarks we have said that functionalism defines the mind as a computing machine. But now the question is at what level does the mind resemble the computing machine? This is where we distinguish between the two levels of a computing machine. The one is the level concerning programmes and computations and the other is the physical system — the hardware that realizes these computational operations. When we are concerned with the former level, i.e., studying only the computations themselves we abstract it from the material nature of the device performing them. Infact, the study of the latter in this respect is unnecessary since it has no bearing on the computational operations as such. The justification of this view can be derived from the fact that two differently constructed physical systems can perform the same operation. They may carry out the same kind of computation. This shows that computational processes are unaffected by the material systems realizing them. To put it alternatively, computational processes can be realized in different computational devices. They are, in other words, multiply realizable.

Functionalists, as we know from our earlier discussion, find that mind may be thought of in the same way because it functions on the basis of the same heuristic principles. Accordingly, mental states can be construed as computational states and mental operations can be viewed as distinct from its physical embodiments. The relationship between the two is the same as that of the relationship between a computer programme and the device on which it runs. Further, since a programme can be always viewed independently of its physical embodiment the same programme we can run it in a device whose material nature is different from the existing one. In the context of human beings, the brain satisfies the requirement of a hardware on which the mental software runs. Considering this, it may be argued that martians though they may be constituted with different hardware may share the same psychology — the same mental software as that of ours. Feeling of pain or thinking of monsoon are not brain processes. They are computational operations being realized through brain processes in its capacity as hardware processes. But what is most important to note here is that like computations all these mental operations are multiply realizable.

The software/hardware analogy has been further extended by functionalists to construct their notion of explanation. The mind which is viewed as a black box is consisting of mechanisms that control human behaviour. The objective of psychological explanation is to give an account of the software which govern the operation of these mechanisms. This shows that there are two levels of explanation involved. The one is the explanation involving the physical nature of the machine and the other is the explanation relating to the software aspect of the machine.

These two levels of distinctions hold not only at the methodological level. There is an ontological level too associated with this distinction. The distinction at the ontological level points out that the properties designated by mental terms are distinct from properties designated by physical/material terms. It is because of this distinction that mental states and properties which are though realized by material states and properties will never be identical to it and thus rules out the possibility of the former to be identifiable in terms of the latter. Take the example of pain. Pain is realized in the nervous system. It is a particular kind of neuron firing, namely, C-fibre firing which is responsible for our being in pain. But being in pain can never be identical with C-fibre firing. The reason is that creatures who do not have the property of C-fibre in their nervous system will never experience pain. On the contrary it can be most rationally maintained that creatures having a different material constitution can still experience pain or being in pain. Hence, being in pain cannot be reduced to the material/biological system that realizes pain.

The last important aspect of the functionalist model of the mind is the idea of causal role — a functional property that an object acquires by fulfilling a particular role. Let us explain the point through examples. Consider the property of being a clock. An object is called a clock not because of its particular internal organization or a mechanical structure that it has. It is called a clock because of the function it performs. In other words, it becomes a clock by its job description. This reveals the simple truth that the property of being a clock is a functional property. To elaborate further the significance of functional property, let us take the example of the property of being an eye. In this respect, we point out that there are two aspects. The one is the biological property and the other is the functional property. The biological property of eye may not be the same across all the species of animals. The biological property of the compound eye of a honey bee is different from the eye of a horse. The eye of a horse, on the other hand, has a different biological constitution than that of the eye of a human being. This means that the biological texture of eyes may be of different forms. But something becomes an eye only if it fulfils the particular role for which it is designated no matter what biological form it takes. Functionalists define this role causally. We don't identify or classify things in terms of what they are made of but in terms of the causal roles that they play.

Functionalists argue that mental states need not be identified or classified in terms of their physical or neurophysiological properties. The same thing can be done in terms of the causal roles that such states play. Consider in this connection the functionalist definition of pain that David Lewis[4] offers. In Lewis's formulation, the concept of pain implies a state "that occupies a certain causal role." It is a state being characterized by a causal structure representing not only a definite cause-effect relationship but also its connection with other mental states. The description of pain thus necessarily involves the description of the causal network associated with it. Roughly the three basic components that constitute this network are: First, the state of pain is caused by a definite stimuli (e.g., tissue damage), Second, it has connection with other mental states, such as, belief and desire (i.e., the belief that you are in pain and the desire to get rid of it); and, Third, the behavioural output (i.e., bodily movement in a particular way) that follows as a result of this connection. As we can see, it is the causal network as a whole that assumes the primary importance while characterizing a mental state. Because characterizing a mental state is done by referring to its place in the causal network. In fact, neither pain nor any other mental state can exist without this causal network. The presence of this network makes the linkages between the various states possible. This gives rise to the idea of a mind as a total functional system.

---

4. Lewis, D. "Mad Pain and Martian Pain," in Ned Block (ed) *Readings in the Philosophy of Psychology*, vol. 2, Cambridge, Mass, Harvard University Press, 1980, p. 218.

But then how could the mind as a total functional system be represented? Adhering to the analogy of computing machines, mental operations can be represented in a similar way. In a computing machine, computational operations are represented in terms of boxes or nodes in flow charts. It is assumed that each box or node represents a function being characterized by a particular kind of input that gives rise to a particular kind of output. For a device to realize these functions it is required that it must have the right sort of causal structure. The same scenario is applicable to the mind where different mental states form separate boxes. Considering this the mind may be thus thought of including a "belief box" and a "desire box," for example. But, how are these boxes represented? and how do they function? Take the belief box first. Suppose, I have a belief that the window is open. To have this belief implies having a symbol expressing the proposition that the window is open. Similarly, if I want a window to be shut, that will imply having such a symbol stored in my desire box. Considering mind as a total functional system, the belief box and the desire box are connected with the rest of the system that the mind represents. This is necessary for the causal interaction among mental states. But how does it lead to the production of overt behaviour? Suppose, there is a symbol being stored in the desire box representing the proposition that the window should be shut. This may quite likely be the cause of my action, namely, walking across the room and close the window. But it will not be done in isolation from the rest of the symbols constituting belief and desire boxes. In fact, it is only in conjunction with appropriate symbols in belief and desire boxes that alone will lead to this action/behaviour. Alternatively, there can be a different behaviour or a resultant state that may be caused due to the operation of different symbols. The same symbol in the belief box while operating with other symbols in belief and desire boxes may lead to a different behaviour.

This conception of mind which is traditionally known as the representational theory of mind has been defended and reformulated in the contemporary time by Fodor in the light of his computational theory of mind. Fodor's version of the representational theory of mind puts forward the demand that a system of symbols which function as mental representations must be postulated as the part of the basic requirement of the theory. These symbols constitute what Fodor calls language of thought. It is a biologically fixed code which functions in the same way as the machine code fitted into a computer. Accordingly, mental states like belief and desire have linguistic/propositional structure having meaning/content of their own. Thus, forming a belief that the window is open will imply having a sentence in the language of thought corresponding to the English sentence, "The window is open." In this way, the representational theory of mind offers a foundation for a new way of thinking about mind, language and meaning. Hence, a brief discussion on Fodor's language of thought hypothesis is in order. This is particularly important to substantiate the view that meaning can be claimed to be a matter of mental mechanism.

III

The Language of Thought Hypothesis

The problem that the language of thought hypothesis (**LOT**) poses is how do mental states like belief and desire represent or have intentional content? The reason is that mental states and mental representations are not identical. Fodor explains this on the basis of his proposal that mental states like belief could get its content due to its relation to mental representations. The language of thought hypothesis makes explicit what is involved in this relationship in order to explain semanticity and intentionality of mental states. Thus, for example, believing that Fido is faithful implies standing in the belief relation to a mental representation that has the content Fido is faithful. Further, mental representations are defined as meaningful symbols having place in the mind itself. It is because of this reason that they are viewed as mental analogues of spoken or written sentences. In fact, mental representations while tokening of intentional states assume the form of linguistic symbols. They belong to a system of language which is not a natural language but the language of thought. Considering this, believing something e.g., Fido is faithful will imply tokening a sentence in one's mind which is corresponding to the English sentence "Fido is faithful."

Fodor's proposal that mental representations belong to a system of language needs explanation. The best way to do it will be to consider it in the light of some of the salient features of natural languages, such as, English. First, English consists of finite number of words which constitute the vocabulary of language. The second important aspect is that it consists of finite number of grammatical or syntactic rules in terms of which words are combined in a particular way to make sentences. The syntactic rules determine whether a particular combination of words of English qualifies to be a legitimate sentence or not. To see how these rules are applied one needs to analyse the structure that a given sentence displays. Each sentence of English has a particular syntactic structure which can be specified by breaking the sentence into its component parts and then show how these parts are combined by the syntactic rules of English.

There is another important feature that natural languages exhibit. English though has a finite number of words and a finite number of syntactic rules can produce infinite number of sentences. This is possible due to the recursive nature of rules. The syntactic rules of English can be applied over and over again. That means the rules which are employed to construct a given sentence can be employed again to construct a more complex sentence with an embedded structure in which the previous sentence will be the part of it. From the recursivity follows the linguistic creativity. A native speaker of a language is able to produce sentences which he has never produced before and similarly he is able to understand sentences which he has never encountered before.

Finally comes semantics. The syntactic rules of English, the syntactic categories to which words belong and the syntactic structure of sentences do not address to the aspect relating to English semantics. Syntax remains unrelated to semantics. But words and sentences are not unrelated to semantics. They are, on the other hand, meaningful. Since they are meaningful the question concerning the relationship between syntax and semantics must be worked out. True, syntax and semantics have a distinct nature, but they are not unrelated because the syntactic properties of sentences influence the meaning that the sentences assume. The reason is that the meaning of a sentence is determined by the meaning of its component words and its syntactic structure. This reveals an important linguistic fact that English has a combinatorial syntax and semantics. This fact leads to the possibility that there can be infinitely many meanings that English is capable of expressing.

Fodor considers LOT to be analogous to English. LOT too has a finite number of symbols and syntactic rules used for the purpose of combining words to form sentences. Over the question of meaning, the semantics of LOT sentences follow the same principle as that of semantics of natural language. The meaning of a sentence of LOT is determined by the meaning of its constituent words and it is thus based on the idea of combinatorial syntax and semantics. LOT is sufficiently powerful to express meaning. In fact, it has the power to express any meaning which a sentence of English can do. How is this possible? How could it acquire this expressive power?

This is possible because the meaning of sentences in English is determined by the corresponding sentences of LOT. We can describe the process involved showing how the semantic connection is formed between a sentence of English and a sentence of LOT. First, to understand a sentence of English, as the language of thought hypothesis puts it, will imply tokening a belief about the meaning of that sentence. Second, tokening a belief implies tokening a symbol of LOT constituted with appropriate meaning. This process leads to the final result according to which, corresponding to every sentence of language that we are capable of understanding, there must be a sentence of LOT having the same meaning.

Due to his commitment to physicalism, Fodor defines LOT as physically embodied. He thus considers the token sentences of LOT being identical to brain states. To explain, suppose I believe that "Fido is faithful," to believe this will involve tokening the LOT analogue of the English sentence "Fido is faithful." Fodor, true to his physicalist stand, claims that this LOT sentence constitutes a particular state of my brain. This is true of all intentional states. For every intentional state there will be a distinct state of my brain being characterized by a relevant sentence of LOT.

In continuation to the above thesis, we will now give a few specific details, regarding how sentences of LOT are being encoded in the brain. Consider the possibility where I token a LOT sentence S. It is a sentence consisting of words placed according to a certain syntactic order. Following Fodor's thesis, this token of S must be claimed to be identical with a particular state of my brain. If we go further into the process it will reveal that each constituent word of the token of S is having identical relation with different components constituting this physical state. This implies that there is a correspondence between the internal structure of this physical state and the syntactic structure of the encoded sentence. Now consider the second possibility where I token another sentence of LOT which may be called S* and contains a particular word W. This token of S* will have the same physical counterpart in the sense that it will be identical to a definite state of my brain. Further, this state will have a component part which will be identical to a token of W: Note that this physical component which is associated with S* and the physical component that encodes W in the token of S both belong to the same physical type. This results in a physical similarity between the tokens of S and S*. It is a similarity exhibited at the level of the word that the two sentences have in common. The general significance that follows from this present case points out that similarity existing at word level or at the level of syntactic structure reflect similarity at the physical level. At the word level, the similarity occurs because tokens of sentences that share words all of them have component parts which belong to the same physical type. At the level of syntactic structure, the notion of similarity is to be sought in internal physical structure of respective sentences. Thus, for tokens of sentences, to be similar in terms of their syntactic structure will mean that there is similarity existing between their respective internal physical structures. The purpose of this description is to give an idea how LOT has its physical basis in the brain. It thus qualifies to be called a biologically fixed code.

We shall now address the question: What is the justification behind the postulation of LOT? What purpose does it serve? To answer this, Fodor relies on two sources, namely, linguistics and psychology. It is the linguistic or semantic reason that provides the fundamental justification for Fodor in accepting LOT. The semantic argument for LOT has the following form: "One cannot learn a language unless one has a language." The phrase "one has a language" is embedded with a definite meaning where the expression "has" implies that which is innately possessed whereas the expression "language" implies the brain's language of thought. They together suggest that learning a language is possible only under the pretext of an unlearned language which is innately possessed by a child. This explains that though Fodor conceives of LOT in the pattern of natural language, such as, English, maintains a basic distinction between the two systems of language. This led Fodor to consider LOT to be a non-natural language which serves as the prerequisite for learning a natural language. We will now give details of the semantic argument.

According to Fodor learning a natural language involves the process of acquiring knowledge of the meanings of the words of that language. But how does this process of acquisition work? For Fodor learning is essentially an activity consisting of constructing and confirming hypotheses that represent the meaning of the words of the target language. Fodor introduces here a condition which for him, is absolutely necessary for language learning to be possible. For to construct hypothesis, the language learner must have a representational system at his disposal because without this he will not be able to form any hypothesis concerning the meaning of natural language words. That means language learning must be inseparably related to the systems of conceptual mechanism that LOT provides. This theoretical commitment led Fodor to put forward the following two theses.

First:

> . . . one cannot learn a first language unless one already has a system capable of representing the predicates in that language and their extensions. And, on pain of circularity, that system cannot be the language that is being learned. But first languages are learned. Hence, at least some

> cognitive operations are carried out in languages other than natural languages.[5]

Second:

> My view is that you can't learn a language unless you already know one. It isn't that you can't learn a language unless you've already learned one — the language of thought is known (e.g., is the medium for the consumptions underlying cognitive processes) but not learned. That is, it is innate.[6]

In this context it may be important to note the structure involved in learning a language. In Fodor's account, to claim that a language learner is having a LOT implies possessing a system of concepts and not of beliefs. In holding this, he, thereby, rules out the necessity of accepting any epistemological requirements in language learning. Acquiring the meaning of words is strictly done through a stock of innate concepts. In this connection, Fodor explicates the logical nature of the hypothesis that are framed by the language learner. As he argues, all these hypotheses take the form of biconditional matching between LOT predicates and predicates of the target natural language. Take the example of learning the English word "dog." Learning this word involves constructing and confirming a hypothesis of the form:

[Dog (X)] is true (in English) iff G (X)

Note that G which is figured here is a LOT predicate. Now the question is how does this hypothesis operate? For a language learner to acquire this word "dog" it is necessary that he must adopt the correct truth rule showing "dog" has

---

5. Fodor, J.A., *The Language of Thought*, New York, Thomas Y. Crowell, 1975, p. 64.
6. Fodor, J.A., *The Language of Thought*, p. 65.

the same extension with G. However, there is one point to be taken into account here. Since the language learner already possesses G by virtue of the fact that it is a predicate of LOT, he understands the meaning of "dog." Currently, the action that he is performing is that of translation — translating the LOT predicate into English. It also amounts to confirming the hypothesis. For a language learner, learning of English involves translating LOT to English. For every predicate that he learns there is a LOT corresponding to that.

It is evident from the above account that Fodor does not bring any epistemological consideration in his analysis of meaning. He draws a strict boundary between the two. On Fodor's view since the meaning of a word is given by a truth rule there is no need to bring such factors like background belief while analyzing or making hypothesis about meaning. In fact, as Fodor's theory states, to know the truth condition for "This is a dog" will by no means entail that one knows that ***this*** particular animal is a dog or knowing how to find out whether this particular animal is a dog. The reason is, as Fodor claims, learning a language has nothing to do with the world. The aim behind forming hypothesis is not meant to determinate what objects in the world fall under the extension of the English word, say, "dog." They are, on the other hand, explicitly directed to specify which representation in the language of thought can be associated with the particular English word. It involves a process where a child, for example, may come up with a wrong hypothesis about a word, say, "bull" and makes the following formulation: "This is a bull" is true (in English) iff this is chair. Later, the child on the basis of disconfirming this hypothesis can form a new hypothesis and this process can go on until he arrives at the correct one which says: "This is a bull" is true (in English) iff this is a bull. It evidently follows that while forming and checking hypothesis epistemological issues are kept far removed from the entire process. The justification that Fodor offers is that these hypotheses that are formed by the language learner are not about objects in the world, such as, dogs, balls and puppies. They are, on the other hand, about English words like "dog" and "bull." But does this Fodor's manoeuvre succeed in removing the presence of background beliefs while acquiring the meaning of words? Can meaning be divorced from beliefs? We will enter into these questions later because some of these questions will form the basis of our critique of the mentalistic account of meaning. But before that there is one more issue to be addressed which is central to Fodor's notion of meaning. This is pertaining to the task of explaining the mental content for the purpose of deciding whether meaning is a matter of conceptual definition of the content or is it a matter essentially based on nomological or causal facts. This takes us directly to the topic concerning Fodor's proposal of naturalizing the content which implies naturalizing of meaning.

Naturalizing the Content:

The problem dealing with naturalizing of meaning must be seen in continuation to the earlier problem dealing with how do we acquire the meaning of concepts. Acquiring meaning implies acquiring the correct truth rules expressed through biconditional. But what has not been explained is the nature of the biconditional. The issue here is to bring out what constitutes the fact that prompts a speaker, say, Fodor to mean *horses* by "horse" or cows by "cow." Does this fact express conceptual truth or nomological truth? Fodor seeks to answer this question by giving an account of intentional/semantic properties of intentional states in physicalist terms. This is how Fodor comes to his theory of content.

Fodor's project of naturalizing the content has been governed by his computational theory of the mind. It becomes a necessary requirement for fulfilling his agenda in philosophy of mind. From our previous discussion, we know that according to Fodor, our intentional states get their content from sentences of LOT. Thus, for example, my belief that Fido is faithful implies that there is a LOT sentence involved in tokening this particular belief and the content of it so conceived has been inherited from the same source. In view of this claim, the next question that arises is: How is content of a given sentence of LOT determined? Fodor's answer is that it is determined by the meaning of the component symbol and the syntactic structure of the sentence. The question that now arises is how to account for the meanings of the simple symbols/ words of LOT? This constitutes the main thrust of Fodor's attempt of naturalizing content.

In carrying out this objective, Fodor finds that his first task will be to give an account of the nature of semantic/ intentional properties of our mental states. Fodor's claim in this respect is that the semantic or intentional properties are real in the sense that they are physical properties of things. Considering this, it may be thus concluded that the contents are physically determined.

However, historically there is an objection against this move. It is the Brentano's problem which poses a threat to Fodor's project of naturalization. Franz Brentano puts forward his well-known argument which may be summarized in terms of the following steps. First, intentionality is the defining feature of the mental. Second, the physical by its very nature cannot generate intentionality. Third, from these two above premises, it follows that mental phenomena lie outside the boundary of the physical realm. The upshot of Brentano's thesis is that intentional phenomena cannot be naturalized.

Fodor along with his other physicalist colleagues of intentional psychology reacted against this Brentano's problem by arguing against the autonomy of the intentional. To this, the strategy that they adopt is to show that physical properties are the ultimate determinants of intentional properties. Such a strategy alone will establish the possibility of a naturalized theory of meaning to be articulated in non-semantic and non-intentional terms. Fodor thus expresses in no uncertain terms the following ideas:

> If the semantic and the intentional are real properties of things, it must be in virtue of their identity (or may be their supervenience on?) with properties that are themselves *neither* intentional *nor* semantic. If aboutness is real, it must be really something else.[7]

For Fodor the naturalistic conditions for representation will imply:

> The worry about representation is above all that the semantic (and/or the intentional) will prove permanently recalcitrant to integration in the natural order; for example, that the semantic/intentional properties of things will fail to supervene upon their physical properties. What is required to relieve the worry is therefore, at a minimum, the framing of *naturalistic* conditions for representation.[8]

In view of Fodor's proposal we now need to spell out the form that a naturalistic theory of content must take in order to be scientifically viable. The one important way through which this theory can be conceived will be to specify the necessary and sufficient conditions that are required for the existence of intentional properties. These conditions, as pointed out earlier, will be framed only in terms of non-intentional properties whose status is well grounded in some specific scientific disciplines. The formulation of such necessary

---

7. Fodor, J.A., *Psychosemantics*, Cambridge, Mass., MIT Press, 1987, p. 97.
8. Fodor, J.A., "Semantics Wisconsin Style," in Fodor *A Theory of Content and Other Essays*, Cambridge, Mass., MIT Press, 1984a, p. 32.

and sufficient conditions will help in bringing out the essential nature of intentional content. The best way to do it will be to construct necessary and sufficient condition naturalistically for the claim, such as "X means Y."

The above discussion suggests that Fodor is primarily interested in arriving at the principle which is of the form:

> X means Y if and only if. . . .

where no semantic/intentional material can be used to fill out the blank ". . ." as indicated in the formulation. Applying this principle, we thus get a naturalistic definition of meaning. To give an illustration, a colour, such as red may have the following definition construed in naturalist term:

> X is red if X reflects light of wave length W.

Alternatively, we can get the meaning of X through a conceptual definition of X which will have the following form:

> X is red if X looks red to normal perceivers in normal circumstances.

The distinction between the two definitions of meaning is that the former expresses a nomological truth whereas the latter expresses a conceptual/analytic truth.

Fodor, of course, is not inclined to accept the conceptual definition of meaning primarily on the ground that he is highly skeptical regarding the viability of conceptual analysis. In various places of his writings, Fodor makes it explicit that philosophers' method of conceptual analysis which seeks to define words in terms of concepts that they express is hopelessly misguided. On the other hand, Fodor is equally unhappy with the way the naturalistic definition has been traditionally formulated. To say that red is identical with certain wave length, or water is identical with H_2O, is stating certain nomological correlations. They are not definitions at all. There is a danger here which is the danger of falling into reductionism. To avoid such danger, Fodor thus suggests that instead of reducing content to something non-intentional we should adopt a different strategy for the naturalization of content. This will be basically consisting in specifying those lower level non-intentional properties responsible for generating contents found in relation to specific intentional states. These properties are thus qualified to be called determinants of intentional contents and, accordingly, they need to be identified. For to do this what is needed is to spell out a sufficient condition for their occurrence. Fodor's theory of content may be viewed as providing a sufficient condition for content. It is by not postulating necessary condition that his theory can be claimed to be saved from reductionism. As Fodor makes it clear:

> I want a *naturalized* theory of meaning; a theory that articulates, in non-semantic and non-intentional terms, sufficient conditions for one bit of the world to *be about* (to express, represent, be true of) another bit.[9]

Later he further liberalized the condition when he says:

> It is enough if I could make good the claim that "X" would mean such and such if so and so were to be the case. It is not incumbent on me to argue that since "X" does mean such and such, so and so is the case.[10]

Fodor's observation makes it obvious the kind of relaxation that he is suggesting. It is pointing out a situation that he is ready to accept as a sufficient condition.

---

9. Fodor, J.A., *Psychosemantics*, pp. 98-99.

10. Fodor, J.A., "A Theory of Content, II: The Theory," in Fodor, *A Theory of Content and Other Essays*, Cambridge, Mass., MIT Press, 1990c, p. 96.

Fodor's naturalization project thus does not reject conceptual definition of meaning. His objective is how to relate conceptual definition with empirical laws associated with it. He too seeks to give a conceptual definition of content where the right hand side of the definition states the relevant causal fact. This implies that a conceptual claim about a content can as well be shown to be a matter of empirical fact. The conceptual definition that Fodor is interested in constructing may assume to have the following structural formulation:

> "X" means Y if it is a law that Y's cause tokenings of "X"

To put it as a lexical definition,

> "Horse" means horses if it is a law that horses cause tokenings of "horse."

There are, of course, predicates whose contents cannot be accounted for through such definitions. The nature of these predicates is that they don't cause anything. But such inadequacies do not defeat the basic purpose for which the definition is constructed. What is attempted here is to consider such cases as "horse" and "cow" where there are no problems involved. The aim is to see that if the proposed definition works well with these simple cases its scope may be further enlarged to include difficult cases. But, suppose, if it does not work well with such simpler cases, it will automatically lose its credibility and will, thereby, be proved to be untenable. This is the rationale provided behind this simple definition.

Fodor's theory has been historically inspired by the approach known as the causal covariation approach to meaning. It says that the meaning of a symbol and the properties that it expresses is a matter of causal reciprocity between the two where the former is determined by the latter. To give the earlier example, the LOT symbol "horse" means horse because it satisfies the causal condition that the tokening of the symbol is caused by horse and horse alone. It may be mentioned here that this causal covariation approach to meaning forms the basis on which the current approach to informational semantics has been constructed. Its main focus is, the information that a symbol carries is causally reciprocal to its properties. Fodor, of course, does not subscribe to the information theory in its present form. His theory though based on it suggests various improvements and thus they lead to a different course of development. However, inspite of the various developments suggested by Fodor, he shows his basic conformity to the tradition which seeks to understand meaning in terms of causal history — a view that is associated with such people like B.F. Skinner, D. Stampe and Fred Dretske.

There are certain overriding reasons that lead Fodor to view meaning as primarily a matter of causal relation. First of all, the causal perspective provides the theoretical framework through which naturalization process is carried-out. The naturalization of content is thus inseparably related to specifying the causal processes involved in meaning. Second, this view conforms to the linguistic behaviour of an adult speaker of a natural language. A competent adult speaker of English, for example, is disposed to utter "horse" whenever the situation so demands. But the same knowledge of meaning we do not attribute it to children or foreigner because they are not so disposed. That is why, it is quite often found that they utter "horse" in response to non-horses. Third, there are cases of meaning which clearly show how meaning is a matter of causal relation. To give an example from the natural world, the rise of mercury column in a thermometre indicates (i.e., represents) the rise of temperature. This indicates the rise of mercury causally covaries with the temperature. If they are not causally interconnected how could the rise of mercury be indicative of the rise of temperature? These are the points on meaning which constitute the common concern between Fodor and the information theory.

The causal explanation of meaning takes atomistic theory of meaning as its essential component. How does it fit in? To explain, when it is proposed that the meaning of a symbol of LOT is causally determined by the properties that it expresses it is assumed that it has no relation with other symbols. This allows the possibility that one can have a symbol in his LOT which means horse without having access to any other symbol in his language. To hold this will be to say that one may have the concept of "horse" and he is capable of thinking about horses without possessing any other concepts and thoughts of his language. This way this whole theory turns out to be atomistic in nature which is diagonally opposite to the non-atomistic perspective on meaning where it is held that a symbol gets its meaning as a result of its relation with other symbols. This implies that the precondition for having a particular concept requires having a battery of related concepts. Without fulfilling the condition of the latter the former will not be possible because language expresses a network of concepts. As a result, as non-atomists argue, for to grasp the concept "horse" one necessarily requires to grasp the concept "animal." This will thus facilitate him to infer from the thought: X is a "horse" to the thought: X is an "animal."

Fodor, of course, placed serious objections against holism (particularly, against conceptual role semantics) as a viable alternative to atomistic theory of meaning. He has two major objections. Holism comes in conflict with intentional psychology and since Fodor is primarily interested in intentional psychology he finds holism to be of no relevance to him. His analysis brings out the negative implications that holism has for intentional psychology. As Fodor argues, one of the implications that follows from holism is that two individuals, in principle, can never share a concept and thus an intentional state. They can never have exactly the same belief, for example, about dogs. There will be some belief which one will have and the other will not have. Suppose, the one person believes that dogs are faithful whereas the other person does not. This implies that the former in his head will exhibit the causal connection between "dog" and "faithful." But the same connection will not exist in the head of the other person. The response of holism is that the symbol "dog" plays a different causal role in the heads of the two people and will thus assume a different content. The same can be ascribed to "faithful." The causal role that the symbol plays in the head of a person believing that dogs are faithful does not have the same role in the other person because in the former case the symbol "faithful" is causally connected to "dog." This is the way how the entire processes will percolate and bring further change. To cut the story short, Fodor's analysis shows that what has been viewed as a minor difference in belief involving a concept shared by two people can lead to various divisions and sub-divisions in the respective schemes of the two individuals. To accept this will imply that if there is a change in a belief or a new belief is acquired by an individual this will bring changes in the content of all of his other beliefs. From this the conclusion that Fodor seeks to derive is that the whole exercise of making intentional psychology explanatorily adequate becomes pointless. The reason is that if two individuals never share an intentional state the laws of intentional psychology will be applicable only to one individual. The effort of intentional psychology will thus result in utter insignificance because there will be no intentional laws. Fodor thus finds holism to be in opposition to intentional psychology. Atomism, for him, is thus the most scientifically viable option.

The second reason for Fodor's[11] rejection of holism is that it denies the central feature of thought. The central feature of

---

11. Fodor, J.A., and Lepore, E., *Holism: A Shopper's Guide*, Oxford, Blackwell, 1992 Ch.6.

thought is that it is always compositional. Fodor puts forward his argument from the point of view of content. He argues that content is compositional because the content of a complex concept is determined by the content of its constituent concepts and there is a mechanism through which they are combined. Putting it in the context of LOT, the content of a complex LOT symbol is similarly determined by the content of its constituent symbols and by the rules of its combination. The meaning of LOT sentence, for example, "The dog is faithful" can be thus known on the basis of the knowledge of the meaning of its constituent parts (i.e. LOT words). The main force behind Fodor's argument that content is compositional is based on the idea of the productivity and systematicity of thought.

In the above, we have given a brief account of Fodor's naturalization project which says that meaning is essentially the result of causal interaction between the symbol and the properties that it expresses. Fodor further claims that this conception of meaning finds its compatibility with meaning atomism and not with meaning holism. But this account will be seriously incomplete if we do not mention the lacuna that this approach has and the modification that Fodor has suggested thereby. This is one major point where Fodor takes departure from informational semantics.

To accept nomological definition of meaning will imply that if there is a law saying that horses cause tokening of "horses" then horses cannot fail to cause tokenings of "horses." But to accept this will be to rule out the possibility of error or misrepresentation. However, we all know that we do make errors and thereby misrepresent the world. I encounter a cow on a dark night but have mistaken it as a horse. This is case which tells us that cow on a dark night causes a tokening of "horse." The information theory does not recognize this as a threat to the cogency of their nomological interpretation of meaning. They construe the whole problem in a different way.

In their reading, cows on a dark night and horses both cause tokening of "horse." Hence the meaning that the symbol entails is not just horse but horse or cow-on-a dark-night. This consideration led them to argue that the symbol "horse" has a disjunctive content. Fodor finds that this disjunctive problem needs to be solved for the purpose of naturalizing the content.

Fodor finds that the prospect of giving solution to the disjunction problem lies in finding out what sort of causal relation exists between the situation, namely, between horses and the symbol "horse" and between cows on a dark night and the symbol "horse." For this, we need to reveal the properties that are found in the former relationship but not in the latter.

To this effect, Fodor explores the various possibilities. One possibility is to appeal to optimal condition. It is possible that cows may cause tokening of "horse." But this happens only when conditions are not ideal to determine the nature of the object as in the present case, when I see a cow on a dark night and misidentify it as a horse. This points out the truth that causal connections can correctly determine the meaning only when it operates in an ideal condition. These ideal/optimal conditions are to be specified in non-semantic and non-intentional terms, such as, illumination condition, spatial relation between the object and the speaker, etc. But appeal to optimal condition does not help solving the disjunction problem. It only says that if it is a law that horses cause tokenings of "horse" then the law can operate only under optimal condition. It cannot resolve the dispute by showing that the tokening of "horse" in the event of encountering a cow on a dark night is false.

Fodor explains the difference between these two types of tokenings. He tries to isolate the two situations in the following way. In one case there is a correct tokening of horse because the symbol "horse" has been tokened in the presence of horses; whereas the other is the case of incorrect tokening of "horse" because the symbol "horse" has been tokened in response to the presence of cows on a dark night. Fodor explains[12] the reason for latter tokening being incorrect. It is incorrect because the causal connection between tokening of "horse" in the presence of cows on a dark night is, what he calls, asymmetrically dependent upon causal relationship between tokenings of "horses" in the presence of horses. In other words, the difference between these two sorts of tokenings is that the incorrect one depends on the correct one but not vice versa.

But the question remains. How does Fodor's asymmetric dependency account of meaning help improving the situation? Does it help us to have a better understanding of the way mental representation actually works? In fact it is not because all that Fodor is saying is that error is parasitic on true belief. But to say this is not saying much since we already know this. But the more important question to be addressed is: What is error? Unless we give some account of error the mere saying that it is parasitic on true belief will not help the situation greatly. Hence, the original question remains unanswered. That is, why does an expression mean one thing rather than another? To elaborate further, what are the properties that an expression must have in order to mean one thing rather than the other? Fodor's naturalization project specifies these properties in purely causal and nomological terms. But obviously there is a demand for further explanation. What sort of explanation are we looking for? This indeed is an open-ended question. It takes to the issues concerning, first, what constitutes the nature of meaning and, second, can meaning be explained in terms of mental mechanism, i.e. the tokening

12. Fodor, J.A., *Psychosemantics*, pp. 107-08.

of LOT symbols? These are the questions which motivate us to critically examine Fodor's idea of mental meaning.

In the next three sections, we will construct a critique of Fodor in terms of the three following questions, first, what is wrong with the naturalization of meaning?, second, can mind be conceived as information processing system? and, third, can meaning be situated in the head? The last question which will be dealt in the last section of the paper will be mostly engaged in working out the constructive proposal of the paper regarding the nature of meaning.

IV

Why Meaning Can't be Naturalized?

As part of our concluding remarks in the last section it has been said that Fodor's attempt to understand meaning in terms of causal or nomological definition cannot adequately explain: Why does an expression mean one thing rather than another? This is where we indicate the need for having an alternative explanation of meaning. Hence, the question comes: Why meaning can't be naturalized? What are the reasons that block the process of naturalization? We will now enter into these questions. Fodor's theory of content has got wide attention. There has been extensive discussion on this problem. We will not go into this debate because that is not our purpose. We will only raise some of the major issues[13] supporting the question why meaning can't be naturalized?

The first problem that Fodor's theory of meaning faces is due to the violation of Frege's sense-reference distinction in semantics. At a conceptual level, this makes his theory counter intuitive. To start with, Fodor has a highly simplified notion

13. Some of the points raised here have been discussed by M.J. Cain in his book entitled *Language, Mind and Philosophy*, Polity, 2002.

of meaning. The meaning of a symbol/concept has been strictly defined in terms of its property that it expresses. Considering this, if two concepts express the same property they will turn out to be equivalent in terms of its meaning. Take the two elements — Water and H_2O. Since they have the same property their concepts (namely, the concept of water and the concept of H_2O) too express the same property having the same reference and thus will be involving in the same mind-world causal sequence. Applying Fodor's theory to the water-H_2O context, we will conclude that these two concepts bear the same content. This gives rise to Frege's celebrated problem concerning identity statement. Frege will argue that "water" and "H_2O" may express the same property and may have the same reference and yet they cannot be claimed to have the same content. This will be evident from such simple instance like the sentence "water is H_2O" is informative whereas "water is water" is not. If the two concepts are semantically equivalent, how could they be different? We can further explore this problem by introducing another dimension to show the difference between the two. We can always, for example, believe that water is sweet and at the same time doubting whether H_2O is sweet. If "water" and H_2O have the same content based on the claim that they have the same property then why this difference arises? There is no way to explain this without introducing an additional component. The additional component is Frege's sense which constitutes the conditions of the applicability of the term. Fodor's theory of content faces this difficulty because of not having the notion of sense in his system.

Fodor, of course, explains his position and rejects the charge. He reaffirms his position by saying that both "water" and "H_2O" have the same content and then allows the conceptual differences between the two. The conceptual differences such as, "water is sweet" and "H_2O is sweet," arise due to differences in belief though both the sentences have the same content. Similarly, why the sentence "water is H_2O" is informative whereas "water is water" is not, can be explained in the light of the same consideration. A person who has the concept "water" can acquire a new belief through the sentence "water is H_2O" but the same is not true of the latter sentence. Hence, Fodor claims that even though the content of both the concepts is same we can explain the difference by introducing the belief element.

Fodor's claim that the contents of the above two concepts are same because they are based on the idea that they must be tokened by the same causal laws. Fodor's analysis assumes a distinction between two levels — the intentional and the computational/syntactic. The laws of intentional psychology which are expressed through computationally governed processes are always supported by lower level mechanisms. This follows from Fodor's methodological position on special sciences. Thus, an intentional law, say X causes Y, must be connected to a lower level phenomenon which causes the linkage between the tokening of X and the tokening of Y.

Fodor's solution does not resolve the issue that Frege's problem posed. It is a logical problem and a causal solution to it implies refusing to see the complexities involved in the notion of meaning. Fodor's plea that meaning is the result of certain underlying mechanism commits the same fallacy of essentialism because it establishes an analytic connection between meaning and a set of mechanism. This is not only a wrong move because meaning by nature cannot be reduced to anything of this sort but also such a perspective fails to give an adequate account of some of the basic conceptual problems of semantics, such as raised by Frege's problem. With this we now come to the second conceptual problem that Fodor's theory of meaning faces.

The second conceptual problem arises due to Putnam's Twin Earth problem. Putnam constructs the Twin Earth which is an exact duplication of the Earth. There is, however, one difference. The liquid that inhabitants of Twin Earth call water though has the same phenomenological properties (such as, colourless, odourless, transparent, quenches thirst, etc.) that water in the Earth expresses a different chemical structure. The chemical structure of Twin Earth water is XYZ and not H_2O. Since the concept of "water" applies only to H_2O, the liquid with having the structure XYZ does not fall under the extension of the concept "water."

The difficulty that Fodor's theory faces is that it will be compelled to consider both XYZ and H_2O as falling within the extension of water. Why should Fodor's theory lead to such a conceptually anomalous position? The reasons are lying in Fodor's theory itself. It has been said that XYZ has the same phenomenological properties as that of water. It is, therefore, superficially the same as water. From this fact, it follows that perceiving a sample of XYZ will have the same effect on me as when I perceive a sample of water. Note the truth asserted here is not a superficial truth. It is based on Fodor's causal principle. If it is a law that water causes tokening of "water" then on the basis of the same consideration it must be admitted that it is also a law that XYZ causes tokening of "water." The only thing to note here is that two laws are asymmetrically dependent on one another. As a response to this paradoxical situation it may be suggested that the only way to overcome the situation will be to snap the connection existing between XYZ and water. But to do this will be to invite a different kind of problem. To deny the XYZ-water connection will mean denying our simple fact of perception. Further, it has a serious conceptual implication because this denial entails denial of "water"-"water" connection. The entire episode, indeed, looks counter-intuitive.

Fodor gave reply to this objection. The essential thrust of his reply is to show that the problem posed above does not really exist. There are two forms of his reply.[14] Fodor's first reply says that there is absolutely no barrier against distinguishing water from XYZ. In fact Putnam's Twin Earth story does not suggest the impossibility of conducting test to separate the two. Fodor's proposal is that since these two substances have different chemical compositions it should be possible to set up a scientifically reliable test to distinguish between the two. Fodor thus assumes the possibility of having a method of test available in Twin Earth too. Such a test can clarify the right sort of causal connection that water exhibits. This will allow people in Twin Earth to distinguish water from XYZ and this will accordingly enable them to apply "water" only to water and not to XYZ.

Fodor's second reply is that we don't know what XYZ is because it is a property which is not instantiated on Earth. Now the property which does not have any instantiation on Earth cannot fall under the extension of "water." It becomes a mere fictitious concept.

Both the replies of Fodor miss the actual force of the objection — the real logical predicament that it poses. Instead of seeing that, Fodor takes it as a practical issue. Regarding the first reply, it may be pointed out that independent of whether there being tests or not, people on Twin Earth will show the same response to XYZ as we do when we are confronted with water on Earth. Hence people on Twin Earth at a perceptual level can never make the distinction between the two. On the other hand, if you follow Fodor's proposal of breaking the "XYZ-water" connection this will lead to a counter intuitive situation. As a result of breaking the relation we can

14. Fodor, J.A., "A Theory of Content, II: The Theory," in Fodor *A Theory of Content and Other Essays*, Cambridge, Mass., MIT Press, 1990c.

no longer apply "water" to the substance experienced by us as colourless, tasteless, odourless liquid. Regarding Fodor's second reply to say that XYZ is a fictitious concept and thus it does not come under the extension of "water" does not seem to be a satisfactory reply at all. Our original problem remains. We thus ask the question: Is there anything in the semantic theory which can block the term "water" being getting attached to both H_2O and XYZ? Hence, we are pushed back to our original problem with which we started.

The question of reference takes us to a general problem, i.e., how reference is fixed in language? Fodor never addressed this question. For him it falls under a rigid structure defined by the associated concept. Sense theorists and those who believe that meanings are in the head take reference to be a determinate notion which is fixed once for all. Such a notion, as Putnam claims, goes against the actual scientific practice. The relevance of the Twin Earth argument is that it shows how two persons though they may be in the same mental state can refer to two different objects due to their difference in respective environments. The environment or what is sometimes characterized as local paradigm or sample of the language user becomes crucial in fixing the reference of kind term.

Fixing of reference, for Putnam, is thus very much a socially determined activity. His justification of this claim is based on his principle of linguistic division of labour. It is a principle which points out that acquiring the meaning and identifying the extension of term constitute the two aspects of language. It is thus possible that an ordinary speaker may have the knowledge of the meaning of a term but may lack the knowledge of the exact extension of the term. He can operate quite efficiently without this knowledge. In the case of dispute only he goes to an expert for identifying the exact referent. These are some of the issues which point out that meaning cannot be naturalized mainly on the consideration that meaning is a social or normative phenomenon. With this we now come to the third objection to Fodor's theory of meaning.

The third objection, as it has been already mentioned, is concerned with the normativity aspect of meaning. An important lacuna of Fodor's theory is that it does not give any account of this aspect of meaning. Normativity, on the other hand is an inalienable property of meaning. To say that a concept or a symbol has a particular meaning is necessarily associated with certain facts regarding how it ought to be used in various possible circumstances. How a symbol ought to be used is not an added element on its meaning. It, on the other hand, defines what meaning is. The meaning of a concept or a symbol thus in its definition includes a set of normative facts. The meaning of a concept and how to use it in a context are inseparably related to each other. A person using a concept incorrectly implies that he is violating the norm — the norm governing the application of the concept. Normativity in this sense is constitutive of meaning.

Fodor does not accept the presence of any meaning constitutive normative facts. For him the only facts that are existing in meaning situation are facts about causal connections. Since causality by nature is opposed to normativity it is not capable of generating any normative facts. But Fodor by explaining meaning as causal ignores the multiplicity aspect of meaning. A concept may have multiplicity of meanings depending on the content of its use. The idea of multiplicity of meaning suggests that the notion of use is embedded in the notion of meaning itself. They form an integral connection so that isolating the one from the other is conceptually impossible. One can probably do this through some reductionistic mechanism. But that will be a denial of the complexities involved in meaning. Meaning will then be the mere skeleton of a dead man. The denial of normativity can, indeed, lead to such a notion of semantics.[15] Suppose a language-learner is presented with a set of objects having the colour red. But the data does not give the sufficient strength to the language-learner on the basis of which he can construct the hypothesis that the English word "red" means the same as the symbol "red" in LOT. The reason is that instances themselves do not relate the word "red" with the LOT symbol "red." In fact, from the same data base, a learner can frame such hypothesis as "red" means "being a physical object or having shape or being three dimensional and so on." There is an inextricable bond existing between concepts and beliefs. Realizing this, Wittgenstein thus points out that we must create place for the concept and that place can be arranged only within a network of beliefs. Later in the sixth section, we will again take up some of the issues while making our constructive suggestions about the nature of meaning. Before taking up this task, we would like to take up the issue of examining whether mind can be conceived as an information processing system? Further, does mind behave in the same way as the computer does? These are the issues which constitute the background assumption of Fodor's theory of language and meaning. Hence, examining of these issues becomes essential.

V

Is Mind an Information Processing System?

As stated earlier, the objective of this section is to examine whether the mind can be conceived as an information processing system. To undertake this discussion is important because the idea that mind is an information processing system acts as a fundamental pre-supposition to Fodor's theory of language and meaning. An attempt to develop a critique of

---

15. Williams, M. "Language Learning and the Representational Theory of Mind," *Syntheses*, vol. 58, 1984.

the latter dealing with Fodor's pre-occupation with semantics will be thus incomplete without providing the critique of some his central assumptions relating to the notion of mind. The major claims of Fodor's theory of meaning derive its legitimacy from the idea that the mind is an information processing system. If it is proved contrary to what Fodor claims about mind then his theory of meaning too will no longer be standing on the same robust ground.

The present critique of Fodor's stand on mind cannot claim to be a full fledged critique. It is mostly based on John F. Searle's[16] critique of cognitive science and the conception of mind that it shares. Note that the present discussion does not go into the connectionist approach to the mind which provides an alternative to the information processing approach to the mind. The reason is the problem that we are posing is a conceptual problem whose objective is to show that the mind does not behave like a computer.

Laying out the Argument

This discussion will primarily focus on the two questions: In what sense does mind process information? Is this processing the same as the processing performed by a computer? The threads of the argument may be stated in the following form:

> First: For human beings to think means processing information;
> Second: Computing machines too process information; and
> Third: Processing here is meant to be transforming the input into the right kind of output constituting information of a new variety.

16. Searle, I. *Minds, Brains and Science*, Cambridge, Mass., Harvard University Press, 1984.

The idea that follows from these steps is that there is something common in the sense in which human beings and computing machines process information. If both are engaged in the same sense of information processing then there is no difficulty to hold the claim made in cognitive science that the mind is an information processing system and it behaves in the same way as the computer behaves.

However, the above claim, as Searle points out, can be contested. It can be contested on the ground that it is simply false. True, thinking implies information processing. But that is not enough. It is necessary to probe further in order to see what is involved in the process. For human beings to engage in information processing implies to be engaged in certain mental processes which may be either conscious or unconscious. But the same is not true of a simple computing machine, such as, a calculator when it is engaged in information-processing. The kind of information processing through which it goes does not involve any mental process. It only simulates the mental process associated with information-processing that human beings do. It is true that the calculator follows the same procedure as we do when we process information. But this procedural similarity is deceptive because in reality the calculator does not do anything which we human beings do while engaged in information-processing. The crucial difference lies over the fact that a calculator does not have any mental phenomena. To cite an example from Searle, the calculator can perform the operation of addition, such as, how to add 6 and 3. But, while it can successfully perform this operation it does not know that numeral 6 stands for number six and the numeral 3 stands for number three. Not only this, it does not even know, strangely enough, that the plus sign signifies the operation of addition. The only explanation for this lacuna is that it does not possess any knowledge. Certainly, they can perform more accurately than what human beings can do. They are also faster in their operation than human beings. But they do it mechanically according to certain formal procedures laid down before-hand. Thus, there is no mental background associated with these operations nor is there any mental effort involved while doing these operations. This makes it evident that human beings and calculating machines don't go through the same sense of information-processing. In fact, they exhibit two different kinds of information-processing.

Considering this difference, Searle distinguishes the two senses of information-processing. In the case of human beings since information-processing involves mental states it may be thus characterized as psychological information-processing. Thinking, which involves processing information, is directly correlated with mental operation. There cannot be any thinking without the mental operation. But in the second sense of information-processing there is no such mental operation involved. There is no mental state assumed in this processing. Hence, in the second sense, as Searle pointed out, it is assumed that as-*if* there were mental processes involved in this kind of information-processing and by virtue of this a claim is made that a computer thinks because the programme constituting it is the same as the mental processes. This is where the fallacy of cognitive science lies. It has failed to distinguish the two senses of information-processing and thus holds a unitary view which lacks any theoretical basis. The unitary view that cognitive science upholds is due to the result of the confusion of the two senses of information-processing. The term "information-processing" is actually the cause of this confusion because it is the same term being used to explain the behaviour of two different phenomena.

In defence, one may argue that when computers are engaged in information-processing they simulate the formal features of thinking and thus on this ground it may be asserted that these are not two different types of information-processing. In reply, it may be said that simulating a mental process is not the same as the actual mental process. In ordinary language, simulating essentially means mimicking. It is mimicking the original. An inevitable gap is thus assumed all through in the process of simulation. True, computer can simulate the formal features of thinking; but from this it does not follow that computer programmes are psychologically real so that they become identical with the mind.

It may be quite instructive here to recall the *Chinese Room Argument* of Searle. The lesson derived from it reinforced the same conclusion derived above. It refutes the basic assumption of cognitive science that the mind is a computer programme implemented in the brain. Instead of going into the details of the argument, we will narrate here only the conceptual import of the argument. The main focus of the argument is directed to show the inadequacy of syntax to capture the full complexities of the mind. The reason is that the mind is also a semantical system expressing its intentional content. Considering this, minds cannot be identical with computer programmes where programmes are defined in purely syntactic terms, that is, in terms of the manipulation of formal symbols, such as Os and ls. This is where the importance of semantics comes while dealing with the operations of the mind. Given these preliminaries the logical structure of the Chinese Room Argument may be spelt out in terms of the following steps:

First: Computer programmes are formal because they are syntactical in nature.

Second: Minds, on the other hand, have semantic/ intentional contents.

Third: Syntax cannot replace semantics.

Hence: Computer programmes cannot be identical (or, replace?) with minds.

Searle, thus, taking semantics as the central clue to the understanding of the mind offers refutation of the computational theory of the mind. The computational theory of the mind, as the Chinese Room Arguments shows, subscribes to a position which is counter-intuitive and thus defies the norms of intelligibility. Accordingly, it is possible that a person who has no knowledge of Chinese language can behave in the same way in which a native speaker behaves on the assumption that as if he understands Chinese by virtue of a certain formal programme. For an outside observer there is no difference between the two situations. But the real story is different. The outside observer fails to distinguish between the actual information-processing and as-if nature of information processing. The actual information-processing is always associated with mental states. Without these there cannot be any information-processing. This is reflected in the present case. Thus, going through a computer programme for understanding Chinese cannot give us, as a matter of principle, the knowledge of Chinese. The reason is that understanding a language is not just manipulation of formal symbols. This is where meaning/semantics comes. Without this there cannot be any understanding of Chinese. This is true not only of language but of all mental states since all of them have semantic contents and by virtue of that they refer. Fodor recognizes the importance of the representational character of the mind. He thus wants to develop a combined theory incorporating the computational and the representational theories of the mind together. But in the process ultimately it is the computation part which dominates over the representation part. Fodor thus pays only lip service to semantics.

VI

Proposing the Alternative

As stated earlier, the objective of this section is to offer a conception of meaning alternative to Fodor's meaning mechanism. This alternative account proposed here is an outcome that follows from a long sequence of arguments advanced against Fodor's meaning mechanism. These critical arguments together suggest the need for an alternative account of meaning. In fact, the essential idea of this account is already contained implicitly in the content of those various arguments directed against Fodor. The present discussion is thus an explicit formulation of those ideas that have been previously lying as implicit. The alternative account proposed here is based on some of the seminal ideas of Wittgenstein which he developed in connection with his own conception of meaning. The proposed alternative is thus the Wittgensteinian alternative on meaning.

The Structure of Fodor's Meaning Mechanism

Fodor's meaning mechanism exhibits a structure which consists of three basic semantic principles.[17] They are interrelated in the sense that one follows from the other. A mechanistic theory of meaning for its operation requires semantic correspondence thesis which involves a picture theory and the picture, in turn, requires acceptance of some form of semantic atomism. As we can see, these principles are mutually dependent and they are constitutive of meaning mechanism. A brief explication of these principles is thus necessary to substantiate the claim.

First: *The Semantic Correspondence Principle.* It is one of the primary requirements of meaning mechanism that there must be correspondence between states of mechanism and semantical states. The semantic correspondence principle follows from the general physicalist thesis which holds that for every mental state there is a corresponding physical state.

---

17. Mcdonough, R. *Towards a Non-Mechanistic Theory of Meaning, Mind,* 1992.

From this, it is further argued that there is a correlation holding between the processing of the syntactic structure of a sentence and the structure of our brain. The semantic claim made on the basis of this correspondence is that elements in the meaning correspond with elements in the brain.

Fodor's thesis that brain is a semantic engine is founded on this semantic correspondence principle. As Fodor makes it explicit:

> . . . . the bedrock upon which the possibility of computational explanation of behaviour is founded is the (presumed) fact that the causal relations among the physiological states of the organism respect the semantic relations among formulate in the internal code.[18]

This passage claims that the idea of computational explanation of behaviour assumes that the causal properties of physiological states correspond with the semantical features being codified in the internal formula of the language of thought. From our earlier discussion on Fodor, we know that, according to him, the propositional attitudes are computational states of the brain and their semanticity is grounded in the corresponding language of thought. Hence, for Fodor, to be in a certain propositional attitude state will imply how that state is being related to an internal formula of the language of thought. Propositional attitudes are thus the result of correspondence holding between the two states. If we notice there are two structures involved, correspondence holds between items in a structure with items in another structure. This is possible when both are structurally similar. Putting it in the context of meaning mechanism, a particular state in a mechanism corresponds with a meaning only when they are structurally compatible in the sense that the former *pictures*

---

18. Fodor, J.A., *The Language of Thought*, p. 78.

the latter. This takes us to the second principle of meaning mechanism.

Second: *The Analogy of Picture.* To hold the claim that there is a correspondence between elements in the brain and elements in the meaning implies that the former pictures the latter. The sense of picturing may be understood in several ways, such as, mirroring, mapping, being isomorphic with, etc. Wittgenstein in his *Tractatus* while elaborating his view that "A proposition is a picture of reality" writes:

> There is a general rule by means of which the musician can obtain the symphony from the score, and which makes it possible to derive the symphony from the groove on the gramophone record. . . . It is the rule for translating this language. . . of musical notation . . . into the language of gramophone records.[19] (*Tractatus*:4.0141)

This passage clearly spells out the relationship between language and mechanism. It tells us the condition for ascribing language to a mechanism, such as, a gramophone in the present context. The condition that requires to be fulfilled is that a mechanism must contain a picture of the thing that it represents. In the case of a gramophone the picture that is embedded within it is the picture of a symphony. In Wittgenstein's observation, the relation between the two is the same as the relation that holds between language and the world. The same is the case with the brain mechanism where meanings are given and thus it represents the same picture which language represents in connection with the world.

Third: *Semantic Atomism*: To hold that the brain contains a physical picture of the meaning raises a question regarding how is meaning to be pictured? Fodor finds that the best strategy will be to break meaning into its component parts. To this effect, Fodor makes the assumption that expressions

19. Wittgenstein, L., *Tractatus*, 4.0141.

in natural languages are formed atomistically. Complex expressions are compounded of simple atomistic expressions. As Fodor[20] points out, "It . . . reasonable to suppose that a system rich enough to express the messages that natural languages convey will have a vocabulary [consisting in] a finite inventory of discrete, meaningful elementary item." Further, with Katz, Fodor[21] holds that the meaning of a sentence is composed of atomic concepts being arranged in a particular structural pattern. Here lies the basic assumption of Fodor's conception of meaning mechanism. Meaning is compositional and it is being formed out of atomic meaning particles.

These are the three principles which constitute the structure of Fodor's meaning mechanism. These three fundamental principles on which meaning mechanism is based are wrong. They are wrong on the ground that meaning is normative, holistic and autonomous. This is the alternative conception of meaning that Wittgenstein proposed.

Wittgenstein and the Alternative Conception of Meaning:

There is one central theme with which Wittgenstein was preoccupied in his post *Tractatus* writing, and it was regarding the issue of how to explain the meaning of a word. What does the explanation of the meaning of a word consist in? Wittgenstein thus puts his problem in the following way:

> The meaning of a word is what is explained by the explanation of meaning, i.e., if you want to understand the use of the word "meaning," look at what are called explanations of meaning.[22]

---

20. Fodor, J.A., *The Language of Thought*, p. 123.
21. Fodor, J. and Katz, J., "The Structure of a Semantic Theory," in their book (ed.) *The Structure of Language*, Boston, Prentice Hall, 1964.
22. Wittgenstein, L., *Philosophical Investigations*, Oxford, Basil Blackwell, 1958. Sec. 560, See also Sec. 69.

According to Wittgenstein, explanation of meaning consists in explaining the use of a word. To talk about the use of a word implies, as Wittgenstein says, *how to go on*. To know the use can also be said to be acquiring the "technique." Explanation of meaning may be given in terms of the use that a linguistic item has; but can it be brought under the purview of a structure so that the former can be pictured by the latter. If this is possible then the semantic correspondence thesis will be applicable to the notion of meaning understood as use.

The notion of "use" can be certainly brought under structure if it is interpreted, as Colin McGinn[23] does, "a kind of behviour which can be described physically." If use is meant to be a physical behaviour it must be amenable to physical explanation. Considering the possibility of physicalist construal of use, McGinn then offers specific interpretation of use by suggesting that it is determined by a "state of the head" which is correlated with behavioural manifestations.

Construal of use in the above manner suggests the possibility of conceiving it as the product of physical mechanism where brain is regarded as the structure. It is a structure connecting to the phenomenon of use and thus functions in the same way as that of the picture representing use. There is a picturing relation between the two which constitutes the corner stone of semantic correspondence thesis.

But none of these attempts or construals can lead to success. The greatest barrier to this is the notion of use itself. The unpacking of this notion on the basis of Wittgenstein's theory will suggest that the notion of use can be even remotely taken as the product of physical mechanism. Use is intrinsically a normative notion that signifies contextually dependent linguistic behaviour. Context defines use. Explanation of

---

23. Mcginn, C., *Wittgenstein on Meaning*, Oxford, Basil Blackwell, 1984.

meaning thus consists in explaining appropriateness of an utterance. An utterance whether it is correct or incorrect will be decided by whether it is appropriate to the context or not. The inseparability of the two notions — context and use — became the basis of understanding the meaning of an utterance. Can this relationship be pictured by a structure? Wittgenstein rules out such a possibility. To this effect, the argument that he offers is of the following nature:

> What belongs to grammar are all the conditions (the method) necessary for comparing the proposition with reality . . . all the conditions necessary for understanding the sense.[24]

The next is conditions. What are the conditions that Wittgenstein is referring to in the above passage? Wittgenstein makes these conditions explicit when he says:

> The understanding of a language, as of a game, seems like a background against which a particular sentence acquires meaning.[25]

This brings us back to the idea of meaning as holistic. A sentence acquires meaning not atomistically, that is, on the basis of its meaning particles. It, on the other hand, acquires its meaning on the basis of its role that it plays in a background language. The meaning of a sentence is thus decided in relation to other sentences in a language game. Meaning, in this sense, is the result of certain holistic connections. Language game represents a semantical system. It is not a system to be understood in terms of certain structures because its inner composition is based on varied nature of properties which are essentially normative and social in nature. A system of language game is thus found to be organized by such elements

24. Wittgenstein, L., *Philosophical Grammar*, Oxford, Basil Blackwell, 1974, Sec. 88, See also Sec. 59.

25. *Ibid.*

like context-involving institutions, norms, procedures, etc. This makes evident that the semantic correspondence principle on which the structure of meaning mechanism is based can be shown to be untenable in view of the fact that meaning is holistic. Holism offers an alternative account of meaning refuting the idea that meaning can be pictured or it is one which is correlated with the structure of mechanism. Meanings are not situated in the head, nor brain can be a meaning machine. The basis of its existence follows from its role in a linguistic whole.

Finally, Wittgenstein's non-mechanistic account of meaning involves the idea that meaning is autonomous. To say that meaning is non-mechanistic implies that, it is not causally determined by any neural mechanism of the brain. Meaning is not caused by what is going on in the neural centre. This, in other words, speaks for the autonomy of meaning. Wittgenstein conceives thought and meaning to be related to the personal level as against, what Dennett[26] calls, sub-personal level which is governed by mechanical laws. The level characterized by the personal can be thus called autonomous because it is not controlled by any mechanism. Meaning and thought since they are organically connected to the personal level, a connection is thus formed between them and a theory of person. Wittgenstein while defining thought says that it is "something specifically human and organic." The same applies to meaning — it is specifically human (i.e., cultural) and

---

26. As Dennett says: Ryle and Wittgenstein are the pre-eminent modern theorists of the personal level. In fact, in their different ways they invent the enterprise, by showing that there is work to be done, that there are questions that arise purely at the personal level, and that one misconceives the questions if one offers sub-personal hypothesis or theories as answers.

    Dennett, D. *Brainstorms*, Cambridge, Mass, MIT Press, 1985, p.154.

organic. It is organically related to the person and not to the mechanical device represented by the brain.[27]

---

27. Mechanism gives a false picture of the mind. As Wittgenstein remarks:

> If one thinks of thought as something specifically human and organic, one is inclined to ask "could there be a prosthetic apparatus for thinking, an inorganic substitute for thought?" But if thinking consists only in writing or speaking, why shouldn't a machine do it? "Yes, but the machine doesn't know anything." Certainly it is senseless to talk of a prosthetic substitute for seeing and hearing. We do talk of artificial feet, but not of artificial pains in the foot.
>
> "But could a machine think?" — Could it be in pain? — Here the important thing is what one means by something *being in pain* [or by *thinking*] *Philosophical Grammar*, p. 105.

Wittgenstein while commenting on Turing's thesis and the idea of mechanism that follows from it says that the attempt to integrate the procedure of computation and the operations of the mind commit a basic fallacy — the fallacy of ignoring normativity involved in rule following. The point that Wittgenstein is making here is that recursive functions which are mechanically calculable cannot be separated from its essential normativity. Turing does not keep any place for normativity of calculation. In this new formulation, rules are "embodied in the brain" and they act as a causal mechanism. Normative behaviour is then reduced to a causal process. Wittgenstein's reply to this is that "There are no causal connections in a calculation" (*Remarks on the Foundation of Mathematics*, Oxford, Basil Blackwell, 1978 VII, Sec. 18). Even a simple calculation presupposes normativity. True, machine's operation is solely based on the causal condition of how machine produced its results. But not on the condition whether or not they are correct. In this way they are antecedent to the machine's operations. On this ground, rules of calculation may be viewed as supplying the criteria by which we can determine whether the result arrived at by a Turing machine is correct or incorrect. Normativity thus becomes an irreplaceable element in mechanism on the ground that calculation which is

→

The mechanistic and organic conceptions of meaning start with different premises. The mechanistic theory assumes that meaning arises out of something that is more basic. Hence, the problem before this theory is how to explain this process — the process through which meaning emerges. The organic theory, on the other hand, does not assume that meaning emerges from something that is more basic. There is thus no need to explain it in terms of some underlying structure. Meaning is something which is given and it is reflected in the linguistic system. This self evident nature of meaning can be seen, as Wittgenstein pointed out, from the fact that even the description of mechanism "itself uses language to describe phenomena." Meaning, in this sense, assumes a new characterization pointing towards its own autonomy.

→ constitutive of mechanism cannot be devoid of normativity. From this, it follows that all the mental cognitive activities, such as thinking, reasoning, using of language, etc. which involve rule-following cannot be devoid of normativity.

See in this connection: Stuart Shanker's *Wittgenstein's Remarks on the Foundations of AI*, London, Routledge, 1998.

11

Kant, Kripke Reading of A Priori

Rakesh Chandra

It is often believed that philosophy is an a priori enterprise and the degree of philosophic purity is measured to the extent of its a prioricity, e.g., the ontological argument to prove the existence of God. Rationalist a priorism however also has been the main reason for criticism of traditional metaphysics by the empiricists. Immanual Kant too is severely critical of a priorism's overenthusiasm but the two editions of his "critique" and the "prolegomena to any future metaphysics" carefully attempt to delineate the limits of genuine a priori knowledge. The notion as well as the term a priori however has not been used by Kant in a single unambiguous way. Though his most favoured use of the term "a priori" replaced often by "pure" is that which forms the precondition of our experience the use of the term to refer to something prior to experience or innate is not entirely avoided.

A rich and a long tradition of discussion exists in philosophy on the question of clarification of interrelationships between the nested categories of truths — the necessary, the analytic and the a priori. There have been questions about whether the analytic and the necessary exhaust each other but I propose to examine in this paper mainly the question surrounding interrelation between necessary and the a priori and to see how the cleavage between a priori and a posteriori is related to the distinction between necessary and contingent propositions? also whether the necessary propositions exhaust the a priori and vice versa? Can one act as the criteria for the other?

We are reminded that for Kant necessity and universality were to be the twin criteria for distinguishing a prioricity. He believed that if a proposition is conceived as necessary then it will be called an a priori judgement. An a priori judgement "in being though is thought as necessary" and is also "thought with strict universality that is in such a manner that no exception is allowed as possible." Necessity is never derived from experience, for experience tells us only what is but not that it must necessarily be so and not otherwise. Kant proposed to characterize a priori knowledge as any knowledge which is "independent of experience" and independent of "all impressions of the senses." He declares "we shall understand a priori knowledge, not as knowledge independent of this or that experience, but knowledge independent of all experience"[1] To understand this independence from experience it is customary to Kant's maxim with which he introduces the epistemological enquiry in the *Critique of Pure Reason* "though all knowledge begins with experience it does not follow that it arises out of experience." The first part of the maxim fairly represents the position often referred to as concept empiricism saying that one cannot gain knowledge temporally prior to experience. In this sense our knowledge begins with experience but Kant intends to emphasize that empirical origin of our knowledge has nothing to do with what may be required for the verification of truth value of the propositions expressing knowledge. Many commentators categorize Kant as a verification rationalist because of his views on the a priori propositions which he holds to be occasioned by experience but not verified by it. The independence from experience that

1. Kant Immanuel, *Critique of Pure Reason*, Trans, N. Kemp Smith, New York: Macmillan Co. 1963 B 3, p. 43.

Kant is speaking of is logical and two judgements are considered to be logically independent if neither of them entails the other, or either is contradictory of the other. A priori judgement is logically independent of all judgements which describe experience or even impressions of sense. As noticed earlier the criteria to distinguish the a priori from the empirical is apparently twofold. First of all p (where p ranges over the class of judgements) is a priori if it is necessary or if p follows from and only from necessary judgements. The second criterion offered is that when a judgement is thought of with strict universality that is in such a manner that no exception is allowed as possible, it is not derived from experience, but is valid absolutely a priori."[2]

It is interesting to notice that "a priori" is used as a term by Kant in more than one way in the sense of prior to experience as well as presupposed by experience. But in both the cases the a prioricity does not seem chronological. It is often believed that in the a priori empirical distinction the positive element is empirical while the residue is swept off by a priori.[3] This implies that the distinction is mutually exclusive and jointly exhaustive.

Much of the recent discussions on the issue seems to question the earlier implication. While there are those like Quine who reject the very idea of a priori truths, there are those like Putnam who accept that there is at least one a priori truth. However the most vexed problems arise in the readings where philosophers like Saul Kripke while accepting that there are a priori truths insist that the very same may be known a posteriori.

---

2. *Ibid* B4, p. 44.
3. Quniton, A.M., "The A Priori and the Analytic," *Proceedings of a Aristotelian Society*, vol. 64, pp. 31-34.

It may be instructive to note that while Kant had taken necessity as distinguishing criterion for a prioricity several positivist writings give an impression that the categories analytic, necessary and the a priori are indistinguishable and sometimes the terms are also used interchangeably. That this is a mistake can hardly be overemphasized. Kripke reminds us "it is certainly a philosophical thesis and not a matter of obvious definitional equivalence either that everything a priori is necessary or that everything necessary is a priori. Both concepts are vague. That may be another problem. But at any rate they are dealing with two different areas, the epistemological and the metaphysical."[4]

The term a priori, believes Kripke, is a concept of epistemology while the notion of necessity is a notion of metaphysics in some "non-persorative sense." Rightly so he reminds us that "the terms "necessary" and "a priori" then as applied to statements are not obvious synonyms. There may be a philosophical argument connecting them, perhaps even identifying them but an argument is simply not required that two terms are clearly interchangeable."[5]

Now the necessary conditions for the identity of the terms or their synonymy of necessary and a priori may be given as follows:

(i) All necessary propositions are a priori without exception.

(ii) All a priori propositions are necessary without exception.

(iii) The above two propositions are not only true but necessarily true.

---

4. Kripke, Saul, "Naming & Necessity" in *Semantics of Natural Language,* ed. Davidson & Harman Dodrecht, D. Reidel 1972, p. 230.

5. *Ibid.,* p. 263.

These conditions are however not sufficient for the identity of the concept of a priori and necessary. This is so because none of the propositions (i) or (ii) are analytic and analyticity of the propositions is also a necessary condition for the identity of the two concepts. The two terms are obviously definitionally non equivalent. To say that a proposition is necessary is to say that its contradictory is impossible while to say that it is a priori is to say that it is not empirical or is independent of experience. In Kant we find necessity defined as "that the opposite of which is inconceivable and a prioricity defined in terms of independence from experience." The former concept, we may agree, marks the metaphysical or ontological modality while the latter is an epistemic operator. Kant is often accused of psychologism and subjectivism for the definition of necessity as opposite of that which is "inconceivable." But this inconceivability is not just a subjective failure to conceive. If the negation of a proposition is inconceivable it indicates there must be something wrong with the proposition itself, i.e., the negation of the proposition in question. We remember that many philosophers have characterized necessary truths as those which are true in all "possible worlds" and their negation is false in all possible worlds. This characterization has been called "ontological" or "metaphysical" for it is given in terms of possible worlds. This nomenclature is misleading as a possible world is more appropriately understood as a picturesque way of talking about logically possible states of affairs. The foremost logicians who speak of possible world semantics too insist that worlds are not to be understood as ontological entities which can be peeped into, and therefore calling the characterization ontological can be misleading. It is of course to be agreed[6] that even if Kant's characterization is not ontological or metaphysical it is definitely not

---

6 Sen, P.K., *Logic Induction and Ontology*, Jadavpur University Studies, The Macmillan Company of the India Limited, 1989.

epistemological and Kant always cautiously set apart the two concepts of a priori and necessary whatever the mode be. The necessary equivalence between "a priori" and "necessary" may be justified by showing that both imply each other and this may be shown thus — to say that a proposition is a priori is to say that the truth value of it can be determined without appeal to experience. And saying that the truth value of "P" can be determined without summoning experience has been sometimes interpreted as saying that mere reflection upon "P" or upon some other propositions say "q" and "r" is sufficient to ensure P's truth value. Where "q" and "r" are themselves propositions one can determine their truth value by reflecting on them alone. Thus the truth value of an a priori proposition is its intrinsic property or that an a priori proposition is one whose truth value is intrinsic to it.

Now necessary proposition when defined as one; if true has its contradictory impossible, and if false is itself impossible. To say this may itself be seen as saying that truth value of such a proposition is intrinsic to it. This is the implication of the property of being a priori and may justify one to maintain that all a priori propositions are necessary, i.e., being a priori implies being necessary.

How is one to show the reverse of this implication, i.e., that being necessary implies being a priori. Perhaps it is plausible to maintain that a proposition, the truth value of which cannot be known without experience, does not have its truth value as its intrinsic property, for, if it is just impossible to determine its truth value except by experience, the truth value depends on some contingent happenings, viz. experiences. This shows that if a proposition's truth value is intrinsic to it, that is, if it depends upon the nature of proposition alone, then it should be possible to decide that truth value unempirically. In other words if a proposition is necessary it should be a priori also.

By another definition of necessity the implication of being a priori by necessity becomes more obvious. For example, a necessary proposition is described as one which is true, whatever be the empirical facts, and if it follows analytically that for determining the truth value of a necessary proposition a consideration of empirical facts, is needless, this amounts to saying that all necessary propositions, are a priori.

On the assumption that the terms a priori and empirical are contradictory of each other, and so are the terms "necessary" and "contingent," the acceptance of the equivalence of a priori and "necessary" commits us to the admission of equivalence between the empirical and the contingent. But about the coextensiveness of the two concepts Saul Kripke forwards considerations in favour of the possibility of both a priori contingent propositions as well as necessary a posteriori propositions.

We will now briefly examine Kripke's notion of "the contingent a priori truths" as discussed in his celebrated "Naming and Necessity" lectures. It would be in order to notice that an appraisal of the issue of contingent a priori does not commit one to a straightforward view on the nature of necessary a priori truths, i.e., if we reject the contingent a priori we are not compelled to accept that all necessary truths are a priori.

We may first examine what Kripke means to say when he says that a truth is a priori. While talking about the epistemic operator a priori what strikes him immediately are questions such as these, who knows a priori? Is it God, Martians or normal human beings with capacities to apprehend like ours. Kripke of course does not dwell upon these questions for long but here we notice the beginnings of a subtle but an important confusion which haunts his entire discussion.

From what Kripke says it appears that he thinks that the epistemic status of a proposition is dependent upon the capacities of individuals to determine the truth of the proposition and that the question whether a proposition is a priori or a posteriori is regarding the capacities of the individuals to apprehend the truth of propositions. This however is misleading. The epistemic status of the proposition is inherent in the proposition itself. In depends on the logical connection between the terms used. The evidential state of an individual who knows an a priori truth would of course be a priori but were there no such individuals even then the epistemic status of the proposition would remain unaltered.

It may appear that the theories such as the Logical Positivistic explanation of Necessity involve an element of individuals, relativity and mention of the capacities of individuals for it says that "Analytic propositions simply record our determination to use words in a certain fashion"[7] or later that "necessary sentences exhibit our determinations to use words in a certain way." It might be well to remember that the positivist were equating the a priori, necessary and the analytic. The theories such as these suffer from obvious shortcoming and in some cases they are even self-defeating, but for the time being even if we accept these theories the element of individual relativism is admitted only in the choice of the notion to be used in a statement which may be called the "preparation of the sentence." But what the logical connections between the terms used shall be and what the epistemic status of the proposition is, is in no way relative to individual arbitration. Alvin Platinga's discussion of the relation between what is known a priori and what is necessarily true is also similar. He rightly believes that the relation is not simple and straightforward but his observations are rather

---

7. A.J. Ayer, *Language Truth and Logic*, Macmillan, 1958.

curious. He begins "It is immediately obvious that not all necessary truths are known a priori, for there are necessary truths, for example Farmats' last theorem or its denial that are not known at all, an a fortiori are not known a priori. Is, it rather that every necessary truth that is known is known a priori? This question divides itself (a) is every necessary truth that is known, known a priori to everyone who knows it? and (b) is every necessary truth that is known to someone or the other, known a priori to someone or the other? . . ."[8]

We must notice here that though the description of necessary truths as those which are known a priori is an inaccurate and an inappropriate characterization, it was never intended that the "known" here be considered as representing its past tense connotation as in a statement, say, "My brother has known me since childhood" nor was it intended as a descriptive statement about either the individual or the collective biography of people.

The a prioricity of necessary truths is a characteristic held by these truths not because everyone or anyone for that matter knows their truth and knows it a priori, but because the interrelationship of the concepts claimed in them requires no justification from experience whether or not the truths are known to someone or not. It is important to notice that not only by a priori proposition or a priori knowledge we do not mean, the knowledge which is not caused by experience, or the knowledge which can be acquired or originated before any experience but also that questions such as who knows it and how does he know (as a question of biographical history) are also irrelevant to determine the epistemological status of the propositions concerned. Questions regarding the origination and cause of concepts or about the temporal order

---

8. Platinga Alvin, *The Nature of Necessity*, Oxford Clarendon Press, 1974, p. 12.

of acquiring them are psychological questions and have no bearing on the epistemological status of a proposition in terms of a priori and empirical which is determined not with regard to its origination or temporal development in one's actual thinking process but with regard to the grounds of its justification. A prioricity like necessity is also a property intrinsic to the proposition as against certainty which may be represented as an extrinsic or a relational one. Just as one feels an intuitive discomfort at the idea of a proposition being necessity for one and not for another person, one may be uneasy to accept that there might be a proposition known a priori to one and not to another, but this needs careful scrutiny and argument. Also it might be felt that just as in the case of necessity use of temporal predicates seem inadequate, so is the case with a prioricity. "Necessary at t_1 but not necessary at t_2" or a priori at t_1 but not a priori at t_2 do not appear to be happy locutions.

Kripke seriously objects to the fact that in the definition of a priori truths as "those which can be known independently of experience" some philosophers have changed the modality in this characterization from "can" to "must." Contrary to the belief that which belongs to the realm of "a priori knowledge cannot possibly be known a posteriori," Kripke holds that "something may belong to the realm of such statements that can be known a priori but still may be known by particular people on the basis of experience."[9]

Kripke gives an example how one may believe that a number is prime when it is given so by a computer and how this belief is based on our knowledge of the laws of physics, the construction of machines etc. The evidence is therefore

---

9. Kripke Saul, "Naming and Necessity" in *Semantics of Natural Language.*, ed., Davidson and Harman Doderecht. D. Reidel, 1972, p. 260.

not purely a priori. Nevertheless this could have been known a priori.

A straightforward counter to this example might be to urge that the content of the knowledge of one who knows a priori that a certain number is prime is different from the content of the knowledge of one who knows that, because of certain laws of physics being operative, laws governing the making of machines being abided, the correct tappings of knobs with marks representing numbers (or their codes) and other mathematical operators, a particular information in computer code reads that a certain number is prime. This is all known a posteriori.

If however we wish to maintain that the knowledge content of the two, i.e., the one who knows a priori and the one who knows through a computer is the same, and the one using the computer is using it like a child's counting beads and that he too knows by abstraction that the number is prime, and not that the laws of physics being so and so the computer code information reads that a certain number is prime and so on, then sure we have a case of a priori knowledge. The aids used are to facilitate our thinking process by perhaps concretizing our concepts but the concepts we are trying to explore have not been derived from them. They are not treated as providing evidence for the truth of the statement. Our evidential state thus is also a priori and this is hardly surprising.

It may however be mentioned that here too Kripke is not alone in holding that certain a priori truth may be known a posteriori by some individuals. Plantinga gives an instance: "Having taken the trouble to understand the proof, you may know a priori that Schroeder-Bernstein Theorem is a consequence of some standard formulation of set theory. If I know that you are properly reliable on these matters and take your word for it, then I may know that truth a posteriori — as I may if I have forgotten the proof but remember having verified that indeed there is one. To learn the value of sine of 54 degrees I consult a handy table of trigonometric functions : My knowledge of this item is then a posteriori. In the same way even simple truths of arithmetic as that 75+36 = 111 can be known a posteriori."[10]

It needs to be pointed that here again either we decide to distinguish the content of knowledge and if not we are clearly confusing evidence for the truth of a proposition with the aids used in understanding or concretising the thoughts or concepts. We must not be misled by the fact that sometimes say in order to come to understand arithmetic we originately required example. Perhaps we have to learn the beginnings of arithmetic in the classroom with the help of examples but once we have so learnt it we do not need examples to grasp further and we can see the truth of many arithmetical propositions, e.g. That 1132 + 2346 = 3478, of which we have never had examples. We have probably never taken 1132 things and 2346 things, put them together and counted the resulting set, but we still know that this shall be the result of the counting and more importantly many would argue that even though we do not know the result we know that whatever it shall be a priori. The need for example is only a psychological matter. In geometry too we stand in need of examples and perhaps here the need is more than in arithmetic. In arithmetic we only need the examples at the most elementary stage but in geometry most people need a drawn figure, or at least an image of one in their minds to see the validity of most truths. But we must distinguish between an illustration and the basis of a proof. If the particular figure were not merely an

---

10. *"The Nature of Necessity,"* Claredon Library of Logic and Philosophy, Oxford Clarendon Press, 1974, p. 7.

illustration but the basis of the theorem, the latter would have to be proved by measuring it. But measuring with a ruler of a protractor never figures in Euclid's proofs, that the proof is not really based on the figure is shown by the fact that we can still follow a proof concerning the properties of right angled triangles, even if the figure used to illustrate them is so hopelessly drawn that it is obviously not a right angled triangle at all. It is also important to mark that if geometry were empirical it would be a very hazardous speculation from the single example before us on a piece of paper or the blackboard to conclude that all triangles had that property. The property in question might well be an individual peculiarity of the triangle and not of others. Ewing adds that the recent developments in geometry have had the effect of much loosening the connection between geometrical proofs and the empirical figure. It is possible to work out non-geometries where we cannot depend on figures. It is interesting to note that while some philosophers quote the development of non-Euclidian geometrical systems to substantiate the idea of the a prioricity of the geometrical proofs and axioms, the same development has been taken by many as an indication of the fact that the geometrical axioms are not a priori. Our sympathy however lies with the a priori characterization of geometry whether Euclidian or otherwise.

Now we come to Kripke's discussion of the so-called contingent a priori truths, a discussion replete with misleading statements. The example he uses is that of the bar at Paris. We are remained of what Wittgenstein says of this bar in his "Philosophical Investigations." There is one thing of which one can neither say that it is one metre long, nor that it is not one metre long, and this is the standard metre at Paris. But this of course is not to ascribe any extraordinary property to it but only to mark its peculiar role in the language game of measuring with a metre rule.

The intuitive idea behind what Wittgenstein says seems correct and in the arguments which we shall subsequently build we shall give reasons why we cannot meaningfully affirm or negate that the rod at Paris is a metre long, if the rod is to work as the standard.

Kripke believes that the bar at Paris "fixes the reference" of "one metre." Even if we precisely stipulate that one metre is to be the length of the stick S at the time t_1 it would not become a necessary truth that "stick S is one metre of length at t_1." He states "Someone who thinks that everything one knows a priori is necessary might think this is the definition of one metre. By definition S is one metre long at time t. That's a necessary truth. But there seems to me no reason so to conclude even for the man who uses the stated definition of one metre for he is using the definition not to give meaning of what he called a "metre" but to fix the reference . . . . He uses it to fix the reference. There is a certain length which he wants to mark out. He marks it out by an accidental property, namely that there is a stick of that length. Someone else might mark out the same reference by another accidental property. But in any case even though he uses this to fix the reference of his standard of length, a metre, he can still say "if heat is applied to this stick S at t_1 then at t stick would not have been one metre long."[11]

Further Kripke goes on ". . . there is an intuitive difference between the phrase "one metre" and the phrase "the length of S at t." The first is meant to designate rigidly a certain length in all possible worlds which in the actual worlds happens to be the length of S at t_1. On the other hand the length of S at t_1 does not designate anything rigidly. In some counterfactual situations the stick might have been longer and in some shorter."[12]

11. *Ibid.*, p. 274.

12. *Ibid.*, p. 275.

Regarding the epistemological status of the statement "S is one metre long at t," Kripke believes that for "someone who had fixed the metric system by reference to stick S it would seem that he knows it a priori. For if he used the stick S to fix reference of the term one metre then as a result of this kind of definition (which is not an abbrevative or synonyms giving definition) he knows automatically without further investigation that S is one metre long."[13]

Kripke's use of the term a priori here is puzzling. For never has the epistemic operator "a priori" meant that which is known "automatically without further investigation" (I suspect even those who identified the a priori with the innate did not hold such a view). a prioricity is in no way relative to the present body of knowledge which an individual possesses. If the suggestion is accepted then most of the empirical knowledge would be counted as a priori. Imagine a position where you acquired some knowledge empirically. Later you deduce some consequences of this empirical knowledge. Would we admit that our knowledge of these consequences is independent of experience since at the time you perform the deduction, you are engaging in a process of reasoning which is independent of the sensations you are having? The knowledge thus obtained is of course without "further investigation" but is it a priori? Well, it may not be. The temptation to say that it cannot be is great in problem cases such as those where an analytic truth is deduced from an empirical promise with the help of the law of addition (e.g., from p infer $p \vee \sim p$) but it must be noted that even in such cases, the reason for calling the conclusion a priori is not that it has been inferred by a deduction and certainly not that the inference is from an empirical premise or a singular statement. (The case of the afore-mentioned curious inference shall be discussed later.)

13. *Ibid.*, p. 275.

It may be repeated that in the classical formulation Kant had stated "we shall understand by a priori knowledge which is independent of this or that experience but knowledge independent of all experience," no definition has yet been proposed which makes the use of the epistemic operators relative to the present body of knowledge which an individual possesses. We need not however hesitate to admit that some experience may be needed to provide us with concepts. Independence of experience is required in the evidence for the logical connection between the terms and concepts not in the acquisition of the terms or concepts.

Kant himself had drawn a distinction between "pure" and "empirical" knowledge and by pure here he had meant that knowledge which is "a priori" but Kant is not consistent in the use of this term and we notice that pure and mixed knowledge have been distinguished by Kant within the scope of a priori. A priori judgements when they involve concepts that are themselves independent of experience are to be called pure a priori judgements. But he was also clear that it is not necessary that a judgement if it is to be a priori must involve only such concepts.

It is important to note that in the example which Kripke uses for the one who fixed the metric system with reference to the stick, "S is one metre of length at t_1" is a declaration and so does not express a proposition to which truth values may be significantly applied. It is also not a knowledge situation to which the epistemic operators such as a priori and a posteriori may be meaningfully applied. The declaration is merely an act of fixation of the reference of the word or phrase "one metre" and once the declaration has been made the question of that very individual's knowing that rod is one metre long at t_1 does not arise.

Suppose I stipulate the definition of "Red" by fixing the reference with the colour of a paper trough ostensively and then later say "This is red" when I am talking about the same paper trough. My sentence has all the appearance of a proposition and I may even ask whether this proposition is a priori or a posteriori or that whether my knowledge that "This is red" is a priori or a posteriori. But my questions are clearly illegitimate. They could have been legitimate if I could know the colour of the t rough but once declared the question of my knowing that is red does not arise. Kripke's argument is of the form : "I declare it to be "Red" so I know that this is red." This is an obviously false and an invalid argument for from any declaration no knowledge follows. The question of truth value can only be significantly raised about "propositions" and sentences may be pronounced as true or false only via the propositions that they express (Wright however finds the talk of sentence truth/falsehood "definitely barbaric"). Moore, we remember, remarked that not all sentences express propositions and he said that he is not sure, whether "an imperative such as "60 away" expresses a proposition at all." Several others too argue that not all well-formed sentences express something which may be associated with a truth value. For example, an imperative sentence like "open the window" or an operative sentence like say "May he come tomorrow?" or an interrogative like "what is you name?" do not do this. Aristotle in his *De interpretations* mentions prayers as examples of sentences which are neither true nor false. Philosophers have not felt tempted to take the above mentioned sentences as constituting exceptions to the law of Bivalence or to say that they express propositions without truth values, but it has appeared obvious to many that they do not express propositions at all. It is often remarked that sentences used for prescriptions such as orders, norms and rules, do not say anything that is true or false. The case of declarations such as "one metre is the length of S at t" is however still more difficult and the impossibility of the application of any truth criteria on them is perhaps more certain. We must remember that though the propositions are themselves not linguistic units yet their availability is only through language and sentences. No proposition can be expressed by a sentence whose words have no already acquired meanings, and a sentence giving the use of a particular "word" cannot be said to be expressing a proposition using the term corresponding to the word in question; in fact no proposition is available here at all. If we ask the question is it true that "one metre is the length of S at t" we have nothing on which the truth criteria can apply since one metre has no previously acquired meaning.

That Kripke believes that reference fixing stipulative definitions or even arbitrary declarations about the usage of a term made by individuals are candidates for truth value and significant use of epistemic operators, is explicit in another example. He says, ". . . even if I should say to myself that I will use "Hesperus" to name the heavenly body I see in the evening in yonder position of the sky, it would not be necessary that Hesperus was even seen in the evening. But it may be a priori that this is how I have determined its referent. I have determined that Hesperus is the thing I saw in the evening over there, then I will know just from making the determination of the referent, that if there is any Hesperus at all it's the thing I saw in the evening."[14]

The inadequacy of the sentence "But it may be a priori that this is how I have determined its reference" can hardly be overemphasized. How a determination or declaration regarding the usage of a "word" can be known a priori or a posteriori is entirely unintelligible. A more sympathetic reader of Kripke might wish to argue that "that" in the quoted sentence must be understood as "because" and we must concede that such a use of the word "that" is not entirely unusual. The argument of Kripke would now read thus "even

---

14. *Ibid.*, p. 290.

if I should say to myself that I shall use "Hesperus" to name the heavenly body I see in the evening in yonder position of the sky if would not be necessary that Hesperus was ever seen in the evening. But it may be a priori because this is how I have determined its referent."

This reconstruction is also of no help for what the argument now says is that a certain proposition "Hesperus is the name of the star I see in yonder position" is a priori for I have determined to refer to Hesperus thus. It is important to notice that what is appearing to be a proposition is the determination itself and is therefore not a proposition at all and all our previous arguments for maintaining so may be repeated.

The case of our knowledge of the length of the rod at Paris is sometimes understood as an example of coming to know a truth on the basis of reference fixing stipulative definition. Kripke has been claiming that one can know a priori that a certain rod (the stick at Paris) is one metre long even though it is contingently of that length.

Colin Mc Ginn[15] compares this to the christening of a ship as QE_2. All present at the ceremony know the contingent fact that a ship struck at t_1 by a certain champagne bottle is the QE_2. But they know this only because they are antecedently apprised of the conventions governing the naming of ships and because they have observed that these conventions have been instantiated in a certain speech act. And these things they know a posteriori. McGinn argues "since a posteriority transmits itself through inference, their inferred knowledge is a posteriori too even though they enjoyed "automatic" and "prior" access to the ship's identity," further he says, "I think the case is similar with the metre rod. One comes to know it is

15. "A Priori and A posteriori Knowledge," *Aristotelian Society Proceedings*, 1975-76.

a metre long on the basis of knowledge concerning the general conventions of stipulative definition and observation (or testimony about) the event of utterance, (etc.) instantiating the convention — these requiring causal commerce with empirical particulars. So I am inclined to say that the sort of knowledge Kripke has cottoned on to is not genuinely a priori."[16]

In the example of the christening of ships we have a social event or function taking place of which striking of the champagne bottle is a part; also there is a linguistic function being performed that of giving meaning to a word or fixing the referent of the word. The conventions of the social function are rigidified intentions of the community of speakers and again normally we do not treat intentions as propositions which are either true or false or are even a case of knowledge to which the epistemic operators may be meaningfully applied. And since conventions are themselves not a priori/a posteriori the transmission of a posteriori modality is not universal. This we shall discuss when we shall take the case of necessary a posteriori knowledge.

But McGinn is only saying that people may be apprised of the conventions governing the christening of ships a posteriori and the instance of the convention is known through experience (There being perhaps no other way) and so the knowledge of the people at the ceremony, that the ship has been christened QE_2 is also a posteriori. This seems to be a fair picture. But what of the rod at Paris? Is the case really similar? Firstly it is not obvious that "one metre" is a name but even if we allow this what does it name? Perhaps we would be told that it is the name of the length of S at t_1.

Now what are the conventions governing such a "naming" (whatever that might mean?). A ceremonial accompaniment

16. *Ibid*, p. 206.

is perhaps not needed. What has been called "the general conventions of stipulative definition" is perhaps that a certain tacit or explicit ostention is required in the case of such definition. These we know empirically and thus when we are dubbing the rod ostensively and "s is one metre of length at t_1" our knowledge is also a posteriori. Our recognition of an act as an act of stipulative definition of naming involves "commerce with empirical particulars." It may however be noted that if by the conventions of stipulative definition we mean the criteria to distinguish stipulative from other forms of definition this knowledge is itself not a posteriori. But this may not disturb the general argument which has been discussed here.

But the problem does not stop here and the rod strikes again. What does it mean to say that the phrase one metre is the length of S at t_1 which we have been treating as a reference fixing stipulative definition, is both contingent as well as a priori? What is contingent is this situation? The stick at t could have had a length other than the one it actually has and under stress and heat it may have lengths other than the one which it actually has. It may cease to be of one metre. But how do we know this? We can know only if we have another standard criterion by which we can measure the stick and know whether it is or is not one metre in length. This indeed is very strange. Stipulative definition sets up a standard of usage. The stipulation that "one metre is the length of S at t_1" should set up a standard for the measure or the metric unit "one metre" but here we have some other standard to measure the standard itself. It seems difficult to call such a case where there are more than one standard a case of genuine stipulative definition.

On behalf of Kripke one might say that we have just shifted the issue. The statement in which the reference of one metre has been fixed with the standard rod at Paris may itself not be a case of genuine stipulative definition for we have an independent definition of "one metre" on which the standard rod itself can be measured but this other definition is really stipulative and this is "one metre is the ten millionth part of the distance from equator to the north pole."[17] Now for the one who fixed the metric system thus the definition or the knowledge of this statement is a priori and the metaphysical status of the statement is that of a contingent proposition. (The devil might punch the earth so as to reduce the distance from the Pole to the equator or the planetary magnetic pull might thus affect the earth so as to increase the distance).

But with such a reconstruction we have obvious difficulties. What is contingent in this case? Only that the distance between the equator and the north pole might not be what it is and thus its one millionth part may also have variable value. But does this make the statement "one metre is the ten millionth part of the distance from equator to the north pole" itself contingent? The answer is "No." For we have no standard measure to measure the metric unit itself. The definition shall stay in Lewis's phrase "come what may."

Now we can say that even if for argument's sake we allow stipulative definitions to act as propositions they are not

---

17. The metre was approved by the French National convention in 1975, was to be one ten-millionth of the length of earth's meridian between the equator and the North Pole.

    To determine this distance, a team of surveyors Rod set out to measure an arc of the meridian between Dankirk in France and Barcelona in Spain. Despite many difficulties — they were plagued by the hostility of peasants and by arrests for treason — the surveyors finally succeeded. The metre was established at approximately 39.37 inches.

    The Keysione was the metre from the Greek metron meaning "a measure." This new basic unit was not divided from the variables of human anatomy rather it was to spring from the universe itself.

contingent and if Kripke wants we may even happily grant him that they are a priori but much better it would be if Kripke spares the rod and the contingent a priori.

It will be instructive to concentrate on Sen's discussion of Kripke's extraordinary examples of the contingent a priori which he thinks arise out of the use of a certain kind of designators, including names.[18] As mentioned before, a designator is sometimes introduced by the help of a definite description which does not give meaning to the designator but only fixes its reference. If this is the only relation between the designator and the definite description that it provides us with only an *independent means of identifying the reference of the designator*, then that a thing which is designated by the designator satisfied the definite description must be a matter of contingent fact. But at the same time it is undeniable that if the designator is *introduced* by the definite description then we know independently of any empirical investigation that the thing does satisfy the definite description. Thus if "N" is the designator and "p" is the definite description which introduces the designator by fixing its reference (and reference only), then the proposition "N" is "p," would be contingent and knowable a priori.

One of Kripke's examples is that the name "Neptune was introduced by Leverrier by the definite description the cause of perturbations in the orbit of Uranus." Leverrier could have introduced the name "Neptune" as an abbreviation of the description. In this case "Neptune" would be synonymous with "the cause of perturbations in the orbit of Uranus," and the proposition that "Neptune is the cause of perturbations in the orbit of Uranus" would be necessarily, because analytically,

18. Sen, P.K. "The necessary and A priori" Appendix I Logic *Induction and Ontology*, Jadavpur University Studies. The Macmillan Company of India Limited, 1989.

true. Secondly Leverrier could have introduced the name "Neptune" as a name of the planet which happens to cause the perturbations in the orbit of Uranus. In that case the description would have just determined (or fixed) the reference of the name, and the same propositions would have been contingent. Kripke believes that the name Neptune was introduced in the latter way and so concluded that the proposition is in order to strengthen his conclusions. He says that the counter-factual proposition "Neptune" might not have caused the perturbation in the orbit of Uranus is not only conceivable but also true. But in any case the name "Neptune," was introduced by Leverrier by means of that description. Leverrier could tell a priori before actually spotting the planet with his telescope that Neptune was the cause of the perturbations in the orbit of Uranus. So we have here a proposition which is both contingent and knowable a priori. Sen holds Kripke's arguments to be inconclusive.

Without doubting that descriptions can be used merely to fix the reference of a name, Sen doubts whether under the circumstances given Leverrier could have done so. It seems to me that we are entitled to say that a description is used merely to fix the reference of a name only if it is not *essential* that that description, rather than some other, should be used to fix the reference of the name. But if Kripke is right about the circumstances under which Leverrier introduced the name "Neptune" it was essential that the astronomer should have fixed the reference of the name by that description. It is not the case that Leverrier, or somebody else had already known the planet in the sky or had been in possession of some other evidence of its existence. He had evidence enough to conclude that there must be some planet or other which is the cause of perturbations in the orbit of Uranus, a planet which is distinct from all other planets hitherto identified by astronomers. In an important sense, he knew when he introduced the name "Neptune" only that some planet must be causing the perturbations and did not know which planet it was. Hence in a very important sense, he did not know anything about the identity of the planet excepting that it was the cause of the perturbations. The kind of knowledge Leverrier had of the planet is precisely what Russell called "knowledge by description." If this is so the description is involved in his knowledge in a more intimate fashion than what a use of the description for the introduction of a name by merely fixing the reference of the name would permit. For under the circumstances, Neptune is nothing but the cause of perturbation and the name "Neptune" or whatever other name is introduced at this point would mean the same as the cause of the perturbations in the orbit of Uranus."

On this account "Neptune is the cause of the perturbations in the orbit of uranus" is necessarily, because analytically, true. Leverrier's knowledge, or the knowledge of anyone else who was initiated in the use of the name in the manner of Leverrier was surely a priori, but it was not a knowledge of a contingent truth.

Prof. Sen presents a perfectly general statement of the principle involved here; if "N" is essentially introduced by "the p" the "N is the p" is necessarily, because analytically true our knowledge that "N is the p" is a priori, but it is so only in the way in which our knowledge of analytic propositions is a priori. Here "N" is the name and the p is the designator.

In course of discussing the other example one metre is the length of the bar at Paris Sen uses the distinction used by Donellon[19] between knowing that a certain sentence expresses something true and knowing the truth which the sentence expresses. He gives two examples to illustrate the distinction.

19. "Contingent A priori and rigid designators," in *Midwest Studies in Philosophy*, II, Marris: Minnesota University Press, 1977.

1. I could learn from a German-speaking friend that a certain German sentence expresses something true but if I do not speak German and do not know what the sentence means I would say I do not know the truth of what the sentence expresses.
2. I could be assured by a qualified mathematician that a certain mathematical sentence expresses a theorem, without thereby knowing the truth of the theorem expressed, if I am ignorant of what the mathematical sentence means.

In terms of this distinction between knowing that a certain sentence expresses a truth and knowing the truth which the sentence expresses we can now formulate our basic objection to Kripke's claim that "one metre is the length of the standard metre bar in Paris" is known by us a priori. The objection is just this : what a priori is not the truth which the sentence expresses but only that the sentence, because of the particular manner in which the designator "one metre" is introduced, expresses a true proposition. (This does not mean that we cannot know at all the truths which the sentence expresses, it only means that truth is not learnt a priori but is to be learnt empirically).

One may try to argue at this point that even this would show that the contingent a priori is possible. Because what is known here is that a certain sentence expresses truth, and that is, being a linguistic matter, nothing but a matter of contingent fact. It seems that this is a point which is ready to concede but Sen thinks that even this need not be conceded. What we actually know in this cause is also necessary truth. What we know is that by virtue of the stipulation governing the use of the designator "one metre" it is necessary that the sentence "one metre is the length of the standard metre at

Paris" should express something true, although what it would express is only contingent. In order to make his point clear, Sen draws a threefold distinction between (i) knowledge that the standard metre bar is one metre long, (ii) knowledge that the reference of "one metre" is fixed, by stipulation, as the length of the standard metre bar in Paris, and (iii) knowledge that given the stipulation governing the use of the designator one metre, what the sentence "one metre is the length of the standard metre bar in Paris" expresses must be true. The first two are cases of a posteriori knowledge of contingent truths, but the third is a case of a priori knowledge of a necessary truth. It is a necessary truth that the sentence in question expresses a truth albeit a contingent one. To put the same thing in a slightly different manner, that the sentence expresses a truth, and nothing but truth, is the consequence of the stipulation regarding the designator. The knowledge we have been talking about here is only knowledge of this necessary consequence, and hence this knowledge is not an a priori knowledge of what is contingent.

Platinga also notice in the passing something similar. He remarks that "suppose I have never seen S and hold no views as to its length I propose nonetheless to use one metre as a "rigid" designator of the length, whatever it is, that S actually displays at t. After thus determining the reference of "one metre," I know that the sentence "S is one metre long at t" expresses a truth in my language; the truth it does express, however, is one I neither know nor believe. So my thus determining the reference of "one metre" is not sufficient for my knowing a priori that S is one metre long.

"What I do know a priori (or so it seems to me) is that if I use "one metre" as a rigid designator of the length of S (and given the appropriate function of the phrase s is long at t) then the sentence "s is one metre long at t" expresses a truth in my language. This conditional, however, is necessary rather than contingent."[20]

Sen goes on to what he thinks is an analogous case. The proposition which is expressed by the sentence "I am talking now" in its use at any time by any person is only contingently, and not necessarily, true. For it will be to the effect that the person who uses the sentence and thereby talks at the moment might not have used that or any other sentence and have remained silent. But on the other hand, it is necessary that the proposition which the sentence expresses in any of its uses should be true because that follows from the rules governing the use of "I," talking," etc. Thus, that I am talking (supposing it is I who is using the sentence at the moment) is not necessary, but that I am talking (in any of its uses) expresses something that is true. This necessary truth that a certain sentence always expresses something true can of course, be known a priori.

Thus, it seems that Kripke has not succeeded in proving the possibility of the contingent a priori.

Sen believes that the thesis that all necessary propositions are a priori is certainly wrong. About the theory that there are certain contingent are priori he thinks Kripke is wrong. Though he believes that the two concepts of the necessary and the a priori are neither identical nor coextensive.

It would be noticed that we have so far desisted from making comments on any other cases of the so-called contingent a priori except for the cases of the reference fixing stipulative definitions. Platinga has presented several such cases. He treats examples such as (i) I know that I exist, (ii) I believe that I exist, (iii) I know that 7 + 5 = 12, etc. all these are known a priori though what they state is contingent proposition. Several others are even tempted to count such

20. Platinga Alvin, *The Nature of Necessity*, Oxford, Claredon Press, 1974, p. 89.

cases as the cases of contingent a priori where a person claims to know something on the basis of his decision. Knowledge of our own decisions and intentions is a priori though contingent.

Let us now attempt to argue that the proposed cases are not really cases of contingent a priori truths. One possible way of denial could be to show that these are cases of necessary truths, and so what if they are a priori? as this combination of the two types of modalities goes well with some of the orthodox intuitions. But this might be hazardous as many intuitively wish to categorize all such statements as "I know that . . ." as contingent as their truth is certainly not immutable viz., they are not true in all possible worlds. (This intuition is however entirely distinct from another according to which if I know something I cannot be wrong. Incorrigibility, we must realize, is neither the same as necessary nor a prioricity).

It is interesting to note that on the construal of a priori truth as those that are "true by virtue of meanings" the quoted sentences are not a priori. Many philosophers have wanted to say that the source of a priori knowledge is some kind of intuition of relations between universals. This intuition, if it exists, is a kind of experience but clearly it is not the kind of experience of which a priori knowledge is supposed to be independent. The kinds of experience that philosophers have traditionally wanted to require this knowledge to be independent of are sense perception memory and introspective sensations. It is extremely difficult to give a list of all the sorts of experience that must be ruled out and regarding certain kinds of experience the decision is extremely difficult. What should we say about introspection? Some philosophers have argued that certain kind of introspection provides us with the characteristic grounds for a priori knowledge is based upon our determining introspectively whether we can imagine a certain kind of state of affairs. S remarked earlier such characterizations in terms of "imaginability" or conceivability are heavily loaded with psychology and we would like to rule out introspection, as the grounds of a priori knowledge. Our knowledge of our own knowledge is not a priori, it may be introspective in which case it is certainly a posteriori or it may be through memory where again it would be a posteriori. Subjectivity of experience or knowledge does not entitle it to the status of a priori knowledge.

We remember that if it is knowable a priori that "p" evidently one's evidential state is not contingent upon the vicissitudes of the world and its ways. In Kripke's fanciful phraseology one could be qualitatively in the same epistemic situation in any world since a priori evidence is constant across worlds, because it is available without observation of the specific properties of each world. Colin McGinn argues that "a priori grounds unlike a posteriori grounds entail what they ground, i.e., provide conclusive reason for belief then one could not be in possession of the very same evidence in a counterfactual situation and yet the statement thus evidentially supported be false . . . (from) independence of evidential state and epistenic necessity of a priori evidence we derive the conclusion that what is known a priori is true in all possible worlds which is to say it is necessary."

A rather conventional point may be reiterated here as a conclusion particularly with reference to what Kripke goes on to say about the contingent a priori. He does not distinguish between the context of discovery and context of justification. His discussion is also laden with the mistaken assumption that question of a prioricity depends on the answer to question such as *who* knows a priori? How does *he* know? Kant never intended his characterization to be so interpreted.

Contributors

Tista Bagchi is holding a PhD degree from the University of Chicago, and is Professor of Linguistics at the University of Delhi. During the academic year 2001-2002, she was the Robert F. & Margaret S. Goheen Fellow at the National Humanities Center, Research Triangle Park, North Carolina, USA. A member of the American Philosophical Association and also of the Linguistic Society of America, she has research publications in syntax, cognitive linguistics, and social epistemology to her credit.

Parameshwar Rama Bhat is Professor of Philosophy in the Department of Humanities and Social Sciences, IIT Bombay. He had his PhD degree from IIT, Kanpur. He has published a number of papers in philosophical journals. He was formerly the Head, Department of Humanities and Social Sciences, IIT Bombay between 2001 and 2004.

Bijoy H Boruah is Professor of Philosophy, Department of Humanities and Social Sciences at the Indian Institute of Technology, Kanpur. He is the author of *Fiction and Emotion: A Study in Aesthetics and the Philosophy of Mind* (Oxford: Clarendon Press & New Delhi: Oxford University Press, 1988). He has published papers in different journals and books on the Philosophy of Literature, Philosophy of Mind, Epistemology and Metaphysics of Value. His latest paper *Consciousness and Virtue Metaphysics* is forthcoming in Chong Kim-Chong and Yuli Li (eds.), *Conceptions of Virtue East and*

West (Singapore: Marshall Cavendish, 2005). He was senior Fulbright Fellow at the University of Texas at Austin in 2000-2001 and Fellow at the Indian Institute of Advanced Study, Shimla in 1997.

Amita Chatterjee is Professor of the Department of Philosophy, Jadavpur University. She is also the Coordinator, Centre for Cognitive Science, Jadavpur University.

Rakesh Chandra is Reader in the Department of Philosophy, Lucknow University. He had his PhD degree from Lucknow University. He specializes in Analytic Philosophy and Philosophy of Language. He has contributed a number of papers to philosophical journals.

Dr. S. Panneerselvam, Professor of Philosophy, University of Madras has authored the book, *The Problem of Meaning with Reference to Wittgenstein and Sankara*, co-edited the *Indian Philosophical Annual*, (vol. XXII,) *A Conspectus of Philosophy, History and Religion* and also published a number of research papers in the leading philosophical journals. He was Indo-Canadian Shastri Institute's Fellow in 2003 and Adjunct Professor of Philosophy, Concordia University, Canada in 2004. He is the Advisory Committee member of the *Sathya Nilayam: Chennai Journal of Intercultural Philosophy* and also the Regional Coordinator of the Council for Research in Values and Philosophy, The Catholic University of America, Washington, D.C., U.S.A.

Ranjan K. Panda secured his Master's as well as PhD degrees from the Department of Philosophy, University of Hyderabad, Hyderabad. His area of specialization is *Philosophy of Mind*. He is currently teaching as Assistant Professor, at the Department of Humanities and Social Sciences, Indian Institute of Technology Bombay, Mumbai.

Ramesh Chandra Pradhan is Professor of Philosophy at the University of Hyderabad. He has his PhD degree from Hindu

University. He specializes in Philosophy of Wittgenstein, Philosophy of Language and Philosophy of Mind. He has authored five books and contributed a number of papers to philosophical journals. He was the Member-Secretary of Indian Council of Philosophical Research, New Delhi in 2000 -2003.

Amitabha Das Gupta teaches Philosophy at the University of Hyderabad. He has published extensively in the areas of philosophy of language, philosophy of linguistics and philosophy of the social sciences.

N. Sreekumar had his M.Phil and PhD from Central University of Hyderabad. Now he is working as Assistant Professor, Department of Humanities and Social Sciences, IIT Madras (Chennai). His areas of research include, Philosophy of Language, Continental Philosophy, Hermeneutics.

C.A. Tomy obtained his doctoral degree in Philosophy from the University of Hyderabad. He spent a year at the University of Goa before joining the Indian Institute of Technology Kanpur as a faculty member. His interests include philosophy of mind, cognitive science and history of philosophy, especially the rationalist tradition.

V. Harinarayanan, currently pursuing his doctoral degree at the Indian Institute of Technology, Kanpur, completed his Master's degree in Philosophy from the University of Calicut, Kerala. He is interested in cognitive science, philosophy of mind and evolutionary biology.

Index